COVENANT

RELATIONSHIPS

COVENANT

RELATIONSHIPS

A more excellent way

A Handbook for Integrity and Loyalty
in the Body of Christ

by Keith Intrater

Destiny Image® Publishers, Inc.
P.O. Box 351
Shippensburg, PA 17257-0351

"Speaking to the Purposes of God for this Generation"

ISBN 0-914903-71-3 paperback
ISBN 0-914903-88-8 casebound

18 19 20 21 / 14 13 12

For Worldwide Distribution
Printed in the U.S.A.

This book and all other Destiny Image, Revival Press, MercyPlace, Fresh Bread, Destiny Image Fiction, and Treasure House books are available at Christian bookstores and distributors worldwide.

For a U.S. bookstore nearest you, call **1-800-722-6774.**
For more information on foreign distributors, call **717-532-3040.**
Or reach us on the Internet: **www.destinyimage.com**

TABLE OF CONTENTS

1

INTRODUCTION

In our circle of friends, believers and co-workers in the kingdom of God, we spend a great deal of time working on our relationships with one another. Occasionally this investment of time and energy seems so great that one would doubt that it is the most efficient way of working in God's kingdom. I can recall a meeting scheduled recently with my dear friends Andrew Shishkoff and Dan Juster; the purpose of this meeting was to work through some areas of misunderstanding that had taken place in one of the ministries that we oversee. As Dan was somewhat late, for a reason that turned out to be quite important, Andrew and I were talking while waiting for the meeting to begin. We began to question whether it was really worth it to continue to work out our relationships to the degree that we had been. After all, we observed, if we had only gone our separate ways, each of us could have had a larger and more famous ministry; there would have been more money, more people, more accomplished for the kingdom of God. And here we were in prime, mid-day time, waiting for a meeting to begin, in which we would once again discuss our unity and our relationships. It hardly seemed worth it!

After a while, we decided that the conversation was getting unproductive and that we ought to pray. The moment we turned to prayer, a prophetic message came very strongly to both of our hearts. The Spirit of the Lord said to us, "I am not in the business of building ministries, but rather of building a Body." We were immediately directed by the Spirit to read **Ephesians 4:16:**

From Whom [Jesus] the whole body, joined and knit together by what every joint supplies, according to the effective working by which every part does its share, causes growth of the body for the edifying of itself in love.

Although we felt slightly chastised for our doubts, the message was clear and supportive. It was a confirmation to continue on in the work of relationship-building, which we have dedicated many years to do. God is not looking so much for a large organization as for an organism that can continue to grow and grow. The group of people who are believers in Jesus are not members of an organization; rather we are, as this scripture shows, interconnected parts of a single body. Each one of us is a joint or a ligament, working and growing together in love; each one of us is a part, and that part is not separate from any other part.

The first lesson of this book might be stated in the following principle: BODY, NOT MINISTRY. So much of the mentality of people who are serving in the Lord's work has been that of trying to build a ministry as if it were simply an organization, or to build a church as if it were a project to be accomplished. If we could see the Lord's work, as one of nurturing and fostering the growth of this living organic body, we would be in a more healthy state. In the long run, the quantitative growth in the congregations would be much greater.

The Real Membership

One might have a large church, one with, let us say, five to ten thousand members. We would have to ask how many of the people involved in that church really have grown to trust one another in love and relationships. Perhaps with a large amount of work, prayer, publicity, projects and programming, the church attendance has grown to a large number. However, it is possible that only a handful of people in the larger group have grown in trust for one another. How many people, therefore, are really in the church. If the number of people in the church is the number of people attending the meetings, we would have to say that that number is very great. On the other hand, if we see the church as an interconnected body of people, the real number of people in that body is the handful of people who have developed more personal relationships.

When a time of testing or trial comes along, large numbers of people not committed personally to the other members may soon turn to flight. We have seen this in our congregation's history. In the early years, problems and divisions caused a shaking in the ranks of the membership. At times even a large percentage of those attending would leave over a given problem or negative event. In the long run, we saw that there was a growing core of people who were more deeply committed to one another. These were the people whom we could trust; they were the actual membership of the congregation.

There is no other way to build a trusting community of faith than to spend real time and effort:

endeavoring to keep the unity of the Spirit in the bond of peace... (Ephesians 4:3).

We should note the word "endeavor." Endeavor means to put forth effort to try to do something. That effort here is directed toward the bond that creates the unity and wholeness within a group of people. The bond is the link or connection between two different people. The bond or link is the relationship. It is the trust. It is the covenant found between the members of the congregation. Therefore, we have a clear scriptural mandate that we are to direct time and effort toward developing the bond that exists between each one of us in the body of believers.

There occurred in 1987-88 a shaking in several of the largest, best-known ministries in our nation. What is surprising is not that there could be sin, greed, immorality or mismanagement among leaders and ministers of the gospel: men can sin, and it is within the scope of our serving together that we can forgive one another. The underlying problem of the ministry has not been the sin itself, but the absence of relationships around those in the ministry. They needed some level of accountability or mutual support to work themselves out of the difficulties. They needed the help of faithful companions. Anyone can sin, and anyone can fall into problems. It is one of the aspects of developing our relationships with one another that we are safeguarded from having years' worth of ministry topple down in a moment because the ministry has outgrown its base of relational support.

Organically Connected

In many places the Bible describes the group of people who believe in Jesus in a way that demands an interconnection between us. One of the most vivid examples is John's description of us together in a vine.

I am the vine, you are the branches; he who abides in Me and I in him bears much fruit. For without Me, you can do nothing (John 15:5).

We in the Body of believers are to be connected as intimately and intricately as the branches of a grapevine. What a clear picture this is! We function within the body only through being connected to Jesus. Similarly, we function within the body only through being connected to one another. As a branch on a vine is attached to the stem, it is also connected to the other branches.

What is alive must be organically connected. For example, if I were working in an auto parts store, I could place various packages on the shelf. The packages would be next to one another. They might even be coded by topic so that there would be a logical order to their arrangement. They would have the same style label, the same number, and the same description, but they would not be organically connected. They would only be separate items, separate objects, sitting next to one another. They must be inanimate or dead if they are separated. In fact, scripturally, the meaning of death is separation. We are separated from God, which is spiritual death. We are separated from one another as a result of our separation from God.

A cut flower, while it may look pretty, is a dead flower; it will soon wither. What is alive must be connected. What is alive must grow. The proper state for a healthy body of believers is to be alive, to be connected throughout its parts, and to be growing.

2

RELATIONSHIPS: THE MEANING OF LIFE

Where does the meaning of life come from? What is the goal of our existence here on this earth? For the believer in Jesus, the meaning of our life stems from our relationship with God and with Jesus. We must remember as well that a relationship between God as a father and Jesus as a son preceded our relationship with them. In a certain sense, the meaning of all of the existence of the universe stems from that preexistent relationship between God and Jesus.

John 17:22-24 explains this idea. At the end of verse 24 Jesus says:

For You loved Me before the foundation of the world.

An essential part of understanding the person of God is to see Him as being in relationship with someone else. God is revealed to be a father, and His primary relationship is with His son Jesus.

God Is Relational

In this sense, we can understand the term God as relational. It is easier to see this concept with the word father: a father cannot be defined alone. To be a father is to be the father of someone. Father implies relationship. Fatherhood cannot be in and of itself. The Scriptures throughout unfold God's central nature as that of father.

In our family, for instance, I am father to my children, and what happens in our lives is an extension of my fathering relationship to them. The children would not even exist had it not been for the relationship between me and my wife; the children are a fruit and extension of that relationship. In addition, the house and cars we own are also an extension of our relationship. I would not have bought this house or these cars, had it not been for the need to provide for my family. My primary interest is not in the house or the cars but in my family members. Likewise, everything that exists in the universe is in some way a product of God's relationship to Jesus as His son. While it may not be apparent, the reason that stars exist, or trees or ocean, somehow gets back to the love that flows from the Father.

Not only what we have, but also what we do is a product of our relationships. For instance, I go to a certain job, and part of the reason for my going is to provide an income for my family. What we do on our weekends and how we sit down to our meals is once again an extension of our relationships with one another. In the same way, we also find that our activities as believers should be an extension of our relationship with God. In reverse, all of the things that God does, acting as God, are expressions of some meaning of His relationship toward us. God does not just do things because He feels like doing them on a whim. Every act of God is a purposeful expression of His love for us.

The First Relationship

Thus, all of what exists and who God is and what God does is an outgrowth of His relationship to Jesus as a father. This relationship existed before the foundation of the world. This fact indicates something about the very nature of God. The Bible tells us that God is love. The statement that God is love means that at the most foundational level of His being, God has a commitment toward relationships.

You have loved them as You have loved Me (John 17:23).

God not only loves Jesus, but He loves each one of us as well. God's commitment to relationship is first to Jesus and then equally to us. The meaning of existence is our commitment to relationship to Jesus. This meaning is also an extension of God's commitment to relationship with us.

That they may be one just as We are one (verse 22).

A network of committed relationships exists among God, Jesus, and all of us. This network of relationships is the goal to which all of our efforts and activities as believers should be directed.

The Goal Is Fellowship

I used to think that among the various activities we have as believers (such as prayer, Bible study, and evangelism), fellowship was akin to a certain break or recess from the more important activities. It was as if one was really doing the work of the kingdom, and then when he got tired, he would take a break to relax with other people. Seen in this way, any strong commitment toward relationship-building is a diversion from the work of the kingdom. However, we now see relationships as the goal and as the very nature of God Himself. This completely reorients our priorities. Instead of our relationships being simply a support mechanism, we find that evangelism, prayer, and Bible study are actually methods and instruments to bring about a certain end. This end is unity, harmony and relationship with one another.

In **I John 1:13** we find: (1 John 1:3)

That which we have seen and heard we declare to you, that you also may have fellowship with us; and truly our fellowship is with the Father and with His Son, Jesus Christ.

All that John bore testimony to and his purpose for writing about Jesus was to bring about a goal: that we might have fellowship with him and the other disciples and the Father and Jesus. Any time a ministry extends beyond the scope of relationships involved in it, that ministry has gone beyond the very goal that it was designed to produce.

This fact, which might appear to limit the scope of ministries, in the long run will make all ministries more effective. Jesus said that it was by our love and commitment to relationships with one another that the world would know that we are believers in Him. Building relationships with one another is the most efficient and effective form of spreading the message of the gospel.

People who are not well grounded in the security of supportive relationships will often turn to outward achievement to try to create an appearance of security. Much of what is done in the world—seemingly great achievements in business, education, and medicine—are really just the outcome of a certain person's insecurity. Insecurity can produce enormous frenetic energy, which can lead to great accomplishments. These accomplishments are false by their very nature.

In **Ephesians 3:17**, Paul says that we must be:

rooted and grounded in love.

Our relationship with God and our trusting relationships with other believers give us a certain rooting, groundedness and security in who we are. When we are secure in our identity, we can then act out of obedience to the Spirit. If we are insecure, our actions come from an energy that is soulish or psychological in origin. Only when we are secure in who we are as a product of our relationships, will our actions be born out of faith, love and the leading of the Holy Spirit.

I have been surprised by meeting many leaders in ministry, whose dedication and zeal for God was an extension of their psychological need for acceptance. Their ministries were not necessarily invalid, but their motivation was not primarily the Spirit of God.

We are to minister the gospel to others without foisting off upon them our own psychological need to be compensated for our insecurity. We must first know who we are in God and receive our security from our relationship with Him and those around us.

The "A" Syndrome

In counseling, I have noticed a certain pattern that I call the "A" syndrome. The "A" syndrome is as follows: For lack of parental Affection, our need for Approval turns to Achievement instead of Acceptance. If we had parents who demonstrated substantial affection in their relationship to us, we would not need to overachieve to make up for the feelings of insecurity. To the degree that the child was well loved when he was growing up, he will find his motivation toward productive labor balanced and wholesome. He will still be achievement oriented, but it will come out of a source of ease and graciousness that does not wear thin on relationships.

If a pastor is trying to win the approval of his congregation by performing to a certain standard, he will find himself falling short. On the other hand, if a pastor knows that he is fully accepted by God and by a circle of trustworthy friends, he will find that a fruit of joy and peace will flow through his congregation. He will reproduce through his spirit and through his preaching the type of trust he has inside of him.

If any believer is to work to achieve God's approval or acceptance, he will soon wear thin his ability to walk in the love of God. We are saved by grace and not according to works of achievement. God is offering us relationship; we can do nothing by way of outward achievement to merit His approval. By understanding that He is a loving God, we can turn back to Him to be accepted and restored to a full relationship. Salvation by grace, or salvation by relationship, is at the center of all our actions as believers.

When I came to the Lord, I was delivered of a subtle problem of anxiety. Inside of me was a striving to accomplish an unknown something that would have merited an ultimate approval or acceptance. No amount of achievement can fulfill the need for acceptance. There is a lack of fulfillment and a striving for approval among those who do not know the Lord. For me, the freedom from that anxious striving resulted in an inner peace that has never left me. We must continue to walk in the acceptance of God by faith; there is always the subtle and dangerous temptation to begin to act again on a performance basis.

Accepted in the Beloved

In **Revelation 2:4**, John rebukes the congregation at Ephesus:

You have left your first love.

The believers at Ephesus were filled with every good form of achievement. They had labor, patience, endurance, maturity and steadiness. They were doing everything correctly. However, they had slipped off the base of their actions. The free acceptance and approval of God must remain as our first love.

I have a certain sympathy for those whom the Bible calls Pharisees. To see them merely as nasty hypocrites would be to miss the depth of their problem. The Pharisees had a strong zeal and sincerity to please God. Paul says in **Romans 10:2** that they acted out of *"a zeal for God but not according to knowledge."* This lack of knowledge is the inability to walk in a sense of God's acceptance and approval. The pattern of the Pharisees is repeated over and over by millions of sincere and well-meaning religious people. Many ministers from every different denomination have fallen into the heart-breaking trap of working harder and harder on a seeming treadmill in an attempt to bring about the purposes of God. This can be frustrating and fatiguing. A renewal of the pastor's or parishioner's understanding of God's acceptance for him is the only way out of such a rut.

For a believer seeking to walk in the revelatory gifts of God, psychological insecurity can lead to a form of spiritual danger. A hidden psychological need may be mistaken for the voice of God speaking through his spirit. A wounded person may justify his motivation to compensate for his insecurities by saying, "The Lord told me." It may become difficult to penetrate that person's confusion.

A believer must be able to distinguish the difference between the wholesome activity of a hard-working person, and the frenetic activity of a person expressing his insecurity through seemingly spiritual feats of achievement. Trying to impress others spiritually to compensate for one's need for identity is a type of self-deception.

A believer who stands up for the Word of God will be rejected by the world around him. If one is to be strong in God, he must have an equivalent strength of his own acceptance by God to resist the rejection of others. If one is caught in a trap of trying to win approval from others, he will soon find himself to be a "man-pleaser." He will lose his footing for moral integrity and spiritual strength. On the other hand, it is often through a set of trusted intimate friends that God ministers healing from past rejection or insecurity. Our acceptance comes from God alone, but it is worked out through the process of developing trust with people. Covenant relationships remove the fears that hinder one's spiritual growth.

The Outworking of God's Love

One can say, "I know that I am accepted in God" to hide himself from making committed friendships. This attitude would contradict what God has said in **I John 4:20:**

If someone says, 'I love God,' and hates his brother, he is a liar; for he who does not love his brother who he has seen, how can he love God whom he has not seen?

If someone says he has received the love and acceptance of God but does not know how to receive the love and acceptance of friends, it is not true that he has really been made whole by the love of God. God loves us. He is our source of acceptance, and His love exercises healing in us. It is through our love of one another, both giving and receiving, that God's love for us is made manifest in our personal lives. **I John 4:12** states how God's love is perfected in us:

No one has seen God at any time. If we love one another, God abides in us and His love has been perfected in us.

The meaning of life has its source in God's love for us. We enter into and experience that love through the development of committed interpersonal relationships. God's process of love is building covenant relationships. Someone who has had a great struggle with insecurity or rejection can still become a vibrant and wholesome minister of God's Word. However, his ability to minister to others is predicated on his receiving healing from past rejection.

Parental Love

No one has had perfect earthly parents; some did a better job of communicating God's love to their children than others. No parent ever did a perfect job. Therefore, all of us have areas, whether great or small, where we need to receive God's love to fill in gaps left by our parents' love toward us. God is called a father to the fatherless; he will make up the gap of parenting in our lives. When we were born again, we entered directly into a relationship with God where we experience Him as a spiritual father. After we are born again, we go through stages of spiritual childhood where we are re-parented by God Himself.

As a father has compassion on his children, so the Lord has compassion on those who revere Him. (Psalm 103:13).

The working of God's love toward us is parallel to the working of a parent's love. God ministers to us in the spirit as our parents did in the physical and psychological realms. **Psalm 27:10** says:

When my father and my mother foresake me, the Lord will take care of me.

To whatever extent our physical parents may have fallen short in nurturing us, God will immediately take up the gap and establish what is missing. Many who are ministering today were orphaned as children; they learned to rely on God as their parent from a very early age. There are others whose parents may have done a wonderful job in bringing them up, but for some small area of parental negligence, they refused to let go of resentment. As adults they may have continued to reject God's spiritual parenting. In this way, through rebellion, they have negated both the earthly and heavenly parenting efforts.

As we take our place as spiritual priests, ministering God's Word to others, we must do so out of a sense of God's parenting to us. Whether the original lack of our physical parents was small or great, we can only minister out of God's direct spiritual fathering of us. In Hebrews chapter 7 we find the description of Melchizedek as an ideal spiritual priest. Verse 3 states:

Without father, without mother, without geneology...but made like the Son of God, [He] remains a priest continually.

This description, actually of Jesus, can also be applied to our own lives, ministering as priests in His stead. Melchizedek was without father or mother, but he was made to be like the Son of God. Regardless of his physical parenting, Melchizedek entered in as a spiritual son of God, receiving the fatherhood of God unto himself. Our priestly ministry in the spirit is an extension of our receiving the relationship of God as a father to us. If this could be done by all ministers, we could avoid the problems of rejection and division that face the ministry today.

I make it a practice to pick up my children and hold them in my arms and rock them while I repeat to them over and over again that I love them. The constant ministering of parental love to a child is the best foundation to prepare him to fulfill his destiny in the kingdom of God.

Bringing Us Back Together

Fear of rejection and insecurity are such prevalent problems because rejection is part of the overall separation of man from God. We were separated from God when Adam had to leave the garden of Eden. We were separated from one another in communication at the Tower of Babel. Mistrust reentered the human race when Cain killed Abel. Rejection, separation and the breakdown of relationships is the overarching pattern of the fallen state of man. It is important to rebuild these areas in our walk as believers. The ultimate plan of redemption is to restore our relationships not only with God but also with each other. This is what we mean when say that relationships are both the meaning and the goal of life.

Paul says that God's plan is:

that in the dispensation of the fullness of the time, He might gather together in one all things in Christ, both which are in heaven and which are on earth (Ephesians 1:10).

As the overall model of sin is a breakdown and fracturing of relationships, so is the fullness of restoration to bring all of these relationships back into unity through the work of Jesus our Messiah. Everything in God's plan and in the function of the body of believers works toward restoring relationships to harmony. Any ministry that goes forward without this goal is not working toward the center of God's purposes.

In **Ephesians 4:13**, Paul also states that the work of the various types of ministry is for the building up of the organic body of relationships in Messiah, *"till we all come to the unity of the faith."* The unity and harmony of our relationships is not a strategic method to accomplish some other goal; unity and restoration of relationships is the goal itself. All of the work of the ministries is for *"the building up of the Body of Christ"* (verse 12).

3

THE NEED FOR COVENANT

Having established the central importance of relationships in the meaning of life, we must now discover God's means for bringing those relationships to pass. How can we guarantee that these relationships will not be broken? What are the terms of any relationship I should enter into? How can I cause the other party in the relationship to be as committed to its success as I am?

The answer to these questions is covenant. Covenant is the agreement between two parties to be committed to their relationship. Covenant is the commitment that lies behind any successful relationship. Covenant comprises the principles of integrity that guarantee a relationship will be preserved.

A Life of Covenant Honor

In the ancient biblical frame of mind, every action a man takes reflects his character. Every interaction between men is a reflection of the relationship between them. Almost every area of life, no matter how small or how large, was then considered a step of covenant. For instance, if I were to trade one of my sheep for another man's goat, the trade would have a lasting spiritual importance beyond the mere exchange of the animals. It would be one step toward determining whether I could trust the other man and whether he could trust me. My honor and his would both be at stake.

Many areas that we would not consider to involve covenant do so from a scriptural perspective. A trade in agriculture is a step of covenant. The circumcision and dedication of a child is a step of covenant. The choosing of a king is a cooperative step of covenant. A man's personal invoking of his god is a step of covenant. In fact, every spoken word backed by a man's personal integrity is a step of covenant.

In this way, every action in life, from a single syllable a man may utter to a corporate decision of a nation to go to war, may be seen as an extension of character and therefore as an act of covenant-keeping. From this perspective no part of life could be considered to be merely mundane or secular. Everything is an expression of love; everything is an expression of conscience and spirit.

Hospitality as Covenant

Let us take, as an example, the offering of hospitality. You may recall an incident recorded in Judges 19 in which a man from the tribe of Ephraim has been on a journey to his home town. He is forced to stop for the night in a town called Gibeah of the tribe of Benjamin. There he waits alone, looking for a place of shelter for himself, his wife and his animals. The people of the town are inhospitable. From a scriptural viewpoint, they are not merely unfriendly but are refusing to act as a covenant-oriented people.

As the sun is setting, an elderly man is returning from a day's work in the fields. It happens that he is also from Ephraim, but has been living in this distant place. When he sees that a fellow tribesman is stranded, his sense of covenant loyalty is stirred within him. He urges the man to lodge at his home. **Judges 19:20** reads:

And the old man said, Peace be with you! However, let all your needs be my responsibility; only do not spend the night in the open square.

At this point, he brings the man into his home and sees to his needs for the evening. In the expression *"...only do not spend the night in the open square,"* we see that this is not a mere offering of social graces; it involves a sense of moral commitment from and urgency from the older man. He knows he will have violated an ethical standard if he allows a co-tribesman to be abandoned. Eating the meal together is an act of communion between the two men that reflects the spiritual bond between them. They have a tribal kinship, even though they have not met personally before this time.

This attitude is also seen in Genesis 18:2 when Abraham offers hospitality to the three men from God who appeared to him. Abraham rushes up to them, insists upon their staying until he can offer them hospitality, and then hurries his wife Sarah to prepare some food. There is more to this hospitality than mere congeniality. It is seen by Abraham as an opportunity for covenant-keeping. He could not by any means let this opportunity pass by.

An Estranged Culture

Our society, being removed from a biblical culture, is by and large unfamiliar with this far-ranging concept of covenant. Interactions between people today often operate on a minimum level of commitment. They are not seen as an opportunity for higher level covenant. In **Ephesians 2:12**, the Scriptures describe such a people and society as being:

strangers from the covenants of promise, having no hope and without God in the world.

Certainly, the world around us has become estranged from the concept of covenant-keeping. If one does not understand covenant, he can have no trust in his relationships with other people. He becomes without hope in this world. God operates with mankind through a process of covenant. If a person is ignorant of covenantal principles, he will find himself unable to approach God or to understand God's desire to interact with him.

Recently, my wife and I purchased a new home. In the negotiations, we struggled with a decision whether to add a basement to the house being constructed.

One of the factors which influenced us toward purchasing a basement was the salesman's promise of an outside access door. As this door would enable us to use the basement for several different purposes, we chose to invest the additional money toward having the basement built. We were surprised to find that when the house was constructed, the access door was not there. When we brought this to the attention of the builder and the salesman, they said that they had not built the access door because of certain construction difficulties. We pointed out that the door had been promised to us. Their answer was that the agreement we signed to have the basement built contained no specific clause about the access door. When I checked with a lawyer, I was told that the law of our nation does not consider binding any verbal statement or contract. If an agreement is not specifically written on paper, it does not exist in the eyes of our legal system.

Lack of awareness of covenantal standards can be seen in people's attitudes toward marital fidelity. It has become in recent years almost socially acceptable for a man and a woman to live together without being married. It is said that they are trying to get to know one another and to see if they are sexually compatible. If they do decide to get married, the level of commitment is such that the marriage will only last as long as both feel good about it. If the feelings of the relationship begin to wane, either party is regarded as free to break the marriage and leave. This is seen by many as mere common sense. They miss the point that there is a commitment and responsibility to protect the intimacy that has been shared by the other person.

Covenant Breaking

In Romans 1:31, Paul lists the many aspects of a sinful character and a sinful society. In particular, he mentions the sin of covenant breaking. In a certain sense, covenant breaking is the foundation of all sin. A man who would father children and then leave the family is a renegade father. He has broken the trust of his wife and children; he has turned away from the covenant responsibility that he made.

Covenant breaking or betrayal of trust is the greatest of all sins. This is what makes the betrayal of Judas against Jesus such a heinous crime. Judas was in the middle of the intimate circle of Jesus' friends. He had been trusted with access to Jesus as a person. His breaking of his covenant with Jesus was not a personal failure on Judas' part, but rather a betrayal of the very soul of a covenant friend.

Vulnerability

A depth of personal relationship results in the beauty of intimacy between two persons. The very sensitivity of that intimacy carries with it the possibility of hurting the other person. Intimacy always bears with it vulnerability. Vulnerable intimacy is a part of holiness.

To protect that vulnerability, there must be commitment to go along with intimacy. To every degree of intimacy, there must be a corresponding degree of commitment. If a man brings a woman to a level of intimacy beyond what he is really committed to, he has violated her as a person. To allow for commitment to be assumed by the other party when it is not actually intended is irresponsible.

Jealousy

One of the primary traits of God's nature is that He is a jealous God. In introducing the ten commandments (**Exodus 20:5** and **Deuteronomy 5:9**) the Lord states:

I am a jealous God.

In **Exodus 34:14** the very name and nature of God as Jehovah is closely related to His characteristic of being jealous:

For you shall worship no other God, for Jehovah whose name is Jealous, is a jealous God.

In the context of Exodus 34, the Lord is renewing His general covenant with the nation of Israel. He is stating His name and nature as *"jealous"* in His position as one partner to this covenant. He presents Himself this way as a jealous covenant partner.

God's view of being jealous is the opposite of the selfish way in which the word jealous is usually taken. Jealousy is commonly understood to involve possessiveness. Being jealous for the covenant is not the same thing as being possessive of and selfish toward the other person. Being jealous for the covenant is actually the highest form of respect for the other partner.

Being jealous in Scripture means that one has a fiery concern to protect the intimacy of the covenant. I am very jealous of the covenant I have with my wife, but I am not possessive of her in a selfish way. A woman would not want her husband to be lacking in this type of jealousy for her. If a husband did not care if his wife were being intimate with another man, he would have devalued the preciousness of his own intimacy with her.

Jealousy is a fiery determination to protect the intimacy of the covenant partners. Biblical jealousy places the same demands on the person being jealous as it does on his partner. It is a jealousy for the covenant. As I am jealous for the single-hearted faithfulness of my wife toward me, so am I also zealous in my commitment toward her. Jealousy is an appropriate reaction to the intense preciousness of the relationship with the other partner. Jealousy sets itself to demand loyalty and to avenge in most horrible terms any betrayal of the covenant.

Vengeance

The Bible says that God will take vengeance. Taking vengeance does not mean that God is an irritable or nasty person. Rather, His commitment to covenantal faithfulness is so total that He must make the same demands on the other partner. The complete consecration of God's willingness to love us demands vengeance on anyone who would break the covenant. God's character as a vengeful God should produce great security and comfort in us. He will never be unfaithful.

Numbers 5 speaks of the judgment that occurs when a spirit of jealously comes upon a husband who suspects his wife of betraying him. At first reading, the law seems unfair to the poor woman who is at the mercy of her husband's emotions. If she is suspected of having done wrong, she is called to stand judgment. When she drinks the *"water of jealousy,"* all sorts of horrible curses are pronounced over her. These are to come to pass if she has actually betrayed her husband.

The meaning of this passage becomes clear once we realize that the husband here is a symbol of God and the woman a symbol of God's people. God's faithfulness is not in question in the law. The law is there to present extreme sanctions against covenantal betrayal. It is intended to guarantee the faithfulness of the people toward God as their spiritual husband. The strong indictments of the law are measures to protect and guarantee the faithfulness of our covenant. Even the most horrible curses and retributions are actually comforting assurances of God's love for us.

The danger of living in an area where there has been much crime produces fear in the local residents. They would experience greater security were righteous and well-armed law-enforcement agents to come through the area announcing that anyone committing a crime would be severely punished. Such legal pronouncements would be a source of peace and safety. In the same way, the curses and punishments of the law of Moses are protective measures to guard the security of the people.

Faithfulness

The purpose of covenant, then, is to ensure faithfulness and commitment to the very relationships that are so precious in God's sight. We live in a world where many people talk about how they love one another in sensual and insincere ways. Introducing the concept of covenant is a refreshing challenge to back up the claims of love. A very poignant verse in this regard is **Proverbs 20:6**, which states:

Many a man claims to have unfailing love, but a faithful man who can find?

Here faithfulness does not mean confidence or boldness so much as the persevering integrity to hold to a covenant without breaking it. What a widespread meaning this verse has for us today! Many people claim to have all love, but those who are really true to their covenants are harder to find.

Jesus makes a similar point at the end of His parable about the unjust judge. In **Luke 18:8**, He says:

I tell you that God will avenge them [the innocent and trustworthy elect] speedily: nevertheless, when the Son of Man comes, will He really find faith on earth?

At His coming in power, Jesus will exercise covenantal vengeance against all who have betrayed the trust of spiritual relationship. He asks the questions whether people who claim to be believers will really be faithful in their covenantal integrity and responsibility. In other contexts, faith means exercising biblical confession and standing in the power of God. In this passage, its more primary meaning is that of being faithful and trustworthy to covenantal relationships.

Sin, then, is the breaking of the trust of another person; one cannot sin in the abstract. Sin is not the failure to accomplish a certain action. Sin is personal, and sin is relational. We sin against a brother, or we sin against God. If a wife burns a piece of toast, she does not necessarily sin against her husband. Even if she does poorly in all levels of performance, she has not sinned against him as long as she is loyal to him. God has never asked His people to perform up to a certain level. He has demanded that we be perfectly loyal and trustworthy to Him and to other people.

The Beginning of Mistrust

Sin releases into a person's consciousness the possibility and fear that a subsequent betrayal of trust may occur. If one partner in a marriage commits adultery, the problem is not so much in dealing with the action itself. The difficulty is reestablishing in each of the partners the assurance and trust that another betrayal will not occur. Had no one ever sinned, there would be no need for safeguards against sin reoccurring. The law is a set of standards that provide safeguards against further covenant breaking. Had there never been sin, there would be no need for law.

Had stealing or murder never occurred, one would not find a law with sanctions against stealing or murder. If there had never been a case of marital unfaithfulness, there would be no need to guarantee one another not to be unfaithful in the future. As sin increases, so must the scope of the law expand to provide further measures or sanctions to prevent those new areas of crime from recurring.

When Adam and Eve first became husband and wife, there was no need for a covenant ceremony or proclamation of an oath for each other's faithfulness. At that time, there were not other men or women around. But as sin increased, a corresponding breakdown occurs in people's trust of one another's word. If there had never been any sin, it would be taken for granted that the words one uttered would be fulfilled. Since we live in a world fractured by the breakdown of covenant, we need a process to ensure that what one party promises will be held true.

How Can God Assure Us?

It is heartbreaking to realize that when God offers mankind a covenantal promise, we have by our sinful nature become so unbelieving of anyone's integrity that it is difficult for us to believe even what God has said. Even though God has never lied and has never broken covenant, He finds Himself in the position of trying to guarantee to us that He will be faithful on His side of the bargain. This is particularly exasperating when one realizes that God is the source of truth and faithfulness. He has nowhere to go to prove His faithfulness since He is the very originator of it. We see here the paradox of trying to have a dialogue between one person who has always told the truth and another person who has always lied. How will the liar ever be convinced within himself that he can trust the words of the truthful one? How can the truthful one contrast or compare himself to anything in the context of the liar's life when the liar does not know what truthfulness is?

This is the case that God presents in **Hebrews** chapter **6:13-19. Verse 13** states:

For when God made a promise to Abraham, because He could swear by no one greater, He swore by Himself.

Abraham is not the parallel of a man who always lied. He was the most covenant-faithful person of his time. But even in God's dialogue with Abraham, we see God's struggle to reassure Abraham of the absolute infallibility of God's promise. **Verse 17** states:

Thus God, determining to show more abundantly the heirs of promise the immutability of His counsel, confirmed it by an oath.

God is making a determined effort to demonstrate to us, the hearers of His word, that He will not break that which He has said. What He has counseled or spoken to us is confirmed by a guarantee. He is trying to demonstrate that He is not doubleminded, that His words will not be changed in the future. **Verse 18** reads:

That by two immutable things in which it is impossible for God to lie, we might have strong consolation.

The consolation here is in our own assurance that the things God has promised will come to pass. The consolation is our being brought to the point through God's twofold guarantee where we see that God's end of the bargain will actually come through.

What are the two unchangeable things in which it is impossible for God to lie? These two things are the promise itself and then the oath of confirmation following it. These two things are similar to a contract and a money-back guarantee given by the seller of an item. The contract is reinforced by the guarantee; the contract and the guarantee are the two immutable things. In this case, God's promise is completely valid and trustworthy. He then adds an oath: He forswears Himself that the promise He originally made is true. The oath becomes the second of the two things, following the initial promise. The promise and the oath guarantee us of the truth of His word.

God has nowhere else to turn to guarantee His own integrity. All He can do is re-promise or re-forswear Himself of that which He has already said. He reiterates what was true in the first place.

For men indeed swear by the greater, and an oath for confirmation is for them an end of all dispute (Verse 16).

The image here is one of two men having an argument in which one is saying that he does not believe the other. At a certain point in the argument, the one trying to make his point says, "I swear that this is true." Even ungodly and untrustworthy men would be awestruck by one of them swearing an oath. Their very vestigial sense of honor would drive them to accept the truthfulness of the other one's statement. Certainly no one could swear an oath to what he just said and have it be a lie. Such lack of integrity would be too horrible to suspect even of one's enemy.

Simple Faith

We ought to be aghast at the depth of our own unbelief which has forced God to this extreme. God has offered us a covenant. He has promised us to keep that covenant true. He has even made an oath over Himself to confirm to us that we can trust the covenant He has offered.

Had it not been for our sin, our response to any statement of God's would have been much more simple and filled with faith. The death and resurrection of Jesus as God's beloved Son is the ultimate measure that God has undergone to guarantee His willingness to restore mankind to a trusting relationship with Himself. God is trying to rescue us out of our distrust through a process in which our souls become more and more reassured. Our thought patterns are renewed to covenantal trust. It is through covenant that our souls emerge out of unbelief into intimacy with God.

This hope we have as an anchor of the soul, both sure and steadfast, and which enters the presence behind the veil (Verse 19).

God has gone to great lengths to restore us to a position where He can share His most intimate presence with us. Trustworthiness is the purpose of covenant-making.

4

HOW A COVENANT WORKS

We have seen that the purpose of a covenant is to guarantee a given relationship. The covenant itself is actually a set of words that are spoken to define the nature of that relationship and set forth the principles of commitment to it. A covenant can be seen as an oath that seals the relationship between two people.

For example: in the case of marriage, a man and a woman have a certain relationship together. This relationship may be deeply felt and understood implicitly between the two of them. The covenant of marriage is when the terms of their relationship are set forth verbally and clearly so that both may be committed to it. The marital covenant is making explicit in word form what their relationship is. In general, the marriage is the relationship between the two of them. The covenant of marriage is the words of oath commitment that pass between them at the marriage ceremony and seal them forever.

The Words of the Covenant

The man states legally before witnesses, before God, and before his wife that "I will be your husband." He has sealed himself by his word of honor into faithfulness to the relationship that he has established with her. The covenant, then, is the words that pass between them. In **I Chronicles 16:15** there is a description of God's covenant with Israel.

Remember His covenant always; the word which He commanded for a thousand generations.

The covenant refers to the word that God spoke. This is why we refer to the Bible as a testament or a covenant. We have a relationship with God. The words which He spoke are the Scriptures upon which we base our relationship.

A covenant is something to be remembered. The purpose of the covenant is to continue to reiterate the set terms by which the relationship between the two people operates. The covenant is permanent and steady, and therefore helps maintain a permanence and steadiness in the relationship between the two people. The people may be subject to change, but the word of the covenant maintains its stability.

Another aspect of the word of the covenant is that it will last on into time. Here it says that this word would be effective for a thousand generations. A covenant may endure beyond the first two parties who originally started it.

There are several general parts to a covenant. The most important ones are: (1) the personal relationship that the covenant is designed to confirm; (2) the specific covenant itself or the words of oath-taking that seal the relationship; (3) the signs of the covenant, some elements that form a graphic impression to remember the covenant; (4) the blessings or positive rewards that ensue from keeping the covenant; and (5) the curses or negative punishments that ensue from breaking the covenant.

The Signs of the Covenant

The signs of the covenant may come in many varied ways. A wedding ring may be a reminding symbol of the marriage between a man and his wife. The ritual of circumcision is a sign of the covenant between God and the descendants of Abraham. All of the worship feasts and sabbaths of ancient Israel were reminder signs of the covenant relationship between God and the nation of Israel.

In the New Covenant, the breaking of the bread for the body of Jesus and the drinking of the wine for the blood of Jesus serve as the reminder signs of the covenant of salvation. This covenant was put into effect through the death and resurrection of Jesus.

The signs of a covenant are valid only to the degree that they reflect the reality of the inward heart relationship that they purport to represent. If the sign reflects something that is meaningful, the sign is meaningful. The sign of a covenant taken by itself has little meaning. For example, if a man has betrayed his faithfulness to his wife in their marriage covenant, the fact that he takes pride in the wearing of his wedding ring has little merit to it. The ring is only as valuable as the relationship it represents.

The power of taking communion for the believer in Jesus is related to the degree in which it reflects for him a deep identification with the death and resurrection of Jesus. If communion is taken without this deeper reality it has no positive effect for the partaker.

Sacrifices of Righteousness

This perspective should help us understand the law of Moses and comments of the New Testament writers in dealing with the attitudes of the people about the law. Let us remember that the temple sacrifices were a system of sign reminders of the covenant relationship between God and Israel. When these sacrifices were done in the spirit of that covenant reality, they had great significance. If not, they became superficial and meaningless. There are many scriptures which indicate this comparison. For example, **Proverbs 21:3** states:

To do righteousness and justice is more acceptable to the Lord than sacrifice.

Doing righteousness and justice was a direct part and extension of the relationship that the people had with God. The sacrifice is a sign of that relationship. The object of what a sign is pointing to is more important than the sign itself. This does not mean that one must reject the signs as reminders of the covenant if the covenant is sincerely in place. This principle is brought out in such other scriptures as I Samuel 15:22, Proverbs 15:8, Isaiah 1:11, and Hosea 6:6. One of the themes of the book of Hebrews is that the ritualistic elements of the law are shadows and symbols of real heavenly things (Hebrews 8:5, 9:23, and 10:1).

This comparison between the signs of the covenant and the heart relationship of the covenant is brought out particularly well in **Psalm 51. Verse 16** says:

You do not desire sacrifice...nor delight in burnt offering.

This shows that the sacrifices that were reminders of the covenant have no value in and of themselves. **Verse 17** adds:

The sacrifices of God are a broken spirit, and a broken and contrite heart You will not despise, O God.

This is pointing to the inner heartfelt reality that the sign of the sacrifice is designed to highlight.

The thought of the psalm does not end at this point. It continues on to **verse 19.**

Then you shall be pleased with the sacrifices of righteousness, with burnt offering and whole burnt offering. Then they shall offer bulls on your altar.

This shows a positive synthesis of the two views. If one's heart attitude is correct, then the signs of the covenant become a valid, beautiful and acceptable expression of that heartfelt reality.

The Sign of the Sabbath

The teachings of both Paul and Jesus were strong and piercing to demand the spiritual purpose of the law. In **Exodus 31**, the sabbath is spoken of as a reminder sign of God's miraculous work in creating the universe. **Verse 13** states:

Surely My Sabbaths you shall keep, for it is a sign between Me and you throughout your generations, that you may know that I am the Lord that sanctifies you.

Verse 17 also states:

It [the Sabbath] is a sign between Me and the children of Israel forever. For in six days the Lord made the heavens and the earth, and on the seventh day He rested and was refreshed."

The sabbath, as an expression of thanksgiving to our Creator, is a beautiful, spiritual vehicle through which to celebrate our relationship with God. If the sabbath is taken out of this context of our personal relationship with our Creator, it becomes void of meaning. This is what Jesus, who was a sabbath-keeper in the best sense of the word, meant when He said in **Matthew 12:8:**

The Son of Man is Lord even of the Sabbath.

In **verse 12**, He also said:

Therefore, it is lawful to do good on the Sabbath.

Circumcision of the Heart

It is also important to see this perspective in the overall scriptural teaching of circumcision. The Old Testament prophets realized that circumcision was an outward sign pointing back to the relationship between God and Abraham. All the spiritual people understood that there was a significance to the circumcision that had to do with an attitude of the heart. Moses stated in **Deuteronomy 10:16:**

Circumcise the foreskin of your heart and be stiffnecked no longer.

Moses was not saying that a physical circumcision could not be performed as a valid sign of the covenant. Jeremiah also states in **Jeremiah 4:4:**

Circumcise yourselves to the Lord and take away the foreskins of your hearts.

The fact that the sign of a covenant pointed back to the issues of the heart was an open revelation known by all the men of God from the very beginning.

Paul writes in **Romans 2:29:**

He is a Jew who is one inwardly and circumcision is that of the heart in the spirit.

He is not presenting a new doctrine that represents a change in the law by the New Covenant. He is expounding the true meaning of the command of the law as it was originally intended. He is defending the true nature of circumcision from the superficial religious hypocrisy of his day. He even had his co-worker Timothy circumcised.

A religious hypocrite, who stresses the outward sign for its own sake, threatens and jeopardizes the validity of those who would walk in the covenant in a sincere manner. In this way ritualistic hypocrisy can be a great enemy to those who wish to use the signs of the covenant. Paul says in **Galatians 5:2:**

If you become circumcised Christ will profit you nothing.

Paul was not opposed to circumcision, per se. He goes right on to state in **verse 6:**

For in Christ Jesus neither circumcision nor uncircumcision avails anything, but faith working through love.

He is not contradicting the entire sweep of scriptures on the dynamics between covenantal relationships and the signs of the covenant. He is, rather, making a strong attempt to rescue certain believers who were in danger of being diverted away from their spiritual relationship with God to a superficial form of ritualism. If people think that through any ritualistic performance they can earn their merit before God, they have lost the entire foundation of what their covenant with God means. Superficial ritualism leads to spiritual death. Signs of the covenant can be used to express one's love to God.

The Heroic Rescue

The main parts of a covenant are the relationship behind the covenant, the words of the covenant, the signs of the covenant, and the rewards and punishments of the covenant. There are many other aspects of the covenant such as the terms, the witnesses, and the seals. There is often a major act of redemption or heroism on the part of the savior figure around which the covenant is constructed. These heroic acts may be seen as an act of faith or love or salvation on the part of the rescuing figure. In Scripture, the act of creation, the exodus, the deliverances of Israel from her enemies, the death and resurrection of Jesus, and many others are seen as the redemptive and powerful interventions of an omnipotent and benevolent king.

In the biblical model of marriage, the husband symbolizes God and the wife, God's people. The husband's taking up the woman to be his wife is seen as a type of benevolent rescue, saving the bride figure from her needy state. In **Ezekiel 16** there is a beautiful parable describing God's redemptive love for His people as a man rescuing a young woman. God portrays Jerusalem as a baby girl who has been abandoned at birth, pitied by no one, and left alone to die in her own blood. God, as the hero figure, causes her to live and to thrive. Under His nurture, she becomes beautiful, maturing into sensual and gracious womanhood. The language of covenant rescue and betrothal is particularly poignant in **verse 8:**

When I passed by you and looked upon you, indeed your time was the time of love. So I spread My wing over you and covered your nakedness. Yes, I swore an oath to you and entered into a covenant with you, and you became Mine.

After this, the savior continues to lavish upon the bride every form of gift and adornment to draw her into the fullness of beauty and royalty. Afterward, she betrays him, and he begins to pursue her to restore his wayward bride to himself.

The point here is that in our relationship with God, our covenant does not start with two people on an equal footing. With God our very relationship of covenant must be preceded by an act of supernatural rescue and recovery. Our salvation covenant with God is not one of co-equality in origin. Our covenant is founded on a powerful act of gracious intervention. We were the helpless party in need of rescue. The offer of any type of covenant is an act of condescending grace on the part of our rescuer, God. The fact that He then offers us bridal co-equality through marrying us to Himself is overwhelmingly gracious.

God's Marriage to His People

Using marriage as a model is helpful in understanding the nature of our salvation covenant with God through Jesus. Despite whatever breakdown there has been in this country in the sanctity of marriage, it is still the best known form of covenant to the mind of Western society. The marriage model is the only one in which most people in our culture have any intuitive grasp of the underlying spiritual issues.

Let us look for a moment at the great passage in **Jeremiah 31** which describes the coming of a new covenant. **Verse 31** states:

Behold the days are coming, says the Lord, when I will make a new covenant with the house of Israel and with the house of Judah.

The image here is one of a man (God), who has married a woman (Israel), and the woman has gone astray. She has broken her marriage covenant with her husband, and it has become void. This is also the message of the book of Hosea. God pursues His people who are acting as a wayward wife. He has the hope of restoring their marriage together and renewing their covenant relationship.

Here the Lord promises that He will be successful eventually in restoring His marriage with Israel and in making a new marriage covenant with her. There will be a renewal of their vows and trust for one another. **Verse 32** states that this new or renewed marriage covenant will be:

Not according to the covenant that I made with their fathers.

What was the primary problem with the first marriage covenant? Did the husband design a wrong marriage? No. The problem with the first marriage was that the wife broke and betrayed the covenant. **Verse 32** continues:

My covenant which they broke though I was a husband to them.

In what way will the new covenant be new, if the same husband is restoring the same wife to himself? The newness of this covenant is that the heart attitude and spirit of the wife figure has been radically changed to allow her to be faithful to the covenantal relationship which the husband had always desired. **Verse 33** states:

But this is the covenant that I will make with the house of Israel after those days...I will put My the law in their minds and write it on their hearts; and I will be their God, and they shall be My people.

When seen in this context, the theological complications about the relationship of the law to the New Covenant are greatly simplified.

The Rules of the Covenant

The set of laws or rules to a covenant are the terms by which the partners set their behavior to facilitate the continuing of their trust and mutual pleasure. Here again the marriage model is helpful. If I were to give my wife a set of rules by which I would like her to run our household, it would be pleasing to me for her to obey those rules; it would enhance the joy of our relationship. On the other hand, were my wife to be unfaithful to me in adultery and break the very foundation of our trust and relationship for one another, it would not matter to me how expertly or perfectly she performed the household rules. No amount of perfect performance or obedience to the law subsequent to a covenant betrayal can ever restore our trust. Making my favorite meal a thousand times in a row would not be able to reconcile our consciences together.

It is impossible by way of the performance of the law alone to establish reconciliation between the partners of a covenant. Reconciliation and salvation can only be effected by an act of personal repentance, atonement, and restitution. The fact that covenant reconciliation cannot be effected by performance of the law does not invalidate the role and place of the terms of that law. The terms and laws of behavior are perfectly valid when seen in their proper limit under the overall covenantal relationship. The communication of the expectations that one party has for the other in the terms of their covenant is always valid whenever that covenant is reciprocal in nature. Reciprocity means that both parties have their part to play.

The laws of the Scriptures have their place when used appropriately. They should not violate the context on the covenant in which they were presented. This is what Paul wrote to Timothy:

We know that the law is good when we use it lawfully (I Timothy 1:8).

There are hundreds of commands in the New Testament scriptures. These commands are applications of the laws of the Old Covenant. They are to be obeyed by anyone who claims to be a believer and follower of Jesus. The fact that we must obey what Jesus says does not contradict the grace by which we enter into relationship with Him. A covenantal attitude sees that laws are good. Laws prevent covenantal breakdown. In no way do they become an obstacle, because we walk in the grace of our personal relationship with the Lord. We have the power of His Spirit in our radically new nature.

Let us summarize the operations of the covenant in this way: First there is an intervening act of redemption on the part of the savior. Then there is a gracious offer of relationship from the savior to the rescued party. This relationship is the heart and the goal of the whole matter. Words and promises of a covenant are set forward to delineate the nature of that relationship. Signs of remembrance are given to make a graphic impression upon both parties of the permanence of the covenant. Terms of expectation between the two parties are set forth in the form of law. The positive rewards (or blessings) for continuing in the covenant are set forth. The punishments (or curses) for breaking the articles of the covenant are also set forward to enforce it. The various parts of Scripture work together to form a composite picture that we call a covenant.

5

CUTTING THE BLOOD COVENANT

In Hebrew the word for covenant is "brit." The word brit connotes a cutting of the flesh in some way so that blood has flowed out; therefore we may take the expression "cutting the covenant," or "blood covenant." Cutting, blood, and covenant are combined together in the word brit.

The word brit today among Jewish people is often used to refer to the particular ceremony of circumcision. The word brit itself simply means covenant. The word for covenant of circumcision would be "brit milah." Circumcision is a cutting away of the excess foreskin off the male organ. It is usually done on the eighth day after birth.

Blood Brothers

In circumcision there is a cutting of the flesh and flowing of blood. It is used as a sign and seal of the continuance of the Abrahamic covenant.

The word brit has also been made popular by the large Jewish social organization called Bnai Brith or B'nai B'rith. B'nai B'rith literally means "sons of the covenant." B'nai B'rith is a modern cultural organization designed to promote Jewish identity and social causes. The B'nai B'rith organization does not quite bring into its spirit the patriarchal sense of cutting blood covenant for tribal unity. The use of the term, however, still connects Jewish identity back to its original unifying point in God's covenant with Abraham.

In its most earthy dimensions, the blood covenant is probably most familiar to the modern mind in such images as the blood brothers of the American Indians or the mingling of blood with the African tribal covenants. Both of these forms are pagan in their mode and origin. They do, at least, bear with them the deeper graphic impression and life-or-death awe in which the covenants of the Bible are presented.

It is worth noting here that the Bible specifically forbids the cutting of any human flesh or drinking of any blood whatsoever. Any form of pagan blood covenant in which a human being's flesh was cut, or in which one of the parties actually drinks blood, would be patently unbiblical. The circumcision of the male child might be a slight exception in this case, in that a certain amount of blood is shed in the act of circumcision itself. The point remains that there are strong biblical injunctions against the direct use of blood: blood is to be shed only by a substitutionary animal, and even in that case the blood is poured upon the ground.

There is something about the nature of a blood covenant that leaves a deeper impression upon the psyche than almost anything else. Even in modern society, the sight of blood evokes a sense of horror and an unsettling in the conscious and subconscious levels. Part of the purpose of using blood to confirm an agreement is that the cutting of the covenant would leave such a strong and fearful impression on the parties involved that they would be seized in their innermost being.

Abram and El Shaddai

The prototype of all blood covenants is found in Genesis 15, where God appears to Abram in a vision. After the promise of the covenant has been made, the Lord instructs Abram how to go about a covenant-cutting ceremony. Abram was to bring several different animals together and to cut certain of them in two. He was then to place the two halves opposite one another in a row, thereby forming a simple aisle down the middle of the pieces. The animals' flesh are being cut and the blood poured out upon the ground.

As Abram beheld this sight he fell into a deep sleep, and a certain horror came upon him (verse 12). This horror was an awe of the holiness of the situation. There was a shocking import and inviolability that this covenant represented. In verse 17 the Shechinah presence of God appears as a flaming torch and passes through the cut pieces of the animals. The Lord had just cut the covenant with Abram. The implications that God Himself would pass through the pieces of the covenant are far-reaching. The God of all creation has bound Himself to a relationship with a human being.

In **Genesis 17** God reiterates this covenant with Abraham. **Verse 4** reads:

As for Me, behold My covenant is with you, and you shall be a father to many nations.

The key phrase here is the words *"as for Me."* God is presenting Himself as one party of a two party contract. He is saying, "This is My side of the covenant, and there is yet left a side for you." This is further shown in **verse 9** which states:

As for you, you shall keep My covenant, you and your descendants after you, throughout all generations.

Individual choice and freedom of will remain with Abraham. A covenant, even when one of the parties of the covenant is God Himself, has two distinct sides to it. The covenant has a side for God to choose; it also has a separate side in which Abraham has the choice.

The Two-Sided Covenant

In God's dealings with mankind, there is a twofold cooperation. The human being, puny in comparison to God Almighty, must himself choose to stand up as a partner opposite God. Covenant has great significance in our understanding of faith. God has offered us a type of bargain or agreement. For this agreement to take effect in anyone's life, both parties have to agree to it. God's intervention into the affairs of man requires an individual's first coming forward to make an agreement with God. God is not running around haphazardly crashing into the course of human events. There is a logic and system to God's ways.

As a covenant partner, Abraham was allowed to be part of the deliberations on the coming judgment on Sodom and Gomorrah. Moses, as a covenant partner with God, was able to intercede with God for the preservation of the Israelites in the wilderness. **Amos 3:7** says:

> **Surely the Lord God does nothing unless He reveals His secrets to His servants the prophets.**

All of God's actions upon the earth are done through the mechanism of covenant. There must be a human being prophetically coming into agreement with God. Through this joint authority, the intervention of God takes place. Without such joint authority, there will be no divine interference.

The concept of a mere man establishing a cooperative alliance with God is one that shatters the classical false impression of man as a passive creature at the hands of a whimsical and capricious creator. God's offering of a two-sided covenant is one that should stir any human being into the deepest kind of action. Anyone will be awakened if he perceives what his options are. The Bible does not portray mankind as the puppets of God. Man has been a delinquent child. He is now under the demands of a father calling him to act in maturity and integrity.

As cooperative covenantal partners with God, we are to take our places as the stewards of God's created garden. We are the sub-rulers over the works of His hands. This is the plan God originally intended for Adam; this is the plan we fell away from. This is the plan we are being restored to through Jesus our Messiah.

In the episode in which Jesus rebukes the wind and the waves during a storm, the disciples react to Him in fear and awe. One might see this awe as a proper religious humility toward Jesus. That reaction, however, missed the point completely. Jesus asked:

> **Why are you so fearful? How is it that you have no faith (Mark 4:40)?**

Jesus was not asking them to revere Him. He was surprised at their lack of understanding of their cooperative partnership with God. He expected them by that time to have understood that they had enough authority to give a command to the wind and the waves. God is challenging man with the freedom to make morally accountable actions.

God Himself comes down to the place of meeting to pass through the cut pieces of the covenant. The slaying of an animal and the pouring out of its blood is an implicit statement that if one of the partners should ever violate or betray the covenant, the slaughtering that was just performed upon the animal should then happen to him. It is as if in the marriage vows of a man and woman, they stated that if either one of them should ever commit adultery, he or she should immediately be executed and have the blood poured out upon the ground.

The Curse of the Covenant

In **Jeremiah 34**, the elders of Israel performed a blood covenant ceremony before God and walked through the pieces. **Verse 18** reads:

> **I will give the men who have transgressed My covenant, who have not performed the words of the covenant which they made before Me, when they cut the calf in two and passed between the parts of it.**

These leaders had passed through the covenant of the pieces of the animal, had made promises to obey a contractual agreement, and then had not done so. They had transgressed and betrayed the covenant. They had forsworn themselves to the point of blood vengeance. **Verse 20** reads:

> **I will give them into the hand of their enemies and into the hand of those who seek their life. Their dead bodies shall be meat for the birds of the heaven and the beasts of the earth.**

In other words, the reverse of the action performed on the pieces of the animals will now be performed upon them. Judicial execution for this highest of crimes will be brought against them. The covenant oath will be enforced.

God is saying that He has made certain promises to us, and should He ever not fulfill those promises, He Himself would be liable to judicial execution. Obviously, that could never happen. God is serious about backing and bringing to pass the promises He has made to mankind.

God has called us in turn to walk between the pieces. We have become partners in a blood covenant. We have sealed ourselves into a holy bond of loyalty, intimacy, and full cooperation with God. Should we ever violate something so overwhelmingly sacred, we would be liable to slaughter.

Drinking His Blood

We can see here how serious a matter it is to take communion in the name of Jesus. Paul could say in **I Corinthians 11:27-30** that:

> **Whoever eats this bread or drinks this cup of the Lord in an unworthy manner will be guilty of the body and blood of the Lord. Let a man examine himself and so let him eat of that bread and drink of that cup. For he who eats and drinks in an unworthy manner, eats and drinks judgment to himself, not discerning the Lord's body. For this reason many are weak and sick among you, and many sleep.**

As we take the cup and the bread of communion, we are passing through the pieces into a blood covenant with Jesus. He is completely bound to loyalty with us, and we are completely bound to loyalty with Him. Should we betray that loyalty that was so lovingly offered and proven at such a horrible expense, we would find ourselves facing a fearful judgment of blood guilt. To enter into a blood covenant with Jesus the Messiah is no light or superficial matter.

To drink of His blood is to become one with Him in a life-for-life, soul-for-soul partnership. In the armies of ancient Israel, cooperating allies would swear allegiance to one another to be equal on the battlefield. In II Chronicles 18:3, Ahab, King of Israel, and Jehoshaphat, King of Judah, make a covenant to go into battle. Their verbal agreement is as follows:

I am as you are and my people as your people. We will be with you in the war.

In this agreement they have set their lives at one stake and one destiny with the other's.

In **I Chronicles 11** we find David separated from Israel and in danger of his life. A group of men come out to him as soldiers to make a covenant commitment to him. They say to him:

Indeed we are your bone and your flesh (verse 1).

This means that they have become one with him in military loyalty. They use the language of being one flesh together even as one might in a marriage commitment. They have spiritually joined their flesh by covenant.

Later in the same chapter, the men are in a warfare situation, and David makes a comment that he would like some water to drink from a well that was on the other side of the enemy line. Certain of his mighty heroes break through the line, draw up some water, and bring it back for him to drink. When David receives the water, he refuses to drink it. Instead he pours it out upon the ground. This pouring out of the water is a covenantal statement parallel to the pouring of an animal's blood upon the ground. The water symbolically represented their lives. When asked why he did this, David responds:

Far be it from me, O my God, that I should do this! Should I drink the blood of these men who have put their lives in jeopardy? For at the risk of their lives they brought it (verse 19).

The language is similar to the new-covenant language of taking communion. David says that drinking the water would be akin to drinking the blood of these men. By this he indicates that they have put their lives in jeopardy for his life. He knows that he is covenantally bound to put his life as well in jeopardy for them. They have drunk one another's blood in that they are committed in this time of war to be willing to give their lives for one another.

Life and Death Loyalty

Jesus said that in order to enter the new covenant, we must all drink of His blood and eat of His flesh. He has indicated here that we must all join our lives into complete covenant unity with Him, our lives for His life and His life for ours.

A blood covenant demands full life and death loyalty. In **Revelation 12** there is a vision of certain men who have given their lives for the sake of the kingdom of God. **Verse 11** describes the fullness of their covenant commitment:

And they overcame him (the accuser) by the blood of the Lamb and by the word of their testimony, and they did not love their lives to the death.

The blood of the Lamb is referring to Jesus' part of the covenant. The word of their testimony is the word of the oath of their covenant with Jesus. That they were willing to give their own lives for the sake of the covenant is the ultimate fulfillment of their own loyalty. The covenant has two sides of cooperative commitment.

This absolute blood liability and loyalty are the principles that stand behind a biblical view of human relationships. Our own viewpoint on how we treat one another should be radically altered. There is a whole new dimension to the statement:

You shall love one another as I have loved you (John 13:34).

6

INTERPERSONAL COVENANTS
Abraham and Abimelech

The model of Jesus having given His life for mankind looms large behind all of our individual interactions with one another. His act of giving His life should be reenacted in some small way in everything we do that touches the life of another person. Each one of our actions should reflect one facet of His great act of love.

Agape Love

Love is the cardinal rule of Scripture; it governs every human interchange. Biblical love is not what the world generally thinks of love: biblical love is the acting out of covenantal faithfulness in regard to each other person.

In the Greek New Testament there are three words for the word "love." The Greek word "eros," from which we get the word erotic, deals with physical attraction, sensual love, and sexual relations. The word "philo," or brotherly love, concerns all areas of emotional, romantic, humanistic, and soulish love. The third word, "agape," means a love that takes its origin from God. Agape love seeks the best for others. Agape works by exercising covenant. For us to act in God's love is to act according to God's principle of relationship. God's principle of relationship is covenant. Therefore, whenever we speak of the command to love one another in Scripture, we may take it to mean to act toward one another according to the principles of covenant.

We may apply Jesus' command in John 13:34 to our own lives in this way: you are to treat one another according to the principles of covenant faithfulness in the same way that I have treated you with covenant faithfulness. From this point on in the book, we will not be so much dealing with our individual relationship with God, but more with how our relationship with God affects our relationships with one another. I John 4:20 states that we cannot say we love God Whom we cannot see, if we cannot love the people of God whom we can see. We demonstrate to God that we love Him by loving His other children. We exercise God's type of love by putting that love into practice with the people around us.

If our love and relationships are to be an extension and expression of our love for God and His love for us, we must study the Scriptures to see how we go about loving in His manner. Our relationship with God operates on the principle of covenant. We must now find those examples in Scripture that demonstrate the operation of covenant between human beings.

Abraham and Abimelech

In **Genesis 21**, Abraham is making a covenant with a man named Abimelech. An interpersonal covenant is known in the secular world as a contract or contractual agreement. An interpersonal covenant is a type of contractual agreement, but it has a more profound spiritual meaning. A covenant is also wrapped up in a relationship with God.

Abimelech sees that Abraham has been blessed and concludes that God must be with Abraham. **Verse 22:**

Abimelech and Phichol, the commander of his armies, went to Abraham saying, "God is with you in all that you do."

The first principle of godly interpersonal relationships is that we should be drawn toward someone else to the degree that we see that person walking with God. It is God inside the person that attracts us to him. Any interpersonal covenant between believers should be God-directed.

When my wife and I were married, we were attracted to one another because we saw that our first priority was to go forward in God. Our goal together in our marital relationship was to help one another fulfill the callings of God in our lives.

Abimelech then says to Abraham:

Now, therefore, swear to me by God that you will not deal falsely with me, with my offspring, or with my posterity, but according to the kindness that I have done to you, you will do to me and to the land in which you have sojourned (verse 23).

Abimelech is desirous of forming a committed relationship with Abraham. Therefore, he presses Abraham to bring that relationship into a definite verbal commitment and confirm it with an oath. Abimelech urges him to *"swear to me by God."* This phrase in the Hebrew could also be translated "allow yourself to be sworn in."

Dealing Honestly

Abimelech wants Abraham to promise that he "will not deal falsely" with him. This phrase could also be translated as "do not lie to me." One way of breaking covenant is to deceive or to lie. Satan, our accuser, is known as a deceiver and a liar because he is by nature a covenant breaker.

If someone deals truthfully with you, even if the subject matter is painful, you are in no jeopardy of being betrayed. When deception or avoidance or lying enters into the picture, there is danger of covenant breaking.

Paul speaks of *"speaking the truth in love"* **(Ephesians 4:15)**. Speaking the truth is an act of love. Speaking a deceptive word, even if it seems to be positive and flattering, is the opposite of love. The beginning of covenant breaking occurs when one is trusting someone who is false.

The phrase "not deal falsely" can also mean to deal justly, to act with justice, and honesty in regard to our exchanges with other people. The primary term of an interpersonal covenant is that two parties must act uprightly with one another. Their actions must be based on obvious moral principles. The equivalent in the business world would be to charge an honest price for an honest product, to report honestly on the label what is actually in the contents, and to do an honest amount of work for an equivalent compensation. A godly scale is an accurate scale.

Abimelech's covenant contains a commitment to carry the benevolence onto the other's children and grandchildren. A covenant, unlike most contracts, goes on from one generation to the next. This is an indication that covenants are God-based. God lives on through the generations, and the covenant should reflect that continuing faithfulness.

Elements of the Covenant

Four elements of interpersonal covenant are: (1) an attraction to a God-centered direction; (2) the formulating of the covenant into words of an oath; (3) the commitment to deal uprightly and with integrity to one another; (4) the continuance of the covenant to the partners' descendants. We have certainly found within our circle of friends that we feel a corresponding commitment to our covenant partners' children. Our children are close friends with our friends' children. We take turns taking care of one another's children. We have a general commitment to see one another's children growing up in the nurturing of the Lord.

Abraham then agrees that he will swear an oath together with Abimelech. Before the oath is actually taken, however, a significant event occurs.

Then Abraham reproved Abimelech because of a well of water Abimelech's servants had seized (Verse 25).

When there is an item of offense or obstacle to the relationship, either one of the parties is directed to go to the other person to present the problem. He must show the other person where he has been wrong and correct him. This correction is done not for the purpose of showing the other person his faults, but rather for the sake of removing any element that is a barrier to the healthy flow of their relationship.

Abraham brings up a practical matter in which one of Abimelech's servants had been involved. Abimelech says that he did not know that this offense had occurred. Covenantal loyalty is not a question of performing up to a certain standard, but of not betraying the other's confidence. Abimelech's response that he did not know about the situation is sufficient justification for the moment, until he can rectify it.

Once this area of disagreement has been taken care of, they go on to finalize the covenant. Abraham then sets forth a sign of the covenant to make an impression on their memories. He does so by taking seven lambs from his flock and setting them aside. The name of the place, Beersheba, which was named for the sake of the covenant between Abraham and Abimelech, involves a play on words in the Hebrew language. "Beer" means "well of water" but "sheba" can either mean "seven" or "oath." In essence "Beersheba" means "the well of the oath of the seven." The seven ewe lambs are a memory device to recall that they had made an oath at the place of this well.

After the seven lambs are set apart, the two of them come together and exchange promises. This swearing of the oath is the covenant proper. They go away with a sure sense that they will not be betrayed by one another.

Isaac and Abimelech

In Genesis 26:26-31, we find a subsequent renewal of this covenant between Isaac and Abimelech. The same elements of the covenant are there: godly attraction, verbal oath, accountability of integrity, and commitment to the other's descendants. The making of the second covenant is in a way a fulfillment of one of the articles of the first covenant. Abraham and Abimelech had a previous promise to continue faithfulness to the other's offspring.

With the offering of a covenant between Abimelech and Isaac, we have a fulfillment of the term sworn to in the original covenant. Isaac and Abimelech share a covenant communion meal together.

So he made them a feast, and they ate and drank (Genesis 26:30).

This eating and drinking is not an insignificant, mundane matter. It may be seen, rather, as the eating of the flesh of a sacrifice (as in the pascal lamb or in a fellowship offering in the temple). The intimacy implied in breaking bread and in sharing hospitality is covered by the protection of the covenant. The elements of the covenant between Abimelech and Isaac are there to confirm and guarantee what is at bottom a fairly simple matter. The content of the covenant is straightforward: they will deal with integrity and without deception towards one another.

7

INTERPERSONAL COVENANTS
David and Jonathan

Of all the interpersonal covenants in the Bible, the most beautiful and personal was the one between David and Jonathan. Their love for one another serves as an ideal for others who would desire that depth of trust and friendship. Let us look at some of the aspects of their covenant that made it so special.

In **I Samuel 18:1,** Jonathan gets to know David as the young hero who just defeated the giant Goliath. The Scriptures say:

The soul of Jonathan was knit to the soul of David.

Any two believers are of one spirit because of their faith in God. However, there is a special calling when two men sense that their own personal identities and souls are to be knit together as one. There is a complementary and mutual appreciation between them. The souls of two men can be so united in vision and kinship that they can be knit together as one.

Knitting Souls

In **I Samuel 18:1** and **20:17** we read:

Jonathan loved David as his own soul.

Here we see Jonathan's love so committed to David that his own emotions, thoughts and desires had virtually become one with his. My friend Paul Wilbur and I have a David-and-Jonathan type friendship. Once, Paul was given a blessing and prophecy over his life that was very meaningful to him. As I watched and listened, my soul felt united with his in the joy of that moment. We ran up to one another and began to sing and play the guitar and praise the Lord together. What a beautiful experience it was for me to have the same joy in my soul that he was experiencing in his! One of the benefits of a David-and-Jonathan kinship is that moments of victory for one can be enjoyed fully by the other.

In **Romans 12:15** Paul says:

Rejoice with those who rejoice and weep with those who weep.

One's soul can have a desire for the benefit of the other's that is equal to his own. This attitude is a fulfillment of the commandment in **Leviticus 19:18:**

You shall love your neighbor as yourself.

Or in this case, you shall be as committed to the welfare of the other person's soul as you are to your own.

Verbal Guarantee

The beauty of the intimacy between David and Jonathan was such that they were driven to bring their commitment to a verbal formality.

Then Jonathan and David made a covenant because he loved him as his own soul (I Samuel 18:3).

Their love for one another sent forth a desire to express that love. They wanted to have the mutual commitment of the other one confirmed and stated. Their friendship was such that they made a covenant to seal their trust. This covenant is reiterated and reconfirmed several times. In **I Samuel 23:18,** Jonathan reconfirmed his commitment to David just before the two of them were to be separated forever:

The two of them made a covenant before the Lord. David stayed in the woods, and Jonathan went to his own house.

Apparently Jonathan's love and godly intimacy with David was so strong that he wanted to make the covenantal guarantee of their faithfulness even stronger. In **I Samuel 20:17** Jonathan makes David take an oath:

And Jonathan again caused David to vow because he loved him.

This oath is referred to again in **20:42** where Jonathan says to David:

Go in peace since we have both sworn in the name of the Lord.

The covenant itself and the double guarantee of the oath provided for a peace between them. No matter how bad any situation might become, they at least had the reassurance of the other's personal loyalty. One of the benefits of having a covenant commitment with a friend is that each party is able to relax and not suffer a fear that the other one might reject him. The strength of a covenantal bond produces a freedom from anxiety over the future of the relationship.

God-Centered

David and Jonathan's friendship was certainly a God-centered one. Their hearts were in mutual agreement because they were both directed toward the Lord. Theirs was not a humanistic or fraternal covenant between two buddies; it was a God-ordained uniting of two fellow servants of the Lord. **I Samuel 20:23** states:

May the Lord be between you and me forever.

Their covenant was not just between the two of them, but included God as a third party. In my relationship with my wife, our marriage is a triangular relationship in which God is as intimately involved with each one of us as we are with the other. If the Lord is the central party in any covenant, whether friendship or marriage, there is always a source of unity. If the Lord is not part of the relationship, whenever the wills of the two human beings might desire to go in a different direction, there is the potential for division. If both of the two parties are committed to the Lord's will first, there is a source of unity, and there need not be a division of the ways.

What David and Jonathan saw in each other that attracted them was the other's bold and heroic devotion to God. When Jonathan saw David's willingness to do bold faith exploits for the Lord in challenging Goliath, Jonathan was drawn to him. David certainly knew of Jonathan's heroic victories against the Philistines. The only way two men can really enter into a David-and-Jonathan type covenant is when each of them see in the other a whole-hearted desire to pursue God no matter what the risk or obstacle. It is only such a daring and reckless abandon to do the will of God that could incite in another this kind of personal devotion and kinship.

Preferring One Another

I Samuel 18:4 states:

Jonathan took off the robe that was on him.

This robe that he took off and gave to David was not simply an article of clothing; nor was it an expensive piece of cloth alone. His robe was a symbol of his position as the king's son and heir to the throne of Israel. In Jonathan's gesture of taking off his princely robe and giving it to David, we see an expression of Jonathan's willingness to yield up his own worldly position for the sake of his covenant brother.

Jonathan had a great desire to share his possessions and his position with his best friend. This does not seem logical to the selfish mind, but anyone who has had a very close friend knows the pleasure of sharing one's possessions with the other. Even as a child might take a playful glee in trading his toys with a good friend, so is there an adult pleasure in being able to see one's closest companion making use of items that are shared.

Verse 4 concludes that Jonathan:

gave it to David along with his armor even to his sword and his bow and his belt.

The spiritual worth of their friendship exceeded these material belongings to Jonathan. We are aware that when one can give money or provide a meal or donate to a needy friend, one receives a greater share of joy. The more hardpressed one is to give, the more he is likely to receive a personal blessing from that unselfish act of giving.

It is more blessed to give than to receive (Acts 20:35).

In addition to giving these things to David, Jonathan makes a beautiful statement of humility and loyalty. In **I Samuel 23:17**, he says:

You shall be king over Israel and I shall be second unto you.

Here we see the wonderful principle of preferring the other person to oneself.

In honor preferring one another (Romans 12:10).

Jonathan is not only preferring David and yielding to him, but is setting himself to seek to establish David's honor, even though it meant displacing himself in the process. This was a great act of faith on Jonathan's part. Not only was he seeking to establish David's honor in making him king, but he also spoke out before him, saying, "I will be second under you." For a man to come forward and state his submission to another is a step of great courage and humility.

Commitment Leads to Authority

Even with the complete equality of their intimacy and love for each other in covenant, there was a greater authority granted to David in the flow of that relationship. The greater the level of intimacy, the more clear the dynamics of authority within the relationship will become. If a man and a woman were to have a light friendship, it would not be necessary for them to come to agreement about the nature of authority between a husband and a wife. If they are planning to get married and live together in immediacy of environment and cooperation for the rest of their lives, each one must understand how authority works. They must be mutually agreed about the level of order within their relationship.

If we were to have a group of ministers who were relating together lightly for occasional fellowship, there would be no need to establish a flow of leadership and authority within the group. If we were to join ourselves in covenant and commitment to work together on a regular basis for the kingdom of God, we would have to seek the Lord to understand the flow of leadership and authority that God would set up among us.

If one does not allow for authority within covenant relationships, he keeps those relationships at a compromised or more distant level. Often the attitude that, "we must all be equal" in our cooperative authority with one another is an excuse for avoiding the commitment that a deeper level of intimacy would bring. When we join ourselves together in closer covenant, we need the humility and yieldedness to allow God to establish others as authorities in relationship to us. Intimacy demands commitment. Commitment, if it is directed toward the Lord, will eventuate in a flow of leadership to be able to pursue God's purposes.

Jonathan in these passages is revealed to be a great man of covenant. His attitude is similar to that of John the Baptist, who, when he saw Jesus, said:

He must increase but I must decrease (John 3:30).

Neither John nor Jonathan were negating themselves by taking this faith action. By yielding, giving and submitting, they were exercising tremendous strength in their own character.

Loyalty and Accountability

Another aspect of interpersonal covenant is to expect the other partner to demand full moral accountability.

You have brought your servant into a covenant of the Lord with you...if there is iniquity in me, kill me yourself (I Samuel 20:8).

While it is not always necessary in everyday affairs to have one's covenant friend be ready to kill him, the covenant friend is to be responsible to bring to one's attention whatever he has done that is morally wrong. If we have covenant brothers who will hold us accountable, then we are protected from going astray without being warned of the problem. There is a safety in being able to say, "I have surrounding me a group of trusted covenant friends who will surely confront me whenever I fall into error."

The covenant brother is expected to remain loyal, no matter what the circumstances are, as long as his covenant brother has not committed a moral wrong. David is saying that if he has not done wrong, then he should not be turned over to his enemies.

Jonathan responds to David's statement by making it clear that he is looking out to protect him. He says in **I Samuel 20:9:**

If I knew certainly that evil was determined by my father to come upon you, then would I not tell you?

Jonathan's purpose to protect David when he has done no moral wrong is of a higher degree of commitment than familial loyalty.

A covenant brother desires to promote a good reputation and name for his partner.

Now Jonathan spoke well of David to Saul his father (I Samuel 19:4).

Jonathan used every opportunity he could to speak well of David and to promote his reputation even among those who did not like David.

Wherever a covenant brother may go, he will always speak well of his partner. Covenant brothers see the positive reputation of each other's name as a high priority.

Faith Comes First

Jonathan was caught in a dilemma of divided loyalty between Saul and David. David represents the new generation with a covenant based on going forward with God's will. Saul represents the previous move of God, and loyalty to that covenant was based on structure and human expectation.

Jonathan made the wrong choice and stayed with his father. Covenants must be based on staying in God's will. To demand covenant loyalty on previous structure as opposed to moving forward with God's will is a tragic mistake. Jonathan missed God's will, and it cost him his life.

Many young ministers are faced with a similar dilemma. Those with a "Saul" spirit will sometimes react against a fresh move of God and demand submission out of envy and insecurity. The Jonathans of today should not submit to those carnal demands but move forward with the leading of the Holy Spirit.

8

FRIENDSHIP:
THE DEVELOPMENT OF TRUST

Perhaps you desire a friendship as close as that between David and Jonathan. The Bible guides us not to keep ourselves alone and separate from others. On the other hand we are not to pour out our trust and intimacy upon the ground only to have it trampled upon. Jesus said:

Do not throw your pearls to swine, lest they trample them under their feet, and turn and tear you in pieces (Matthew 7:6).

The pearl of your life should not be trusted into the hands of an unfaithful person.

Perhaps you fear to enter into such a close relationship. "What if the person rejects me? What if the person betrays me? How will I know that I will not get hurt?" you may be asking yourself. With close friendship comes intimacy, and with intimacy comes vulnerability. Vulnerability is the possibility of getting hurt. The principle of developing a close friendship is to groom oneself and the other person to be trustworthy not to hurt one another.

Trust Versus Love

If one does want close friendship and intimacy, he must develop the character of trustworthiness so that the potential of being hurt does not come to pass. A startling statement is made about Jesus in **John 2:24-25:**

But Jesus did not commit himself to them because He knew all men, and had no need that anyone should testify of man, for He knew what was in man.

The word "commit" here might also be translated as "entrust." Jesus did not entrust Himself into the hands of all men. He did not trust just anyone. He did not do so because He knew that most people were untrustworthy. He wanted to entrust Himself into everyone's hands, but He knew He could not. He would have entrusted Himself to anyone who was trustworthy, but He could not find anyone to receive such trust.

Jesus, having seen there was no one to whom He could entrust himself, chose a number of people who at least had the potential to be trustworthy. He spent His time training them to get them to the point of being able to receive His trust. Not only would Jesus have been willing to entrust Himself to anyone who was trust-worthy, but He was willing to train anyone who even had the potential or willingness to be made trustworthy. The whole method and goal of discipleship is to take someone who has the potential of being a trustworthy friend and developing him to that point of trusted friendship.

God so loved the world that He gave His only begotten Son (John 3:16).

How is it that God could love the whole world? He loved every person in the world. How can this be if the Scriptures just said that Jesus did not entrust Himself into the hands of men? There is a difference between loving someone and entrusting oneself to him.

The essence of love is to give. I can give something to someone; I can even give myself to that person to a certain extent. I can help him and minister to him. However, I do not risk through vulnerability destroying the potential to continue loving others by opening my inner self to someone who is not trustworthy.

Blocking Fiery Darts

I can love and help someone who is antagonistic, treacherous or untrustworthy, but I must do so while wearing spiritual armor:

Above all taking the shield of faith with which you will be able to quench all of the fiery darts of the wicked one (Ephesians 6:16).

This shield of faith is a spiritual shield that protects us from the attack of evil spirits and from the attack of negative thoughts.

The shield of faith is also to protect us from negative and nasty words which are spoken at us by other people. The person who may have spoken something nasty is not the wicked one, but at the moment he was yielding his tongue to such a negativity, he allowed the fiery darts of the devil to come through him. The primary way that fiery darts attack us from the enemy is through the spoken or written words of other people. Demonic verbal attacks use the human tongue as a vehicle.

If the other person who says something nasty has come within one's inner sphere of vulnerability, that fiery dart may stab right to the heart. It will hinder one from going on to love others. We are called to love everyone. To the degree that the other person is trustworthy, we take him into our trust. To the degree that people are untrustworthy, we continue to love them just the same; but we do so with the shield of faith firmly in place to protect us from any negative words.

No Coarse Joking

The fiery darts of the devil are primarily spoken at us through other people:

Like a madman who throws firebrands, arrows and death, is the man who deceives his neighbor and says, "I was only joking" (Proverbs 26:18-19).

The fiery arrows come through a fellow human being. The fiery darts of a neighbor often come through the mode of joking. What makes most jokes funny is that they are causing pain at the expense of another person. This is not true every time, but in most situations it is so. One definition of laughter is a feeling of intense relief from something that would have been very painful. When one watches a slapstick comedy routine in which the comedian is slipping and falling and hurting himself, it strikes one as being so funny. Why is it irresistible not to laugh when someone walking outside on an icy day slips and falls down? Laughter often involves the pain of someone.

Those who are going into ministry, or have positions where many other people's feelings are hanging onto their words, should avoid all coarse joking (Ephesians 5:4). Sometimes this can be misunderstood as not having a sense of humor. However, there is a difference between good humor and joking. When one makes a joke very lightly at another person's expense, everyone may laugh and say, "Don't worry, we were only kidding." The person who was the object of the joke goes away not only hurt but will have a difficult time removing the negative thought from his memory.

Another verse about the darts of the devil through the words of another human being is **Proverbs 25:18:**

A man who bears false witness against his neighbor is like a club, a sword and a sharp arrow.

Again it is through the untrustworthy words of a fellow human being that we can be attacked as if by a sharpened arrow. **Proverbs 25:19** continues:

Confidence in an unfaithful man in a time of trouble is like a bad tooth and a foot out of joint.

God does not call us to deliver our personal trust into the hands of someone who is unfaithful and untrustworthy.

Biblical Definition of a Friend

At the beginning of Jesus' ministry he took the attitude that He could not entrust Himself into the hands of men because they were untrustworthy. At the very end of His ministry, however, He makes this statement to His disciples:

Greater love has no one than this, than to lay down one's life for his friends. You are My friends if you do whatever I command you. No longer do I call you servants, for a servant does not know what his master is doing; but I have called you friends for all things that I have heard from My Father I have made known to you (John 15:13-15).

Here we have a summary of the final results of the years of Jesus' ministry and discipleship with the twelve. That process of discipleship was done by taking a group of people who were untrustworthy but had the potential of becoming trustworthy, putting them through a training period to develop trust, and ending up with a group of people who were trustworthy. They went through the three stages, from potential to training to friendship.

The biblical meaning of the word "friend" is much deeper than our modern usage. We should replace the word "friend" in our minds with the word "covenant friend" or" covenant companion" or "faithful partner." In verse 14, Jesus indicates that these disciples have become His covenant partners because He has trained them to do whatever He commands them. In verse 15, Jesus says that He did not always consider or call the disciples His friends. At first they were strangers; then they were servants; finally, through the process of training and discipleship, they became His friends. One must go through a process before earning the position of trusted friend. That process of trust building is new-covenant discipleship.

God refers to *"Abraham My friend"* in II Chronicles 20:7, Isaiah 41:8, and James 2:23. We must realize here once again the depth of covenantal commitment that is involved in the word friend. What might be said is, "Here is Abraham, My covenant trusted friend." This covenant friendship between God and Abraham was demonstrated in Genesis 18 when God shared with Abraham the fact that He was preparing to destroy Sodom and Gomorrah. Abraham had the right to enter into deliberation about the judgment. Abraham was a friend to God through proven character and faithfulness to the covenant.

Fathers, Friends and Disciples

The process of discipleship for Jesus was to bring this group of men to the place of trusted friendship. This is the model I personally go by in my attitude toward fathering my own children. I see fathering as a type of discipleship, and discipleship as grooming someone to be your close friend. When I look at my young children, I have a great love for them. Certainly while they are very small, they are in no position for me to be able to entrust my own life to them; that would be foolish.

I demonstrate love toward my children even though I do not entrust myself into their hands. I demonstrate my love toward them because as an act of faith I see the invisible potential in them to become my best friends. This has helped me a great deal in my own attitudes toward love and fathering. My purpose in training my children is not to get them merely to obey me whenever I tell them to do something. I train them to obey me so that I can bring them to the point of being my best friends. Whenever I am with my children, I visualize them in the future as adults being my closest and most trusted companions.

Keeping the goal of friendship in mind will help us in parenting not to become legalistic. I am not training a robot, I am grooming a friend. This goal will also help avoid becoming legalistic or project oriented in the process of discipleship. We should always look at new disciples as potentially close companions for the future. We are grooming them for the purpose of fellowship and relationship. This has the side benefit of making the whole process of discipleship much more enjoyable.

An act of discipling or discipline becomes an act of love, reaching out to draw the person closer into relationship. We correct a disciple's bad habit or weak area, not for correction's sake, but because it represents a stumbling block to our being able to grow closer in friendship. We are not pushing someone away, but are extending ourselves in humility in the hopes of drawing closer together.

What a different spirit this will generate into the works of the ministry! *"Speak the truth in love"* (Ephesians 4:15). A truth, even if a difficult word of correction, will be more readily received when spoken under the motive of love and for the purpose of drawing a person closer in relationship.

Training to Be Trustworthy

The model of discipleship is that of building faithfulness into a group of friends.

Things you have heard from me among many witnesses, commit these to faithful men who will be able to teach others also (II Timothy 2:2).

The process of discipleship is getting these men to be faithful. The first step of discipleship is to discern which men have the potential to be faithful. The second step is to choose them to be trained. There are four generations of disciples in II Timothy 2:2: Paul, then Timothy, then the faithful men, then the other faithful men. If discipleship is not seen as developing faithful friendship, it will become a production-line mechanism devoid of intimacy. Paul had an intimate, trusting friendship with Timothy. He was calling Timothy to reproduce that same kind of companionship with the future disciples.

In II Timothy 2:2, the things that are being committed to these faithful men are words: *"the things that you have heard from me."* The process of discipleship involves speaking to the new men. We train men to be faithful, sharing with them words of truth and watching how they react to these words. What someone does with a message of intimacy clearly reflects the degree of his faithfulness. Growth in discipleship enables one to share increasingly more intimate words of truth with the companion.

Secret Revelations

Jesus teaches about the use of parables for discipleship in **Matthew 13:10-13:**

And the disciples came and said to Him, "Why do you speak to them in parables?" He answered and said to them, "Because it has been given to you to know the mysteries of the kingdom of heaven, but to them it has not been given. For whoever has, to him more will be given, and he will have abundance; but whoever does not have, even what he has will be taken away from him. Therefore, I speak to them in parables, because seeing they do not see, and hearing they do not hear, nor do they understand."

The disciples noticed that Jesus spoke in a different way to them than He did to those outside the inner group. Apparently He was more candid and frank with His own disciples. Noticing this distinction and realizing that it had some significance in the process of disciple-making, His followers asked why He did so.

Jesus told them that, as His chosen group, they were granted to know the mysteries of the kingdom. These men, having earned a certain level of trust, were now being allowed by Jesus to know some more intimate aspects of revelation.

Jesus says that to a person who has, more will be given. He is describing the communication of increasing levels of intimate revelation according to one's response at handling previous revelation. He is saying that to those with whom He has shared more intimate truths about Himself, and who have proven themselves trustworthy with those intimate words, He will share even more. If Jesus shares an intimate truth with a person, and that person betrays Him, he will not be given further levels of intimate truth. The unreliable person will even be removed from his previous level of trust. Not only the process of discipleship, but also the teachings of Jesus, may be seen as gradations of developing trust.

The granting of spiritual revelation is also a matter of trust.

I speak to them in parables because seeing they do not see and hearing they do not hear, nor do they understand (Matthew 13:13).

As we are faithful to God, our spiritual eyes are opened to more and more revelation. If we are not being faithful, our minds may continue to fill up with certain seeming truths about scripture, but they will be only of a superficial nature. If we are not trustworthy, our spiritual eyes will be blinded to the inner meaning of the Word.

The revelation of God through the Scriptures is written on more than one level of meaning. If someone's heart is hard, he can read the same words but miss the deeper revelation. The greater revelations of Scripture are the ones that reveal more of the intimacy of God and Jesus. It takes intimacy and trust to grasp the revelations of intimacy.

Paul says in **I Corinthians 4:1-2:**

Let a man so consider us, as servants of Christ, the stewards of the mysteries of God. Moreover, it is required in stewards that one be found faithful.

Paul feels privileged to have received great revelations from God. He says that in order to receive mysteries and secrets, one must prove himself faithful in character. True revelations from God are preceded by a corresponding trustworthiness.

In **John 16:12** Jesus says:

I still have many things to say to you, but you can not bear them now.

Jesus did not mean that they were not smart enough nor courageous enough, but that they still had much yet to learn of trust and intimacy. When we so open our hearts to God's in our own vulnerability, His very Spirit comes to dwell in us. Intimacy and revelation come together in completion with the indwelling of God's Spirit in ours. Jesus' answer to the challenge He gave the disciples was to say:

However when He the Spirit of truth, has come, He will guide you into all truth (verse 13).

When the Spirit of truth comes, He takes up residence in that most intimate of places, heart to heart. God's Spirit mingles with our spirit. As a husband and wife mingle themselves into one, so do we become one with God in perfect intimacy. Discipleship is a process of developing trusted friendship. The teaching of Scriptures and the yielding to revelation from God depend on trustworthiness to receive new intimacy.

There is a difference between being friendly and being trustworthy. What the world calls being friendly is often soulish or carnal socializing and the outward appearance of friendship. The difference between socializing and true covenantal friendship is what the Scripture refers to in **Proverbs 18:24:**

A man who has many friends must show himself to be friendly, but there is a friend who sticks closer than a brother.

The showing forth of the outward appearance of friendship is not the same thing as being a real friend. We should use discernment to see who will be a consistent companion over time. Discernment will see through mere socializing.

In a fellowship of believers there is sometimes a person who seems to be the "life of the party." The subtle entrance of a partying spirit in the guise of fellowship can be dangerous. Such a person can draw toward himself a great circle of friends; he can be a dynamic force for socializing within the community. One indication of this false type of friend is that he will come to life during the lighter period of fellowship but may be somewhat deflated or distracted in moments of intense worship or devotion.

The danger of this type of person to the fellowship is that he may gather around him a circle of loyalty in the flesh. Should he become offended at something that goes on in the congregation, he may cause a division that will tear up many young plants. The opposite of appearing to be friendly is sticking closer than even a physical brother. True covenant friendship does not try to make a show of sociability to wide numbers of people. It is more concerned with being committed and faithful to those whom God has placed in relationship. A few friends out of many will stay close and loyal for the longer period of time.

There is a difference between intimacy and socializing. There is a difference between friendship and fraternizing. I am an intimate and trusting person. I was blessed to have parents who were affectionate and intimate with me. My closer friends know that I am committed to our friendship. They are allowed to approach the most intimate parts of my life. On the other hand, I do not always come across as a person who generates a lot of socializing and light mixing. My preference for committed friendship tends to steer me away from any superficiality or social maneuvering.

Proverbs 16:29-30 describes as a dangerous man, one who brings carnal elements to covenant fellowship. The verses speak of a violent man, but can apply to one who manipulates social situations.

A violent man [or carnal socializer] entices his neighbor and leads him in a way that is not good. He winks his eye to devise perverse things; he purges his lips and brings about evil.

People with a partying spirit may be quick to pat you on the back with a "hail fellow," or quick to wink their eye in some secretive joke. They may draw people away to a direction that is not good. Discernment of spirit is important for the promoting of healthy and sincere fellowship among believers. This discernment about worldly socializing will prevent future divisions.

Paul, in his letters to Titus, urges him to train his disciples to be sober in their attitude. **Titus 2:2** urges:

that the older men be sober, reverent, temperate.

Verse 3 encourages:

the older women likewise, that they be reverent in their behavior.

Verse 5 urges the younger women to:

be discreet and chaste.

Verse 6 directs Titus to:

likewise exhort the young men to be soberminded.

These verses promote sincere friendship and discourage counterfeit socializing. They are an expression of loving discipleship. These wholesome exhortations should not be mistakenly interpreted that God is against fun and enjoyment of life. There is a difference between a joyous spirit and a partying spirit. One can be sober and yet quite joyful. One can have partying enthusiasm and yet lack true joy on the inside. We should avoid being hurt by the wrong kind of people during our quest to develop deeper, trusted friendships.

9

DISCIPLESHIP: GROOMING FRIENDSHIP

Discipleship is the grooming of friends who can be trusted. The training is a series of experiments in which a disciple is given ever-increasing areas of trust in which to respond. If one is faithful in a certain sphere, he can be given the next stage. If one is faithful with little, he is likely to be faithful with much. A potential future leader should be given first a small area of responsibility to steward.

Stages of Responsibility

One is given an area of responsibility which serves as a trial run for the next area of greater responsibility. That area in turn serves as a trial run for the next. Jesus taught on this increasing stewardship in the parable of the ten talents.

Well done good servant. Because you were faithful in a very little, have authority over ten cities (Luke 19:17).

The same statement is quoted with a slightly different emphasis in **Matthew 25:23:**

Well done good and faithful servant. You were faithful over a few things; I will make you ruler over many things. Enter into the joy of your lord.

One proceeds from smaller to larger. Each task represents a test for the next stage. The type of responsibility varies in quality through the process.

Notice the use of the word "servant" in these passages. In John 15:15, Jesus said that He used to call His disciples servants, but they had passed out of that stage and entered the stage of being His covenant friends. In the parable of the ten talents, Jesus says, *"Well done, My faithful servant. Enter now into the joy of the lord."* The meaning of the two passages is to say, "Well done, you who have proven yourself to be faithful during your stage of doing service activity. Come now and enter into the better stage of our joy and relationship together. You will receive a wider scope of service, responsibility and authority."

A change in type of responsibility is given. The first area is one of service in objects, money and practicalities. The later stage is one dealing more with authority, people, governance and teaching. One is first a servant with objects. Then he may be granted governance with people. Here the people are described as a city, which could be parallel to a home group or a pastorate in the ministries today. Some people have the godly calling to work with the practicalities more than with counseling or teaching. They can also continue to grow in authority and intimacy in their sphere of anointing. There is unlimited possibility for growth in either direction.

Discerning in Whom to Invest

In working with a new group of people, to discern who will emerge as the more trustworthy stewards, it is appropriate to assign small tasks of practical service to all involved in somewhat equal fashion. The way the different members of the group respond to assigned chores will be one indicator as to their motivation. Being helpful in service will show their likelihood to be faithful in teaching.

A pastor needs to be able to discern where to invest his time. Many people in the group may desire to have personal time with the pastor. If one starts the pattern that small areas of service are made available to all members right from the beginning, it will become evident which members are seeking counseling for wrong reasons. Some want to go in the downward cycle of self-pity, less responsibility, and more counsel. If a person responds constructively to a simple task of service, it is likely that when he seeks pastoral counsel, he is doing it out of the right motivation. He will use that counsel for the purpose of productivity and improvement, rather than wallowing in attention getting. He will not be energy draining on the pastor. Setting the tone of positive, constructive service keeps everyone moving in the right direction. It makes the counsel of the pastor to all the members more effective and fruit producing.

This gradation of responsibility serves as a protection that an emerging leader will respond to authority over people in the right motivation. If a person who does not want to help out in practical service sees himself as governing others, he has a wrong motivation. Authority over others is an extension of the same motivation to be helpful in practical service.

If one is counseling another person with the goal of helping him, the experience is similar to that of doing a chore. Casting out demons and counseling personal problems can be similar to taking out the trash and cleaning a toilet bowl. If a person sees himself as a counselor over others, but not a helpful servant in practical chores, his counseling has become a way of flattering himself. His pride is being reinforced by the submission of the counselee. He has lost the primary motive of helping the other.

Laying On of Hands

Paul wrote to Timothy saying:

Do not lay hands on anyone hastily (I Timothy 5:22).

The laying on of hands here can be seen as ordaining someone into his next wider scope of responsibility and authority. If the laying on of hands is done prematurely, it will create problems in the exercise of authority.

The laying on of hands represents the setting in of a faithful servant to the next stage of responsibility. The laying on of hands should therefore only be done at the end of a successfully completed period of practical service. It is that period of practical service which guarantees right attitudes for the person as he is sent into the next level of authority. It is the training of practical service which will help him to approach people's needs with the same motivation of constructive helpfulness. It will help the new leader not to be tempted by flattery and pride in giving direction and advice.

If the person has not been prepared to avoid the subtlest temptation of the devil to puff up his pride, he will be subject to the *"snare of the devil"* (I Timothy 3:7). If the laying on of hands comes prematurely, the very ordination of increased authority that was meant to be a blessing to him may become a stumbling block and a source of problems. It would have been better if he had not received the ordination at all.

Intimacy and Confidentiality

The first pattern of discipleship is to engage the potential covenant partner in areas of practical service. The second area is to see how the covenant partner will respond when words of intimacy are shared with him.

There is no better test of faithfulness than to share with someone an intimate bit of information. If that person runs to tell everyone he knows, he is probably not the best candidate for further trust. If, on the other hand, he is able to maintain confidentiality, one's trust in him is likely to increase rapidly.

We have all experienced the temptation of having had a close friend share something that is intimate and confidential. Immediately, something inside of us wants to broadcast that information through every available channel. It is worth the effort to exercise control over that temptation to maintain the confidentiality of a friend counselee.

When someone has shared something confidential, it should not be told to anyone. Afterwards, when the person discovers the news has not been shared, he may be surprised. After the surprise wears off, trust will immediately be engendered. "You mean you really didn't tell anybody?" is the usual response. We can then say, "Well, you asked me not to." Their response then becomes, "That's right, I did." When others realize that we intend to keep our word and keep matters of confidentiality, there spreads an assurance of trust and covenant keeping.

Paul said, in II Timothy 2:2, that Timothy was to find friends who were faithful and trustworthy to receive and keep the words that he was going to share with them. In Matthew 13, Jesus told His disciples that He could not reveal to all the masses but only to the circle of His more trusted friends the secret meanings to the parables. The ability to keep a shared word is similar to the ability to keep a covenant. To the degree in which one has strength to hold in confidentiality a secret is the same degree in which one will have strength not to break a covenant directive. It requires the same strength to hold a word inwardly as it does to perform the word outwardly.

Guiding the manner in which a person responds to words is the primary method of developing faithfulness of character. Samson was a great man of strength and covenant faith. His strength to destroy the Philistines physically and to keep his covenant promise to God was exactly equivalent to the amount of strength he had not to divulge his secret to Delilah. Using the words of Samson to Delilah to test her character, we see she flunks the test. No sooner were the intimate words of confidentiality and vulnerability out of his mouth than she was plotting to reveal them to his enemies, receive a financial reward for her betrayal, and gloat at the destruction of her potential covenant lover. But it was also Samson who failed the test to the degree that he was not able to resist her nagging to reveal his secret. His strength to resist her nagging was the same as his strength to conquer personal temptation and was the same as his strength to act on the covenant with heroic deeds of faith.

In the previous episode in Samson's life, where he had killed many Philistines, he justified his actions by saying that the Philistines had discovered his riddle about the honey in the lion by violating his confidentiality with his betrothed wife. The modern mind might say that it was unreasonable to go about killing people for having lost a riddle, but to Samson's perspective, he was completely justified in killing these men who had broken covenant confidentiality with him. They had proven themselves to be unfaithful, untrustworthy, and thereby worthy of death.

Receiving Instruction

The ability to respond appropriately to words that are shared is the primary area of character development to prepare oneself for faithfulness to covenant friendship. The Proverbs spend much time instructing us about our lips and our tongue and how our words affect our relationships with other people. The book of Proverbs should be meditated on over and over again by anyone seeking to grow in covenant character. It has divine guidelines on how we are to relate to one another.

Let us look at a few examples to set a pattern as to how the book of Proverbs may be used. Here is a sample of proverbs about the trustworthiness of a friend. **Proverbs 1:8, 2:1, 3:1, 4:1, 4:20, 6:20,** and **7:1** all share the same concept that a son should keep the words of his father:

> **My son, hear the instruction of your father and do not forsake the law of your mother... My son, if you receive my words and treasure my commands within you... My children, hear the instruction of a father.**

The way to grow in character is to receive wisdom. The way to receive wisdom is to keep the words of one's parents or one's parent-figures. As the principal of a covenant high school, I have had many opportunities to analyze the motivations of teen-agers. One excellent method is to gather the adolescents together, speak sincerely to their hearts with words of wisdom and correction, and then allow them freedom within limitations to make choices. They will follow those words of wisdom or reject them. Within that sphere of freedom to choose, one can observe how the adolescents react to the words of direction. Some will be foolish and miss the point. Some will perform the absolute minimum required by the letter of the words. Some will rebel and break the instruction. Others will seek to understand what was said and fulfill the heart of the wisdom contained in the words.

It is the struggle with the words of instruction, to digest the spirit of what was intended, which demonstrates a high level of motivation and character. When a young person can be seen meditating on the words and seeking to fulfill them, as he grows into adulthood he will be a likely candidate for a trustworthy covenant friend. The reaction to words of instruction is the test of character.

The Bible describes nobility of character in the example of the people in Berea by their willingness to go through the inner struggle of meditation and study about the words that were shared with them by Paul:

These were more noble than those in Thessalonica, in that they received the word with all readiness and searched the Scriptures daily to find out whether these things were so (Acts 17:11).

Receiving words of instruction too easily from any new source may indicate a gullibility and lack of conviction on the part of the listener. A response of irritation to words of direction would indicate a heart of rebellion or stubbornness. A reaction of investigation with the commitment to come to an agreement on what is right reflects the heart of one who has a willing spirit. He will stand by his individual convictions in the face of difficulty once they are made. The wisdom to receive words of instruction indicates character potential inside the person.

No Gossip

We find in **Proverbs 11:13** this statement:

A talebearer reveals secrets, but he who is of a faithful spirit conceals the matter.

One "who is of a faithful spirit" or a trustworthy character has the ability to hold inside himself words shared in the confidentiality of friendship. A talebearer represents the opposite type of character from that of covenant faithfulness. To the degree that one will reveal secrets is the degree to which one is unable to be a covenant keeper.

In a similar vein, **Proverbs 17:9** states:

He who covers a transgression seeks love, but he that repeats a matter separates best of friends.

If a person will maintain a word shared with him, he keeps covenant. A person can go beyond that and actually seek to cover the weak points of another person. He is, to that extent, seeking to create covenant love and establish trust. Not only is one who spreads gossip unable to maintain covenant, but he may also cause a division between other people who were standing in covenant friendship.

Good Report

One important community concept is to maintain a good report and not to spread a bad report. All the members of a group should agree to protect the positive reputation of the other members of the group. They should be committed not to spread a false rumor. They should also be committed that when something negative happens, even if it is to some measure true, not to go around broadcasting the fact. Bad news and gossip can take care of itself in getting spread around and finding enough ears to be heard. The members of a group should agree not to be party to the further spreading and thereby aggravating of an already difficult situation. This is called a covenant of good report.

Spiritual Murder

If there is to be positive covenant within a group, all negative gossip must be purged out. From a scriptural viewpoint, words are extremely powerful. The old adage that "sticks and stones can break my bones, but words can never hurt me" is not necessarily true. In the world, words are the most powerful things that exist. To say something negative about someone else is to have broken covenant with him and even to have spiritually murdered him.

Jesus applies the commandment not to murder to mean not to say negative or mocking words of someone else.

You have heard that it was said to those of old, "you shall not murder," and whoever murders will be in danger of the judgment. But I say to you that whoever is angry with his brother without a cause shall be in danger of the judgment. And whoever says to his brother "Raca!" [or empty-headed] shall be in danger of the council. Whoever says, "You fool!" shall be in danger of hellfire (Matthew 5:21-22).

The command of the Law says, *"Thou shalt not murder."* Jesus turns to His followers and says, "This means for you that you are not to speak mocking words at one another." We try to train our children at an early age that they are not to use a sing-song, teasing voice or to direct mocking words at one another. Considering the spiritual power of words, any sense of covenant must firmly establish that negative words are not to be said about one another.

Ecclesiastes 10:20 gives this recommendation:

Do not curse the king even in your thought; do not curse the rich even in your bedroom; for a bird of the air may carry your voice, and a bird in flight may tell the matter.

In World War II, the naval expression had it that "loose lips sink ships." The idea is somewhat the same. I once joked with a staff member about a person we had not seen in months. My office door was locked, no one was around, and all was quiet. As I opened the door to leave, the person about whom we had joked was standing in the doorway. The odds were one in a million against such a coincidence. I was shocked, embarrassed, and convicted of my sin. I made a commitment never to speak negatively about anyone behind his back, no matter how sure it seemed that no one was listening. A bird might have heard. Our words must have a sovereign integrity that does not depend on circumstance.

Power Words

Mark 11:23 states that if one:

believes that those things he says will come to pass, he will have whatever he says.

Supernatural power can be released through the Spirit when we know that every single word that comes out of our mouth is backed by absolute covenantal integrity.

As we are trained in our relationships with one another to exercise integrity in our words, our words will then reach a new dimension of power release in the Lord. As we are faithful to train our tongues not to violate covenant in our interpersonal relationships, God will then release through our tongues the power of faith. Faith, even faith for miracles, comes through our ability not to betray the spiritual covenant that we have with God. When we are faithful in the little words of everyday life, God will grant us the greater power of faith in the larger words of spiritual authority.

"Faith works through love," says Galatians 5:6. Faith power works through covenantal love. The charismatic faith-power of God works through us when we are loyal to character and covenant in our relationships with others.

10

CHARISMA VERSUS CHARACTER

The believer lives in a steady state of wholesome tension between character and charisma. By charisma here, I mean all of the aspects of the revealed power of God and faith confession; by character, I mean the whole realm of integrity and mature personality of godliness that is developed in each person. Charisma, for instance, would include the release of all the gifts of the Spirit, whereas character would include the growth of all the fruits of the Spirit.

Most people tend to emphasize one side or the other. They are usually more charisma-oriented or character-oriented. Whichever side one is on, he tends to be biased toward that side and to lean away from the other. Both sides are fully necessary without exception. It is the healthy state of a believer to find himself pulled in both directions. This is not double-mindedness, but rather the paradox of being a new-creation person living on this earth with other people.

The Two Pulls

Paul experienced this sense of this dual pressure when he said in **Philippians 1:21-25:**

For to me, to live is Christ, and to die is gain. But if I live on in the flesh, this will mean fruit from my labor; yet what I shall choose I cannot tell. For I am hard pressed between the two, having a desire to depart and be with Christ, which is far better. Nevertheless to remain is needful for you. And being confident of this, I know I shall remain and continue with you all for your progress and joy of faith.

The pull toward charisma flows out of the love of God. It is the spiritual desire to be with God and experience His Spirit and all of His manifestations. The pull toward character, on the other hand, stems out of a desire to love one another as we are commanded to do. Character would see love of God without a demonstration of that love toward others to be invalid.

It is necessary for every believer to develop fully both of the aspects of charisma and character in his life. Each one should examine himself to see which area he is lacking and move to see that any deficit is fully restored.

We Must Have Both

Paul said that he was pressed toward being with God in the spirit and he was pressed toward acting in this life while in his body to love and help others. This is the way it should be. We are commanded to love God and to love our neighbor; he experienced both. A person who is more charisma oriented may make excuses for not developing character in his life. He might justify some area of personal irresponsibility by pointing to the grace of God. He might feel that to develop character is worldly, soulish, or humanistic.

The person, on the other hand, who is character oriented may point out that faith without love and without works is void. He may have a subtle feeling that people who walk in the charismatic gifts all of the time are flighty and undependable. He may then begin to doubt whether these gifts are valid, and even see some of the life of the Spirit as phony. When urged to release more charismatic power, he may answer that he has known people who walked in the gifts of the Spirit who were insincere.

We need to have both areas fully developed in our lives. If one walks in the charisma of God without integrity, he is a phony and a loud-sounding cymbal. If he continues to seek supernatural experience without the guidelines of moral character, he can be soon led off into false prophecy and self-deception. If a man were to grow in the principles of faith for prosperity but not also have ingrained in him the principles of ethical spending and accountability, he may find himself easy prey for the devil to be led into the deception of spending money on his own lusts and luxuries.

Character Alone Falls Short

On the other hand, if a man says he is developing character because it is more important than charisma, his character may not be filled with the life and love of God. He may say love is more important than faith, but the love of neighbor stems out of the love of God, which comes first.

If one truly is developed in character, he will be brought more and more to an awareness of his absolute inability to do anything outside of the full spiritual power of God. His very character and integrity will lead him to see his own need for more than just character. If his character is truly genuine, it will catapult him into the life of charisma. If one pleads his case always for character to the avoidance of charisma, that character is either not genuine or it has not been developed to its full extent. True character must cross the line into depending on the miraculous power of God.

This is one aspect of what Jesus meant when He said to Nicodemus:

That which is born of the flesh is flesh, and that which is born of the Spirit is spirit. Do not marvel that I say to you, "You must be born again." The wind blows where it wishes, and you hear the sound of it; but you cannot tell where it comes from, and where it goes. So it is with everyone who is born of the Spirit (John 3:6-8).

Jesus is talking to a highly educated and disciplined man of nobility, stature, and standing. Nicodemus was strong in his knowledge of Scripture and well-developed in his own integrity. Jesus in effect tells him that even his relatively well-developed moral character will fall short of its goal. There must come a time when he crosses the line into the miraculous realm of God's Spirit; he *"must be born again."*

Jesus is saying that what one develops out of his own character is simply that—his own character. The development of the character of God involves the gracious intervention of the Spirit of God. The renewed, godly character continues to draw the person even more into the realm of the Spirit. Jesus said that the workings of the Spirit do not stay within the bounds of what human logic and natural character can grasp. The Spirit is more like the wind which one may perceive how it is moving, but the way in which it blows is beyond one's ability to comprehend.

Charisma without character is void, insincere, and deceptive. Character without charisma is lifeless, vain, and falls short of the true character of God. Charisma without character is illegitimate. Character without charisma is not sourced by the Spirit of God. Charisma without character is not really charisma at all but a counterfeit of it. Character without charisma is not true character at all but a form of humanism.

By charisma, we are referring to all of the revelation of the dunamis power of God. Character includes all of the disciplines of a person committed to God. Charisma would involve the gift of the word of wisdom while character would involve receiving wisdom and counsel. Charisma would include the gift of the word of knowledge, while character would include studying to show oneself approved in the knowledge of God's Word. Charisma includes the revelation that we have become the righteousness of God. Character includes acting in righteousness and honesty toward others.

Character Demands Charisma

While the purpose of this book is to emphasize the development of covenant character in the believer, these qualities must be seen in the context of full conjunction with the power of the Spirit of God.

Let me give as an example how I came to use the gift of speaking in tongues. At the time, I had several obstacles keeping me from releasing this gift of the Spirit. I was attending a church which, although it was evangelical and Bible-believing, was not encouraging the gifts of the Spirit. I had no teaching to go in that direction. Secondly, my own academic background was one which contained training in linguistics. This area of analytical skill in my life was tending to make me critical of something that seemed so irrational. Thirdly, I had been introduced to a few counterfeit charismatics who had given me a bad impression. Even with these obstacles, it was clear to me from a reading of Scriptures that the gift of tongues was described in the Gospels, in Acts, and in the Epistles.

Here is how character led me to charisma. I had at that time a disciplined Bible study which led me to see speaking in tongues in the Scriptures. Secondly, I had a commitment to a daily time of prayer intercession which opened an opportunity for the gift of tongues to be manifest. The primary covenantal characteristic, however, which led me to speaking in tongues was my love and loyalty for my parents. I had been spending an extended period of time in fasting and prayer for my parents' salvation. It was during this period of intercession that there grew up within me a desire to pray for them on a deeper level.

A covenantal command of Scripture led me to honor and love my parents. The character of love and commitment led me to pray for them. It was the discipline of continued intercession that awakened in me a desire for additional spiritual power in my prayer life. Out of sincerity to see them come to salvation, there arose within me an urgency that was more than words could express.

This desire led to a groaning in prayer for their salvation from within my spirit (Romans 8:26). This groaning led to emitting syllables which were articulate, but which my rational mind had no ability to interpret. Although my intellectual pride fought releasing this form of speech for quite a while, commitment toward my parents and the integrity of my desire for them to be saved broke through these barriers, allowing for the gift of tongues to flow through me.

True Charisma Produces Fruit of Character

When I had experienced God's miraculous grace to be speaking in tongues, I was then led in response to a more redoubled effort to improve my character, discipline and Bible study to match this new-found reality. After character produces charisma, charisma will, in turn, produce an even greater etching of character into a person's life. This is how it should be.

A tree with good roots will produce good fruit. A tree with good fruit must have good roots. True charisma will always demand more character, and true character will always produce charisma. Character that does not bear the fruit of charisma is really not character at all. Charisma that is not grown out of the roots of character is really not charisma at all.

Daniel's Example

Both of these elements are demonstrated in the life of the prophet Daniel. He was a man of sterling character. He was able to exercise discipline in his own eating habits. He successfully applied himself to the tasks of his academic training. He developed a disciplined prayer life in which he would pray three times a day on a regularly scheduled basis. He searched the Scriptures and meditated on them in detail to the point of recognizing specific promises to be fulfilled from the prophecies of Jeremiah. He held a highly placed job and bore much worldly responsibility. He was trained in the skills of administration, law, and government.

Daniel was a man in whom even his enemies, after much careful searching, could not find even one speck of moral impropriety. He was a man of courage and integrity, who was willing to risk his life in order to refrain from denying his religious convictions. He was willing to maintain his integrity in the face of personal opposition and possible public disgrace. He was a man who showed undying loyalty and submission to the authorities over him. He was a dedicated and patriotic civil servant.

It was to this man of undisputedly covenantal character that were granted some of the most unparalleled charismatic and miraculous experiences in the entire history of the Old Testament. He was given a clear supernatural vision of Jesus in heaven (Daniel 7). He received far-reaching revelations of the future that were to span many generations (Daniel 2). He was visited by and spoke to some of the highest commanders in the ranks of angels (Daniel 10). By miraculous intervention, he was able to overcome the laws of nature to be rescued from the jaws of hungry lions (Daniel 6). How clearly do we see the necessity and complementary nature of character and charisma!

Love and the Gifts

The clearest exposition of the interaction of covenantal relationships with supernatural manifestations is found in I Corinthians 12-14. The nine gifts or manifestations of the Spirit of God are listed in I Corinthians 12, a chapter whose overall theme is the unity, cooperation, and interrelationships within the body of believers. The entire presentation of the gifts of the Spirit is done in the context of community life. This is not a coincidence. The very purpose of the gifts is to edify the group. The very nature of how these gifts operate is a cooperative one. The exercise of the charismatic gifts as an expression of one's independent, albeit spiritual life is inappropriate and unwarranted. The purpose of the gifts of the Spirit is to promote love, unity and edification.

The manifestation of the Spirit is given to each one for the common good (I Corinthians 12:7).

Although each person receives from God individually, what he receives is then expressed through and for the good of the community.

The original Greek text contains no chapter divisions. First Corinthians 13 is intricately connected with chapters 12 and 14. The teaching on the gifts of the Spirit in chapter 12 and the teaching on the gift of tongues in chapter 14 are linked together by that magnificent exposition on God's love in I Corinthians 13. The gifts of the Spirit cannot be divorced from our love for one another. Neither, on the other hand, can a teaching on love be separated from the expression of the gifts of the Spirit and speaking in tongues. The supernatural gifts are manifestations of that love itself. The context for the gifts of the Spirit in I Corinthians 12 is the cooperation between the different members in a congregation. The context for love in I Corinthians 13 is understanding and exercising the gift of prophecy. The context for speaking in tongues in I Corinthians 14 is order and discipline within a local congregation.

Miraculous manifestations of the Spirit and the cooperative nature of congregational relationships are linked together. Trying to exercise order and discipline within a congregation where there are not the expressions of tongues and prophecy is incongruous. The purpose of authority within a congregation is to promote and facilitate the flow of the Spirit, not to quench it. To say that one believes in congregational order but does not believe in the exercise of the gifts of the Spirit is an illogical statement. The propriety and decency ordained for the flow of prophecy and tongues within a worship service is designed to facilitate the flow, not to establish justifications for disqualifying and eliminating it.

On the other hand, any flow of charisma can and should come under the governance of character.

The spirits of the prophets are subject to the prophet (I Corinthians 14:32).

Although the Spirit is as the wind that blows where it will, whenever the Spirit is to be manifested through another human being, it is always under the control of the will of that human being. By definition, the Spirit can always be subject to the ability of that human being to act in cooperation with the other human beings around him. A spirit that forces itself upon a person is of the devil, not of God.

Misuse, Disuse and Proper Use

Imbalances do occur in the manifestation of the supernatural and in the exercise of discipleship, as in other aspects of New Testament life. The answer to misuse is proper use, not disuse. To put it another way, "Do not throw the baby out with the bath water."

Test all things; hold fast to that which is good (I Thessalonians 5:21).

If there is some aspect of life in the Spirit which is being done improperly, our response must not be to abandon it but to find the appropriate and most genuine way of expressing it. If we do not have this approach, we will be easily diverted every time we encounter a demonic counterfeit of something that God genuinely desires to incorporate into our lives. We will turn away and abandon the very thing which the counterfeit is trying to do away with or pervert.

If some have erred in the way they operate in the miraculous gifts of God, it is incumbent upon us to be a demonstration of the genuine use of the same things. If others have erred and abused authority or discipleship, it is incumbent upon us to be an example of the proper use of authority and discipline. What we need is wholesome authority, not the avoidance of it. This route takes courage, patience, and sincerity. Covenant obliges us to embrace the good qualities of both the miraculous manifestations of the Spirit as well as the characteristics of integrity.

11

THE COUNSEL OF A FRIEND
Part 1

When we realize that the words uttered through the mouth of a human being are imbued with supernatural power, we gain a drastically different perspective on whom we should allow to speak into our hearts. From a biblical viewpoint, words can be likened to the blade of a knife. In the hands of an enemy, the word-blade can be a lethal weapon. In the hands of a trained and trusted surgeon, the very sharpness of the blade makes it a tool to excise with exactness any poisonous growth in one's life. We must block with a protective spiritual shield any words that were meant to harm us. In contrast, words that come by God can be sharp to the point of discerning intricate aspects of our thoughts and imaginations. We are to be undergoing at all times the delicate surgery to remove ungodly elements in our lives.

We are not to give access to our heart to everyone. The role of the friend can be seen as one who has earned a trusted position to speak the delicate words of surgery to us. The friend is the one who has earned the privilege to give us intimate counsel.

A person is given tools and vehicles of power to the extent that they have demonstrated the maturity and responsibility to use them. A child is given a tricycle and then a bicycle. When he becomes an adult, after passing a test, he is given license or permission to drive an automobile. That license is an extension of covenant on the part of the civil authorities toward the individual driver. The age requirements and the driver's test are a form of covenantal approval of his readiness to drive.

A child may be given a plastic toy gun. An adult, under certain restrictions, may be given license to own a handgun. A soldier is commissioned to bear arms for the covenantal purpose of defending the innocent citizens of his country. A criminal is arrested and brought to covenantal justice for illegal use of a weapon.

Accepting or Rejecting Words

When a word is spoken at us, we have the option to receive that word or reject it. Not every word that is heard is received. We have the choice as to what depth we are willing to take a word inside us. Even such a powerful set of words as a vow to be married can be rejected or overruled if it is dealt with immediately. **Numbers 30:5** states concerning words uttered toward a marriage agreement:

If her father overrules her on the day that he hears, then none of her vows

or agreements by which she has bound herself shall stand. The Lord will forgive her, because her father overruled her.

This bit of ancient law contains within it the spiritual principle that words have an effect upon us to the degree that we either accept or reject them.

The words of the marriage vow were spoken. If the father, who is the figure with spiritual authority, allows the words to stand, they will have a powerful effect. If the father chooses to overrule the words, their authority will be canceled. Curses and blessings can be broken or established depending on the will of the people. We have the personal authority to accept or reject words spoken by others.

There is a biblical expression "to speak unto the heart." It means that a word is shared in an intimate way to touch the inner being of the other person. The covenant friend is one who is given the access and privilege to speak into one's heart. We do not take counsel from everyone. The role of the friend is to give that heart-received counsel.

The sweetness of a man's friend does so by hearty counsel (Proverbs 27:9).

It is important to develop the ability to discern what counsel should be rejected. We should know the type of person from whom we should not receive counsel. We should also be developing discernment about which people are appropriate to receive counsel from.

Giving and Receiving Counsel

We must develop the humility and openness to be able to receive advice and counsel from another person. A covenant friend must also develop the wisdom to give trusted counsel and advice in a timely manner. These ins and outs of giving or receiving counsel are important spiritual techniques to be able to grow toward trust and intimacy.

Some people are very good at giving advice but are closed to receiving it. Other people are too open to receive advice from anyone and have not developed a maturity to close off at the right time. Others need to acquire the boldness and exercise the patience which it takes to be able to give wise counsel. Still others need to learn simply to keep their mouths closed and listen.

As Proverbs 27:9 states, one of the sweetest aspects of intimate friendship is those moments of being able to give and receive counsel. The verse can also be taken to mean that the sweetness of intimate friendship is developed through the process of the giving and receiving of wise counsel.

Many a man will claim unfailing love, but a faithful man who can find (Proverbs 20:6).

There are many people who are willing to offer you their opinion as to what you should do, but there are few who have gained the discretion to be able to give the kind of wisdom that one can count on. It may take time to find and develop wise counselor friends, but they are certainly worth the effort.

In the world's view, receiving direction from another human being can be taken as a sign of weakness. This is not so. A person who is weak and insecure will easily fall into a defensive posture and guardedness that does not allow him to receive input. One who has developed the ability to hear correction from others should be seen as a person of strength and self-confidence. He does not feel that he is jeopardizing his self-image by receiving counsel. One who easily takes corrective advice in his stride can be marveled at by his peers as having uncommon self-confidence and resourcefulness.

Loving Reprover

One who is bold enough to come forward to offer a reproof to another is often seen to be arrogant, pushy or domineering. This again is not necessarily so. It is usually an uncomfortable experience to offer someone a bit of correction when one does not know how he will respond. It is much more easy, lazy, and cowardly to avoid or postpone the confrontation. It is necessary to overcome the fear that the other person might reject you if you try to show him a change of direction.

Like an earring of gold and an ornament of fine gold is a wise reprover to a prudent ear (Proverbs 25:12).

The giving and taking of advice is like an ornament of fine gold. It is very precious, it must be refined, and it must be delicately placed upon the ear. The dynamics of wise counsel require two players. There must be the wise reprover, and there must be also an obedient ear. If we are to play ball with one another, both to throw and to catch, we need to learn the skills of being a wise reprover as well as having an obedient ear. This is how we train ourselves both to be and to have a covenant friend.

Not Receiving Wrong Words

Recently, the wife of a ministry leader called my wife to say that she had been hurt by words that someone had spoken to her. She asserted that this other person was one who had clearly demonstrated himself over the past year to be a person of irresponsibility and selfishness. She knew that she should not have listened to such a person, but she had allowed herself to be hurt. After some loving prayer and comfort, my wife counseled her on these techniques for not receiving wrong input. If she, as a leader's wife, allows someone who is obviously untrustworthy to cause her tremendous hurt, then she has allowed Satan a certain access to hurt the ministry in which she is involved. If the ministry is hurt, the progress of the kingdom of God has been hindered. Therefore, it is an important principle of covenant to learn not to receive unwise counsel.

In another instance, a young man recently called me to ask for my advice because he had felt confused over a prophetic word that someone had given him. A certain false prophet had recently come into a congregational worship time. The eldership of the congregation correctly restricted this divisive person from interrupting the service. Afterward, however, another person who was an assistant to this false prophet had come up and shared a supposedly prophetic word with my young friend. The young man said that he could clearly discern the wrongness of the spirit of the false prophet, but there was a certain aspect of what the assistant had shared with him that he thought was insightful. In pondering this prophetic word, he wondered if it was really from God and fell into confusion. Here again we found it necessary to go over the principles of receiving or rejecting counsel.

Individual Conscience

Another young man said that God was directing him to set out in a certain direction to start his own ministry. Those around him who were concerned for his welfare, perceived a confused and reactionary nature to the decision. They tried to surround him with counsel that this was not God's best for his life. Since counsel is effective only to the degree that it is received, the friends offering the counsel realized that they were not getting through to him. Eventually, he was released to pursue his direction and deal with his own consequences.

Each person has ultimate responsibility of conscience for his own actions. Counsel, when given, whether confirmatory or confrontative, is still only of an adjunct nature. Sometimes a person is given an independent call in God that will be misunderstood even by his friends. He must obey that call. More often, however, an independent spirit, due to past hurts, will lead a person to miss God's best for his life.

Prophecy and Free Will

The apostle Paul was one who was given an authoritative and independent call by God to move in a new direction, even though it would be often misunderstood by those around him. When he went to spread the gospel so predominantly among gentile nations, it was not understood why he was moving away from the emphasis on ministering to Jewish people that was found in the ministry of Jesus Himself.

Paradoxically, when Paul came back to Jerusalem to bear witness before his own people in a very Jewish way, it was again misunderstood. People thought that he had mistakenly yielded to the sway of religious, cultural influence. As the Jews of Paul's time had trouble understanding Paul's universal call to the gentile nations, so it is that most theologians have had difficulty understanding Paul's testimony in Jerusalem. They have not been able to see him as a Jew with a calling and commitment to the Jewish people. Prophetic counsel and influence must be contrasted with the independence of allowing each person to hear from God on his own.

Paul's friends, led by the prophet named Agabus, believed he was making a mistake to go up to Jerusalem, and they tried to dissuade him. Here is how the event is recorded in **Acts 21:11-14**:

When he [Agabus] had come to us, he took Paul's belt and bound his own hands and feet and said, "Thus says the Holy Spirit, 'So shall the Jews at Jerusalem bind the man who owns this belt and deliver him into the hands of the Gentiles.' " And when we heard these things, both we and those from that place pleaded with him not to go up to Jerusalem. Then Paul answered, "What do you mean by weeping and breaking my heart? For I am ready not

only to be bound, but also to die at Jerusalem for the name of the Lord Jesus." So when he would not be persuaded, we ceased, saying, "The will of the Lord be done."

Agabus said under the anointing of the Holy Spirit that Paul was to encounter great difficulties in his testimony in Jerusalem. Notice that he did not say under the anointing of the Holy Spirit that Paul was not to go. After he gave his prophetic word, Agabus and the rest of the people joined together in human and brotherly compassion for Paul and naturally assumed the warning meant Paul should not go. However, this assumption and deduction was not the truth. The only anointed word of the Holy Spirit was that trouble was to ensue.

The people then surrounded Paul and pled with him. They tried to counsel him as friends not to do what he was intending. Let us leave the question as to who was right in this situation aside for a moment. After they pled with him, they realized that Paul was firmly convinced in his own conscience that he must do this.

Notice here that they carried out the covenant confrontation only to a limited degree. They did not go forward to try to order him to obey, or to take disciplinary action against him. They were dealing here with a case of counsel and advice as to direction; they were not dealing with a rebuke for sin. Neither Paul's going to Jerusalem nor his refusing to go to Jerusalem would be a case of transgressing a biblical injunction. It was within the sphere of his freedom to do either option. They were only counseling him as to which one they felt would have been the better of the two.

There are certain things that are sinful and cannot be allowed. There are other things that fall within the realm of choice of the individual. Even though there may be better options or worse options, even God respects the freedom of choice of the individual. If God does not necessarily dictate to us every exact detail but leaves room for choice within an approved range of activity, so should we as counselors and friends be willing to defer to a certain point.

Paul's friends realized this, and in the end they did defer. They resorted to telling him that their only prayer was that God's best will be done for his life. Given the fact that they could not come to an agreement as to which was the best direction for Paul, the only wise thing they could have done here was to finish giving their advice and then defer to Paul himself. They had clearly communicated to him in love what they perceived to be the better option; having done so, they had fulfilled their covenantal loyalty to him. In the case where there is no absolute right or wrong, nor an absolute directive from God, the counselor-friends would have been presumptuous to press their case further. We need to learn when we are dealing with a biblical moral imperative and when we are dealing with wisdom for a better choice among several non-sinful options.

Paul's Testimony in Jerusalem

So who was right in Acts 21? A spiritual technique for developing wisdom is the ability to put yourself in the shoes of the person you are trying to counsel. Theologians have underestimated Paul's personal commitment to the Jewish people, the importance of an orthodox-oriented testimony of the Messiah in Jerusalem, and the nature of the Jewish calling on Paul's life in his ministry to the Gentiles. Paul said that he would be willing to be accursed himself if some of his physical kinsmen could be saved (Romans 9:3). Paul said that he was to give a testimony to those under the Law as one himself also under the Law (I Corinthians 9:20). Paul further said that his motivation in ministry to the Gentiles was to make much of its success so as to reflect back upon his testimony to the Jews (Romans 11:13-14).

Did God really instruct Paul to do that? **Acts 20:22-24** reads:

Now I go bound in the spirit to Jerusalem, not knowing the things that will happen to me there, except that the Holy Spirit testifies in every city, saying that chains and tribulations await me. But none of these things move me, nor do I count my life dear to myself, so that I may finish my race with joy, and the ministry which I have received from the Lord Jesus, to testify to the gospel of the grace of God.

Can we see this from Paul's perspective? The Spirit here is not telling him not to go, but rather warning him of the costs that he must pay to make such a testimony. Warning Paul of the costs of his ministry is an appropriate action for the Holy Spirit, since the Scriptures say that when we go out to tackle a certain task, we ourselves are the ones who must weigh the costs to determine whether or not we can finish the task (Luke 14:31). The Spirit of God is communicating to Paul the costs of the task. Paul has weighed them in his heart and has determined that he will be able to complete it. This is his decision to make.

In verse 24, Paul describes his testimony in Jerusalem not only as finishing his own race but also as fulfilling the ministry that he directly received from the Lord Jesus in a vision. Not only did Paul receive a vision before he started to go to Jerusalem, he also received another vision directly from Jesus afterward which confirmed to him that he had done the right thing.

But the following night the Lord stood by him and said, "Be of good cheer, Paul, for as you have testified for Me in Jerusalem, so must you also bear witness at Rome"(Acts 23:11).

Paul had counted the cost, and he had completed his testimony in Jerusalem. Jesus Himself then came and stood next to him and talked to him. Notice that Jesus said, *"as you have testified in Jerusalem..."* indicating that both the manner and content of what Paul did was approved by Jesus. Jesus then said, *"so you must also bear witness..."* indicating that in the approved manner in which he had just given witness in Jerusalem, Jesus wanted him to continue.

We can conclude, then, that it was God's best will for Paul to bear witness in Jerusalem in the way he did. Paul's friends missed this perception by drawing a humanistic conclusion. They added to what they had indeed heard from the Spirit. Theologians have misunderstood Paul because of their difficulty to surmount their own cultural assumptions to see Paul in his Jewish context. Counseling and prophetic input to a friend must leave room for the person to follow his own conscience in obeying the Holy Spirit.

12

THE COUNSEL OF A FRIEND
Part 2

We have been examining how covenant friends go about offering counsel to one another. It is important for us to spend time on this issue because in congregations where people are trying to be covenantal and spiritual with one another, there is often confusion among the believers because contradictory advice is given. This crisscrossing of the flow of counsel can cause hurt among some of the most sincere believers. If we can understand the principles of when to give advice, who should give it and how far that advice should go, we may be able to eliminate much pain and confusion among our dearest friends.

Respecting Lines of Counsel

It is important that we allow counsel to flow along certain lines of authority and that we respect the lines of communication that have previously been established. Counseling usually continues over a period of time. One must be attentive not to butt in on counsel that has already been in process, thereby unwittingly causing a contradiction to the original advice. The second counsel may not be substantially different from the first, but since it interrupts the previous flow, it may be taken out of context and misunderstood. This misunderstanding may create distrust in the person being counseled for the very person who has invested the most time in giving sound wisdom to him.

If someone comes to us to be counseled who is under someone else's pastoral care, we should refuse to do so unless there is a well-communicated invitation from the other pastor. Pastors, leaders and counselors must be very attentive not to allow themselves to be manipulated into giving a second opinion that will be assumed by the person being counseled to be a contradictory word.

A person who is seeking to avoid doing God's will often wants a second opinion for the very purpose of having it contradict what was already told him. Using this manipulative technique, he can then say the second advice invalidated the first one, and therefore neither of the two was of God. In this way he has successfully removed himself from the witness of wisdom into his life and has found a flimsy excuse to justify himself for not doing exactly what his conscience is telling him to do. Most of the time the two sets of advice were really not contradictory or inconsistent at all, but the mere fact that the second advice was given allows the person being counseled to interpret it as he will and to manipulate it into a seeming inconsistency. Not only will this frustrate God's input into that person's life, but it will also create a source of division and offense between the two pastors.

Faith to Hear God's Counsel through Others

Let us not take this principle too lightly. Experience has proven how true it is. When we are in the position of seeking godly advice, we must do so in an attitude of faith projection. It is an act of faith on our part to believe that God will use the dialogue with the person counseling us to communicate His will. We are not so much seeking that person's particular human advice as we are believing that God Himself will use the situation to speak to us. Sometimes it even happens that the human advice is the exact opposite of what God is speaking, but the nature of the dialogue confirms in our very conscience the rightness of God's direction to go the other way. God may have used that advice to make it clear what circumstantial obstacles our faith has to overcome.

We are believing that God will use the other person as a vehicle to communicate with us. If we succumb to the need to hear many other people's opinions, it may be that we are not really trusting our ability to hear from God. We should not seek advice for a mere humanistic consensus; the primary flow of wisdom is from God Himself directly.

The seeking out of many counselors can be a step of unbelief, tantamount to doubting our ability to hear from God. If we find ourselves pressing the person who is giving us counsel in a pleading, manipulative or desperate fashion, we have placed too much faith on that human being himself instead of our own ability to hear from God through him.

We are not to go to the extreme in pride of doubting the ability of another to counsel us and the possibility of his being used by God to minister to us. Nor are we to go to the other extreme of helplessly casting ourselves upon another human being, as if that other human himself were our very savior. When we go in to seek counsel from someone, we must first pray and be assured of the fact that we can hear from God through him. The Bible says that God can direct the heart of the king (Proverbs 21:1), and that divination is on the lips of a king (Proverbs 16:10). If I am feeling doubtful of another person's capacity to advise me, I should pray before the dialogue that God will put sovereignly upon his heart and lips the right answer for me, even if it was not the advice the person naturally would have given. When we ask for wisdom from God, we must do so single-mindedly. To seek a second opinion can sometimes be a step of double-mindedness, not believing that God was able to use the situation. James said about seeking wisdom and counsel:

If any of you lacks wisdom, let him ask of God... and it will be given to him, but let him ask in faith, nothing doubting (James 1:5-6).

James goes on to say that if a person continues to seek in this double-minded or second-guessing manner, he will end up not receiving anything at all.

On the other hand, the Bible certainly directs us to seek counsel in manifold ways. The more counsel we have in the planning stages, the less likely we are to make a rash mistake.

In the multitude of counselors there is safety (Proverbs 11:14).

Also:

Without counsel plans go awry, but in the multitude of counselors, they are established (Proverbs 15:22).

This is not a directive to seek more and more humanistic opinions in a double-minded way; it is rather a clear warning to avoid the independent kind of spirit that says that God cannot speak to me through other human beings.

Hearing God Together

I can remember a time sitting with a group of covenant brothers seeking direction for a certain ministry. When we prayed, God spoke to us seemingly unanimously about a certain direction through the Spirit. After the word was shared in prayer and then shared again in dialogue after the prayer, we were confident of having come to the agreement of God's will. Surprisingly, one of the leaders then said, "What you have all said sounds nice, but I do not know if it is from God. I need to hear it for myself. But now, since you have told me in person, I will never know if it was really God telling me or just the thought you have placed in my mind through having said it."

This type of response shows a lack of understanding of how to hear wisdom from God when it pertains to a cooperative decision. In these cooperative decisions, the Lord does speak in times of corporate prayer to the group as a whole. Secondly, we must believe that it is possible to gain a clear sense of agreement and confirmation in having reached the mind of Christ (I Corinthians 2:16). Thirdly, hearing the word of God coming through another human being is indeed a valid form of hearing from God. **I Thessalonians 2:13** states:

When you received the word of God which you heard from us, you welcomed it not as the word of men, but as it is in truth, the word of God, which also effectively works in you who believe.

The attitude that responds to anointed counsel by saying, "I just don't know. I still haven't heard from God. I'll have to hear for myself," is often a smoke-screen that disguises an independent and uncooperative spirit. God is speaking, and has spoken well enough. A person with a non-relational spirit will not be able to deal with the implications that what God said and how He said it demands an inter-working with others.

Some people who claim to be charismatic may have a surprising difficulty in hearing from God on even a simple matter when it involves teamwork and relationship. The charismatic guise may have been an excuse to justify himself going his own way and doing what is right in his own eyes. A truly charismatic person will flourish in being able to hear God in the midst of other related brothers and sisters as they seek the will of God cooperatively. Those are times of high anointing and great revelation.

Spiritual Solutions

One indication that we may be pressing for a humanistic solution in counseling, as opposed to trusting in our ability to hear God through the counsel, is the tendency to demand the specific practical details of the solution instead of receiving the spiritual principles of guidance that lie behind the question being asked. Generally, the anointing of wisdom comes to a person to draw him to the spiritual dynamics behind his problem. The Spirit of God wants not so much just to drop an answer in the person's hand, but to equip him with principles of spiritual wisdom so that he can handle similar situations in the future. A person who without patience wants only to know the final outcome of the practical decision, shows that he is lacking a heart for the wisdom that wants to know why and how to arrive at the solution. Counsel involves a spiritual version of the adage that "it is better to teach a man to fish than to give him a fish." The spiritual principle of wisdom is the fishing line; the particular decision is like the single fish.

When giving counsel, one ought to prefer communicating a spiritual principle to making a decision on behalf of the counselee. Ephesians 4:12 says that we are to equip believers with their own ability to do the work involved in any ministry. It does not say that we are to do it for them. Making a decision for another person is treating him like a child. Drawing the person into the perspective of the solution is treating him like an adult. The subtle temptation on the part of the counselor to make the decision independently on behalf of the counselee is a form of pride in which the counselor sees himself as high above the lowly state of the one being counseled. It is a loving act not to allow the counselee to wallow in a position as a helpless child. It is an act of faith to call him up into a level of maturity where one is helping him make his own decision. A profound verse with widespread application in this regard is **Proverbs 20:5**, which states:

The counsel [or purposes] in the heart of a man is like deep water, but a man of understanding will draw it out.

Since each believer has the Spirit of God inside him, the counsel and solution for any possible problem is already there. Jesus has become the source of all wisdom inside us (I Corinthians 1:30). It is the purpose of a counselor to help the counselee draw out of the resources of the Holy Spirit that is in him the wisdom that he needs to solve his own problem. This is a great technique of covenant friendship counseling. Even if the counselor is sure he knows the solution long before the counselee will ever arrive there, he should take the time to present it to the person so that he comes to his own conclusion about it. This takes more time than just slapping the answer on him, but in the long run it will be much more time saving.

By helping the friend come to his own conclusion, the counselor has edified him instead of magnifying himself in the counselee's eyes. The counselee has been trained in the techniques of helping himself the next time. If this is not done, the counselee may become dependent, and the counselor will be trapped in a non-productive, repetitive cycle. Whenever a person makes a decision, he must be fully convinced that it is his own will to do so, even if the solution was originally presented by the counselor-friend. If this is not done, the counselor may find himself liable for the blame of anything that may go wrong in the future, even if it was not a result of the counsel he gave. This technique of gently leading a person to draw out his own solution to the problem is a capacity that indicates great wisdom on the part of the counselor.

Many profound principles on the dynamics of friendship making are found in the book of Proverbs. Various proverbs can be used to guide us in the specific techniques of developing deeper levels of covenant.

Hushai, David's Friend

Let us look now at the figure of Hushai, who is an archetypal counselor and friend to King David. Hushai was a man who had gone through the process of trust building with David. He had earned David's intimacy and had proven his loyalty. Hushai's greatness is indicated by the fact that he won the prized but simple title of *"David's friend"* (II Samuel 15:37) and the *"King's companion"* (I Chronicles 27:33). What a testimony that brief description is!

When David was forced to abandon his throne during the insurrection led by his own son Absalom, he had two high-ranking counselors. The first was named Ahithophel, who betrayed him, and the second was Hushai, who remained loyal to him. David sent his beloved friend Hushai into the camp of Absalom and Ahithophel to feign allegiance to them in order to defeat the counsel of Ahithophel. Hushai won Absalom's respect over Ahithophel, thereby thwarting Absalom's attempt to kill David. Ahithophel hanged himself because of his disgrace. Absalom was defeated in war, and David was eventually safely restored to his throne.

What is significant here is not only David's trust and dependence on his friend Hushai, but also the spiritual battle surrounding the giving of counsel. Counsel and wisdom is much more than simple human advice. Wisdom and counsel is a release of the anointing of God that can win spiritual battles by defeating evil powers and principalities (Ecclesiastes 9:15 and 18). The ministry of counsel and wisdom is grounded in the covenant relationship of friends; it releases an anointing that is powerfully effective in the spiritual realm.

When the Going Gets Tough

The ministry of a friend and covenant counselor shines through in moments of difficulty. There is an adage that says, "A friend in need is a friend indeed." People also say, "You can tell who your friends really are when you are down and out." **Proverbs 17:17** states:

A friend loves at all times, and a brother is born for adversity.

In other words, when times get tough, one knows he can count on his covenant brother.

When I see someone whom I would like to befriend, I look for an opportunity to develop closer trust with him. I try to put myself in his shoes and ask myself when he might most need a friend's help. By waiting for the moment when the need is greatest, you can establish a deeper kinship than you would in a lighter or more normal situation. We should delight in the opportunities that allow us to extend ourselves beyond what is convenient in order to help a friend. We should look to show ourselves faithful when it really counts.

As we gain trust, we can establish more intimacy and then extend the trust even further. A spiritual trust is built between two people that will be a blessing to all involved. The counsel of a trusted friend is sweet indeed.

13

LOVING CONFRONTATION

The overall model for the sinful state of mankind is that our relationship with God has broken down.

Our iniquities [or our sins] have separated us from God (Isaiah 59:2).

Therefore, we can define sin as that which causes a relational breakdown between us and God.

Therefore, a sin which is committed against a fellow human being is that which causes a break in relationship between one person and the other. Whatever creates an offense, barrier or separation between me and another human being is that in which I have sinned against him.

Repairing Fractured Relationships

An extension of our overall sinful separation from God is the fracturing of all the relationships between individual human beings. Sin is essentially relation breaking. Love is the opposite of sin; love is the repairing of a breach between two people; it is the restoring of the relationship which was broken. Love is the work that counteracts the effects of sin. Love is a positioning of oneself toward another human being in such a way that the full relationship is maintained.

The Bible says that all of the Law can be summed up in the commandment to *"love one another."* All of the individual laws of Scripture are an extension of that single command to love. Love can only be seen as the summation of the principles of Scripture if sin is fully encompassed by the definition that sin is a breaking of relationships. **James 2:8,9** and **11** state:

If you really fulfill the royal Law according to the Scripture, "You shall love your neighbor as yourself," you do well; if you show partiality, you commit sin. He who said, "Do not commit adultery," also said, "Do not murder." Now if you do not commit adultery, but you do murder, you have become a transgressor of the Law.

Sin, then, is not so much an act unto itself, but a thing done unto someone else. It is similar to the word *"debt"*. A debt cannot exist in a vacuum; a debt is owed to someone. One does not just transgress, but one transgresses or violates the covenant with God or a fellow human.

Therefore, it does not matter so much whether I commit adultery against one person or murder another. By doing either one, I have become a violator or breaker of covenant law.

In ideal conditions, love would be a state of bliss in which the perfection of our relationships was maintained and protected. Since we do not exist in an ideal state, love becomes an action by which a fractured relationship must be sought out for the purpose of being restored. Love is a reversing of the act of fracturing. Love must pursue the other party which has been separated. Love must restore the covenant. Love must go directly to the item that caused the relational breakdown and deal with it. Love must seek out the source of offense and overcome it. Love must go to the other person and make restitution for the article of the covenant which was broken.

Seek and Restore Mission

The first step of love is to seek out the other party. Jesus said that He came to seek out and save that which was lost. He came personally to all of us, who had been alienated and separated by sin and offered to restore us back to a relationship with Himself. This attitude affects how we deal with other people.

A beautiful definition of love is described by Paul in the example of Onesiphorus.

The Lord grant mercy to the household of Onesiphorus for...when he arrived in Rome, he sought me out very diligently and found me (I Timothy 1:16-17).

This is a fine model for the first stage of active love: seek out the other party.

In a world with fractured relationships, love is an act of facing and dealing with sources of relationship breakdown. Love, by its very nature, must involve a degree of confrontation. This may seem foreign to the modern mind, but the essence of love is that of confrontation. Confrontation for the sake of removing stumbling blocks is the primary action of love.

Love's objective is always to overcome the breakdown of covenantal relationship. Therefore, love must deal with the source of the problem; it must address the issue. Love is communicating to the separated party how a point of offense can be removed. Love is an act of communication whose essential context is an area that is offensive to one party or the other.

Love is compelled by a desire to restore relationships. Love is, therefore, with heartbreakingly merciful motives, forced to start confrontations. Love, with coverage and selflessness, stands up to communicate to the other party that which the person often least wants to hear. As a doctor must deal with the area of sickness and as a surgeon must bring his knife to the infected area, so must love with sensitivity and firmness deal with that which is wrong.

Love is compelled to seek a perfection of relationship. Love cannot accept a speck of infidelity to violate one's trust for the other. I love my wife so completely that I could not bear for the tiniest flaw to separate us. Our relationship must be whole, complete and perfect. I am not a perfectionist in requiring legalistic standards of performance. Far be that from the truth. Rather, my love for my wife could not bear for anything to cause a separation between us. Any item that would cause division or mistrust, no matter how small, I would seek to remove. We can be widely divergent in many of our tastes and opinions, but our trust and affirmation of one another cannot be impaired. My wife and I are extremely different types of people, yet we are absolutely united in our bond with one another. Love will seek to maintain that bond at all costs. Love's very forcefulness of desire for one another cannot tolerate any violation of trust.

Rebuke: The Choice of Love

The great command to love one another is originally stated in **Leviticus 19:17-18**:

You shall not hate your brother in your heart. You shall surely rebuke your neighbor and not bear sin because of him. You shall not take vengeance, nor bear any grudge against the children of your people, but you shall love your neighbor as yourself.

Love cannot take vengeance, nor can it hold in resentment. Love's only option is loving confrontation. In the gospels, Jesus seemed to be confronting and rebuking His disciples and others with an extreme forcefulness. Jesus was driven by tenderness and compassion to deal forthrightly and convincingly with any issue that might have separated His loved ones from Him. In Leviticus 19:17 the parallel clause to *"you shall love your neighbor as yourself"* is the clause *"you shall surely rebuke your neighbor."* The rebuking of the neighbor is the fulfillment of the command to love him. Love put into action is a step of covenantal confrontation.

If someone did not have a great love, he would never be able to muster the courage to face the risk of rejection or hostility for the mere sake of restoring the other person. There are two ways in which one can err in not acting in covenantal love. The first error would be the counterfeit of loving confrontation: to voice a petty and nasty criticism of the other person not for the purpose of restoring him to relationship, but to inflict pain or condemnation. That kind of critical motivation only causes a further separation. A critical spirit is the opposite of covenantal love.

The second error is to avoid any covenantal confrontation at all because of fear. Avoidance allows a potentially restored relationship to slip further into separation, possibly being lost forever. It is the lack of real love for the other person that will allow fear to keep one from going to that person to confront him. Hope in restoring the relationship will drive the loving person through the barrier of fear.

Galatians 5:6 says that the only act in this world that avails anything at all is *"faith working through love."* It takes faith to perform the act of love. It takes courage to overcome the barrier of fear of rejection and go to the other person first. It takes belief in the invisible possibility of restored relationship to be able to approach the other person. Faith requires love, and love requires faith. The communicating of loving confrontation requires courage.

As the principal of a covenant high school, I was often faced with having to confront a teenager on an area of misconduct or disrespectful attitude. This was the last thing my flesh wanted to do. It was usually a moment of discomfort. It would have been easier to avoid the situation. It was only by reminding myself how much I loved and cared for that young person that I would be able to continue through the process of facing down his rebellious spirit. If I had allowed myself not to be concerned for the well-being of the student, I would simply not have taken the trouble of doing him the service to challenge his attitude.

Who Goes First?

The onus to initiate the dialogue is always on both sides of the relationship, regardless of who was at fault in the original problem.

Therefore if you bring your gift to the altar, and there remember that your brother has something against you, leave your gift there before the altar, and go your way. First be reconciled to your brother, and then come and offer your gift (Matthew 5:23-24).

If it is the case that you yourself have wronged someone, you must halt any other spiritual activity and seek out the person to effect a reconciliation. Love is the first priority of all spiritual activity. One can move no further in the Lord wherever there is lack of reconciliation. The scripture here says that your brother has something against you. This may not mean that you actually did something wrong, but that the person perceives you to have done so. The scripture does not say "If you wronged the other person, go to him." It says, *"If he has something against you."*

The issue is not whether the charge of violation against you is valid or not. It is, rather, the breakdown of relationship that the offense or the perception of offense has caused. For whatever reason, when the offense resides in the other person and is directed at you, you must be the first one to go to him to start the reconciliation process.

On the other hand, **Matthew 18:15** states:

Moreover, if your brother sins against you, go and tell him his fault between you and him alone. If he hears you, you have gained your brother.

Here the scripture outlines the reverse situation, and yet the responsibility to start the dialogue is still upon you. Even if it is the other person who did the sinning, it is up to you to go to him to try to be reconciled. Perhaps it is your own perception that it was the other person's fault, when he actually did not wrong you. Or perhaps he is unaware that he has sinned against you. The only issue at stake is restoring the relationship. It does not matter what the events were that led to the breakdown of covenantal trust. If that breakdown exists, it is the immediate moral responsibility of either party to initiate the action of going to the other person to communicate the problem.

14

THE MECHANICS
OF CONFRONTATION

Matthew 18 (verses 3 to 20) is the central passage of Scripture that describes the process of confrontation, discipline, and reconciliation. Its practical applications in the lives of a group of believers are widespread and touch almost every area of life. The Bible is saturated with the theme of love, but this passage in Matthew 18 illuminates the practical process of how to bring about covenant reconciliation. It is the diagram of the gears that turn the mechanism of covenant love. Matthew 18 is applicable to an individual, a group of individuals, a community, or even a nation.

I am indebted to my friend Thurlow Switzer for many insights about covenant confrontation. It is not so much his teaching but his example from which I have learned the meaning of this passage.

Overcoming Selfishness

Before a person can enter a covenantal dialogue, a spiritual wrestling must take place on the inside. When the selfish mind thinks of a dialogue of confrontation, it is primarily concerned with defending its own rights. A person who sees covenantal dialogue as protecting what belongs to him or gaining what he deserves, misses the purpose of being reconciled to the other person. Covenantal dialogue has nothing to do with getting something for yourself. Its motivation is to restore relationship and to seek the other person's good. If this is not understood, a covenantal dialogue may become an argument. It would be preferable to consider oneself unjustly wronged if that could somehow effect the greater good of causing a reconciliation between the people involved.

In I Corinthians 6, Paul is addressing a problem in the congregation at Corinth. Apparently two of the believers had fallen into such a state of disagreement that they had brought a lawsuit against one another in a secular court. Paul has heard of the two individuals' claims for their own righteousness. He is trying to explain to them that the greater issue is not who was right in the cause of the division, but rather that at all costs the division should be mended.

Now therefore, it is already an utter failure for you that you go to law against one another. Why do you not rather accept wrong? Why do you not rather let yourselves be defrauded (I Corinthians 6:7)?

What a challenging principle! Paul exhorts us rather to allow our own selves to be unjustly accused and wronged than to allow for a lack of reconciliation to continue between us and another person. In almost any situation where we have been part of a division, if we would be willing to admit our wrong and assume responsibility for the blame, the division would likely soon be ended and mended.

A brother recently took offense at something I had done. Understanding the situation from his perspective, I realized how he must have felt. Yet I also realized what aspects of the situation were his fault. Some of what I had done he had not understood. The situation really had to do with a lack of communication that was no one's fault at all. There was, from my perspective, a larger issue of truth in which I was right that he could not see. I felt that were he not able to see my viewpoint, the truth would not have won out. If my side of the issue had not been justified, we would have missed God's will for us (or so I reasoned in my pride).

When I realized that this brother was offended, I made an effort to contact him, and we were able to come to a certain level of reconciliation. Later, however, I found out that he was still offended, and we needed to come to review matters before a third person. While everything inside me wanted to prove the righteousness of my case, I realized that the greater good for all was to come to reconciliation without insisting upon who was right. As I turned to the Lord in prayer, I sensed the Spirit of the Lord say to me, "Why would you not rather be wronged in this instance? Why would you not rather let yourself take the blame if it would bring peace?"

After more prayer and an inner struggle that felt as if I were invisibly biting my lip to keep from spilling out what was inside me, I went to the next meeting. I brought myself into his viewpoint as much as possible, admitted myself to be in the wrong, and accepted the blame for having created an offense. From this point on, our dialogue grew more relaxed and a new sense of favor for one another grew up between us. We continued to dialogue and affirm our acceptance and support for one another. We discussed ways of improving communication in the future. By the time we left, we could see that a greater bond had been produced between us than had been there before the division. In our new sense of reaffirmation, an expansion of our ministries in cooperation began to emerge. Much gain was won against the territory of Satan. The principle is that interpersonal reconciliation takes priority over personal rights. If we can grasp this, the body of believers as a whole will become unfettered and be able to do great exploits together for the kingdom of God.

The Law of Perspective

Matthew 7:1-5 is a clear description of the kind of inner preparation that must take place before any covenantal dialogue. Matthew 7 serves as an introduction to the more detailed explanation in Matthew 18. **Matthew 7:1-5** states:

Judge not that you not be judged. For with what judgment you judge, you will also be judged; and with the same measure you use, it will be measured back to you. Why do you look at the speck in your brother's eye, but do not

consider the plank in your own eye? How can you say to your brother, "Let me remove the speck out of your eye"; and look, a plank is in your own eye? Hypocrite! First remove the plank from your own eye, and then you will see clearly to remove the speck out of you brother's eye.

We are instructed here not to judge our brother. This means that we are to avoid having a critical spirit. We are not to sit in a lofty position, looking down upon others. We are not to allow a spirit of condemning others to affect us in our covenantal dialogue. This does not mean that we are not to exercise discernment, nor does it mean that at the end of a patient process of confrontation that there cannot be discipline exercised. We are to use discernment. We are to use discipline when dialogue has fully run its course. We are not to be critical; we are not to be judgmental; and we are not to be condemning. A judgmental and critical spirit is the satanic counterfeit of godly discernment.

From a self-centered perspective, each person can only see a situation from his own viewpoint. He will always be naturally inclined to think that his side is right while the other is wrong. If two people stand at a distance, each one obviously has a closer view to his area of the situation. The factors that more closely affect each person will loom larger and seem more important to him than to the other one. Two objects that are the same size will appear larger or smaller depending on the distance and the perspective from which one is viewing them.

When we look at the fault in another person, here described as "a speck in his eye," our natural inclination is to see his fault as the main source of the problem. When considering our own portion of the fault or what is in our own eye, our natural inclination will be to minimize, justify, and rationalize it away. The issue here is not so much that one's own fault is greater than the other's, but that each person's perception of what is right and wrong depends upon his angle of viewing it.

Taking Responsibility for Wrongdoing

A useful measure is for each person to take 100% responsibility for all of the problem that he can affect. Even if the other person is 99% wrong and I am only 1% wrong, my 1% is 100% of my own area of responsibility. My attitude should be that my part of the fault is 100% my responsibility. What is another person's fault and another person's responsibility is up to him.

There are a few standard remarks that are heard when a teenager is confronted with wrongdoing. "This is not fair. There were others who were doing the same thing. Why aren't they getting in trouble as well? The other person started it. I was only doing the same thing that everyone else was. You are just picking on me. It's not my fault. I didn't mean to do anything wrong. You don't understand me. You always think I'm to blame." Does that sound familiar? Blame-shifting is a temptation that affects us all. Taking covenantal responsibility overcomes that tendency.

I often give teenagers the example that if they were to be driving a car over the speed limit, they might be stopped by the police and given a ticket. If they respond that all of the other cars were also going over the speed limit, the policeman would merely say that had nothing to do with it. The policeman can only deal with one car at a time. It is not a question of being fair; it is a question of being just. If a person went over the speed limit, he is 100% at fault. The fact that ninety-nine other people also went over the speed limit does not make each one only 1% at fault for the total problem. Each person is 100% responsible for his own driving speed. Each person can be held 100% accountable for his own wrongdoing, even if no one else is dealt with.

If the policeman were to ask to see the driver's license and registration, and these documents could not be displayed, a more severe citation might be given. The response that these documents were really in good order and had just been left on the kitchen table would not bear any sway with the police officer. The citation would be for driving without the documents in hand. It is not a question of whether the driver had left them behind by accident or on purpose.

Changing Ourselves First

The Bible says that we are to judge ourselves and to examine ourselves. We are to change that which is found wanting.

Examine yourself as to whether you are in the faith (II Corinthians 13:5).

For if we would judge ourselves, we would not be judged (I Corinthians 11:31).

Before we can enter into a covenantal confrontation with another person, we must first judge ourselves and change any wrong attitudes. This is what is meant in **Matthew 7:5** when Jesus said:

First remove the plank from your own eye and then you will see clearly to remove the speck out of your brother's eye.

Jesus is not saying that we should never deal with another person's fault. He is saying that if we do not deal with our own wrong attitudes first, we will not have the perception or grace to handle the situation justly. On the other hand, if we do exercise self-judgment, we have the promise of being able to have godly discernment in dealing with the other person. Jesus is not saying that we should wallow in unrighteousness or self-condemnation. He is stating the principle that there are two stages in dealing with the discernment of fault. The first stage is to deal with our own faults thoroughly and absolutely. The second stage is to move forward with sensitivity toward the other person.

Confrontation Should Be Reconciliation

The attitude and spirit with which we approach a covenantal dialogue makes all the difference. The whole passage in Matthew 18 is dedicated toward gentleness, sensitivity, forgiveness, patience and reconciliation. In that context, one finds the clear dynamics of confrontation and eventual discipline. This confrontation must be firm and decisive when necessary, but it must always be absorbed within the larger picture of reconciling love.

The two moral imperatives to be established in our congregations are (1) that members understand and are willing to cooperate with covenantal confrontation and discipline, and (2) that all of our relationships remain warm, caring, supportive, and personal. The two respective dangers that we must avoid are (1) that there would be such a loose atmosphere of fellowship that there was no ability to confront carnal attitudes or drive immorality from our midst, and (2) that the confrontation toward covenant values might become mechanical, unloving, judgmental and unresponsive. A congregation with no discipline or authority is not a congregation at all. It is a loose association or meeting place. On the other hand, the congregation whose authority has become defensive, impersonal and performance oriented has become a dead congregation, lacking the very love that gave it life in the first place.

The actual mechanics of covenantal confrontation are simple and straightforward. **Matthew 18:15-18** states:

> **If your brother sins against you, go tell his fault between you and him alone. If he hears you, you have gained your brother. But if he will not hear you, take with you one or two more, that by the mouth of two or three witnesses every word may be established. If he refuses to hear them, tell it to the church. But if he refuses even to hear the church, let him be to you like a heathen and a tax collector.**

The first principle is that one must literally get up and go to the person to establish communication. *"Go and tell him"* (verse 15). It is often at this very spot that one falls short, and the process never begins. One can make a phone call, set an appointment, drive over to the other's house, or contact him in writing. In any case, a clear act of initiation and invitation to dialogue must take place.

God often tells us to go to someone in readiness of communicating a message before we know the full content of that message. If a problem arises between me and another person, I may not know what to say or how to approach the problem. I do know that I have an immediate responsibility at least to establish contact and see what spontaneous dialogue might arise. If contact is not made, one will find himself in a second breach of covenant, in addition to the initial mistake that started the division. Not contacting a brother after an offense is itself a further offense.

In **I Kings 18:1** God directs the prophet Elijah to initiate a covenantal confrontation with King Ahab:

> **The word of the Lord came to Elijah saying, "Go, present yourself to Ahab, and I will send rain on the earth."**

At this point, Elijah does not know what is later to happen at Mt. Carmel. He does not know how Ahab will respond, nor what the outcome will be, except that there will eventually be rain. With the animosity of the government leaders against Elijah, this simple command to go and present himself before them was not an easy one. It took courage and a firm resolution to obey the will of God to go to make contact with his opponent. When an individual goes to start a covenantal dialogue with another person, he must fight off feelings that the other person is his opponent or adversary. He must fight off any emotions of fear or antagonism. He must overcome his insecurity.

Privacy

The first stage of dialogue should be carried on without involving other people. *"Between you and him alone"* (verse 15). There should not be another person present at the first meeting. Rumors should not have been spread to other people. A defense of one's own position should not have been given to a third party. No talk of the other person's fault should be allowed until it is presented to him first.

The privacy of this first meeting contains the problem in its initial stage to a very small area. If different people's versions of the incident have spread to others in the community, it will be a long and difficult task to draw in all of the various loose ends. We want to contain the problem. The other person has the covenantal right to be the first person to be told his fault. If he finds out that he has been spoken about to any other person, there will be another offense generated.

This does not mean that if one of the persons involved is unfamiliar with covenantal process that he is not allowed to seek the advice of a pastoral figure to find out what is the right thing to do. Going in private to obtain counsel from a pastoral figure on how to go about initiating a covenant dialogue is not at all the same as sharing one's side of the story with any available friend in an attempt to receive affirmation. People often try to prejudice the sway of others' opinions to justify themselves.

The next step is to tell the other person in straightforward terms what the problem is. *"Tell him his fault"* (verse 15) indicates a certain frankness and honesty that does not involve hinting or beating around the bush. We want to be as objective and direct as possible. The mere communicating of information can go a long way toward clearing up misunderstandings. Talk to the other person about the problem.

These steps constitute stage one of the covenantal confrontation. There will be one of two outcomes: either he will receive the input or he will not. If he does receive the input, the two people should be reconciled immediately, and any past hurts should be forgiven and forgotten.

If he refuses to receive this input, the confrontation may then escalate to stage two. There is no time limit mentioned on stage one. People often need to be given a little time to receive input before they can repent. Only go on to stage two when all the possibility of being reconciled in stage one has been exhausted. The two parties can stay in stage one for a relatively long time, as long as there is still willingness to dialogue and some progress is being made. A premature escalating of the confrontation to stage two may itself be a source for another offense. Patience prevents a judgmental attitude.

At any stage of confrontation, the only goal is to gain the brother back in reconciliation. Any of the rest of the mechanism may be yielded, if the people can be restored to one another.

In the Mouth of Two or Three

Stage two of Matthew 18 is to bring into the dialogue a third party figure. Hopefully, this third party is someone who can be mutually accepted by both people. He may also be someone who wants to add to the witness and verify to the person doing wrong the need to recognize his fault. So the third party may be either a neutral mediator or an additional witness. One or two additional persons may be brought in depending on the discernment of what is appropriate.

If he will not hear you, take with you one or two more (Matthew 18:16).

The addition of one or two outside mediators or witnesses brings a certain gravity to the dialogue. One should do everything possible to avoid the sense of putting someone on trial. At the same time, it does need to be communicated that the issue of reconciliation is a serious one. The extra witnesses help to bring the other party to an awareness of the importance of continuing the dialogue. A non-covenantal person may not count the reconciliation process as very important and will tend to avoid coming to a meeting. He may try to pass over the fact there is not reconciliation by pretending that, from his point of view, reconciliation has already taken place. Evasive tactics hurt the effort to keep covenant. Either stubbornness or avoidance can keep the covenantal process from reaching its desired end.

One must be careful not to convey a spirit of bullying or intimidation. The dialogue should be well-lubricated with affirming remarks toward the other person since it would only be natural for him to feel somewhat insecure and defensive. The dialogue should not be vindictive toward the person as a bad individual. It should be in the mode of solution seeking, so that both parties are brought together toward the goal of helping one another do what is right.

Before moving on to stage three of the confrontation, every opportunity should be given to exhaust the possibilities of reconciliation on stage two. By the time the confrontation reaches stage three, the issue is likely to have become much more complicated than it was at first. What will emerge is that the underlying problem is not so much the sin that was first committed but the unwillingness of the other party to be reconciled. Usually the original offense is not even being discussed anymore. There may be a varied assortment of maneuvering to avoid coming into compliance with the real reconciliation. Most of the dialogue will now have been shifted onto the difficulties and improprieties that were being exercised in the process of reconciliation.

This avoidance tactic on the part of the person being confronted reveals that the real issue is a lack of understanding of integrity in covenant relationships. Covenantal breakdown is more the root of the sin than the sin itself. Any sinful act can be forgiven and forgotten, but if there is not a sense of covenant keeping, the people cannot be reconciled.

Technical Foul

In the American legal system, the bulk of a jury trial does not center on whether the crime was committed. The trial has become a struggle over the process of proper jurisprudence and prosecution. The reason for this is simple. If the person is guilty, his only way to escape punishment is to try to invalidate the case of the prosecution on a technical point. Even if a criminal is guilty, if he can show that the government violated some technicality in its process of apprehending him, his case will be dismissed and he will be released without charge. There is a key here for discerning whether a person has sinned.

The nature of a guilty spirit, when confronted with any system of justice, is to respond in a legalistic manner. The calling of "technical foul" or "technical violation" is the only way for the guilty spirit to escape. The guilty spirit tries to divert attention from what he did. The very nature of religious hypocrisy is to focus on legalism, detail, and ritual. The Pharisees focused their attention on what day of the week it was and on whether or not the disciples washed their hands, instead of dealing with forgiveness and healing. The emphasis on technicality diverts the attention from the basic issue of heart attitude. Satan himself already knows that he has done wrong; he already knows that God knows that he has done wrong; he knows that judgment is awaiting him. In the meantime, the only thing Satan can do is to press the issue of technical violation in the hopes that his case before universal justice may become disqualified. Likewise, the response of any heart which has not been made right before God will be to look for technical violations of procedure when faced with issues of right and wrong.

By this time if the person is averting reconciliation, he will probably be directing a lot of energy toward trying to prove that those who are bringing covenantal confrontation to him are violating some procedural point. They have, therefore, disqualified themselves from being capable of any moral judgment as regards to him. Often those that are in authority in the congregation are bending in any way they can to help facilitate reconciliation but cannot seem to get the other party to meet and deal with the issues squarely. A person convinced of his innocence will welcome any examination. His thoughts and actions are free and open. An innocent heart will not be defensive or reactionary.

Tell It to the Church

By the time the confrontation reaches stage three, the only issue is the refusal to deal with the issue and be reconciled. The refusal to operate covenantally is the foundational problem more than whatever the original sin was that initiated the offense. **Matthew 18:17** states:

If he refuses to hear them, tell it to the church.

The matter can then be taken to the authority of the congregation to be resolved. The issue is told and explained to the elders in the hope that some solution can be found. If reconciliation cannot be brought to pass, the elders must inform the members of the congregation.

Disfellowshipping

Since the person insists upon continuing in a covenant-breaking attitude, his presence threatens the very fabric of the congregation's interrelationships. The poison of pride and resentment must be removed. If the person will not yield and listen to the authority of the entire congregation, he should be removed from the communion of that congregation. He must be disfellowshipped from association with the rest of the people. The disfellowshipping is not so much an execution of punishment as it is taking note of a fact that has already taken place. The person has refused to be reconciled to the covenant body of people in the congregation. Disfellowshipping is a statement indicating that fact so that no one goes on in the pretense that the unreconciled person is part of the body.

Let him be to you like a heathen and a tax collector (Matthew 18:17).

This means let him be to you as anyone else who is not within the covenant of unity of the congregation. The man has brought this definition upon himself because he refused to cooperate with the process of reconciliation. If he refused reconciliation, then he is not reconciled. Disfellowshipping is a clear, authoritative statement to preserve unity with the general membership.

The congregants must be convinced that putting this man outside the boundaries of the congregation is a biblical step. **Titus 3:10-11** says:

Reject a divisive man after the first and second admonition, knowing that such a person is warped and sinning, being self-condemned.

Here we see in capsule form basically the same process as outlined in Matthew 18. There is a series of attempts at reconciliation through stages of confrontation. If this process fails, the person must be removed from the inside of the group.

I Corinthians 5:4-5 also refers to the same steps of discipline:

In the name of our Lord Jesus Christ, when you are gathered together, along with my spirit, with the power of our Lord Jesus Christ, deliver such a one to Satan for the destruction of the flesh, that his spirit may be saved in the day of the Lord Jesus.

In verse 4 when he says, *"gathered together,"* he is referring to the end of the third stage of Matthew 18 confrontation. The phrase *"deliver such a one to Satan"* means to remove him from the ranks of the congregation with its corresponding covering and blessing. There can be no doubt that the disciplinary action of disfellowshipping is a biblically mandated one.

I Corinthians 5:12-13 also states:

> **Do you not judge those who are inside [the church]? But those who are outside God judges. Therefore, "put away from yourselves that wicked person."**

The purpose of disfellowshipping is to remove the unreconciled elements from the greater body of people who are reconciled.

Disfellowshipping for Reconciliation Sake

Even the drastic nature of this step is done in the hopes that the person can be later reconciled. If he is defined as being outside the church, a new process of bringing him back in may be initiated, similar to the process of evangelizing an unbeliever. If he is outside the congregation, the offender will be able to deal with the realities of who he is and what the consequences of his sin are. This leaves room for the person to repent, protects the integrity of those within the covenant congregation, and allows for a future reconciliation whenever he is ready. **I Corinthians 5:5** says that dealing with the destructive consequences of sin may give the man the opportunity to turn around in his attitude and be restored:

> **Deliver such a one to Satan for the destruction of the flesh, that his spirit may be saved.**

When a person is not reconciled to covenantal principles, he cannot be tolerated within the community. Once, however, the man is on the outside of the community, he no longer threatens the principle of covenantal integrity. All of the members are now free to reach out to him as an outsider and attempt to bring him back in. The beauty of the disfellowship is that it allows for the people to start over again in a process of love for the renegade brother. If he is not disfellowshipped, then they have no means to reach out to him. If no disfellowshipping takes place, everyone is stuck in an unrighteous position, and there is no hope for future relationship.

Being outside the church, the offender is now equivalent to an unbeliever and can be treated with witnessing love. He is no worse than anyone else and can still be an object of our prayer and love. Only he cannot be considered to be part of the congregation when in reality he is not. We cannot pretend to have covenant with someone who is not in covenant. That would make a mockery of the foundation of our integrity.

> **I have written to you not to keep company with anyone named a brother who is a fornicator, or covetous, or an idolater, or a reviler, or a drunkard, or an extortioner—not even to eat with such a person (I Corinthian 5:11).**

This injunction takes place only while the person is named "a brother." The purpose of disfellowship is to have him not named a brother any longer. Once he is not named a brother, the members of the congregation are free to reach out to him in witness.

Paul writes in **I Corinthians 5:9-10:**

I wrote to you in my epistle not to keep company with sexually immoral people. Yet I certainly did not mean with the sexually immoral people of this world, ...since then you would need to go out of the world.

The fact that he is a sinner presents no threat to the congregation once he is not named among the covenant brothers. Paul says we are free to keep company with people who are outside the congregation in a way of bearing witness to them of God's love. As long as we are not deceiving ourselves as to who is under the covenant, there is no problem.

The punishment which was inflicted by the majority is sufficient for such a man, so that, on the contrary, you are rather to forgive and comfort him, lest perhaps such a one be swallowed up with too much sorrow. Therefore I urge you to reaffirm your love to him (II Corinthians 2:6-8).

The *"punishment which was inflicted by the majority"* is referring to the step of corporate disfellowshipping that was taken upon the man mentioned in I Corinthians. Once the step of disfellowshipping has taken place, the integrity of the covenant has been restored, and everyone can move back into the mode of reaffirming one another.

While these times of covenantal discipline are painful to all involved, it can also be a time of tremendous dedication, purity, commitment, and dependence upon God. Discipline and disfellowshipping are not actions that have any humanistic footing. Anyone involved in them must throw himself with abandon upon the mercy and wisdom of God. After such a discipline is complete, there will be a beautiful air of relief in the congregation and a release of the Spirit of God. A new sense of safety for the flock will emerge for the faithful remnant who have been able to stay through the difficult process of discipline. There is nothing else that Satan can throw at that remnant of people who are so committed to their covenant with one another. At that point, the congregation will begin to grow again in a lively way.

Spiritual Authority

The well-known verse about binding and loosing is part of this passage. Taken in context, binding and loosing actually have to do with the authority within the congregation to effect discipline upon its members. There is a parallel between the authority on earth and the authority in heavenly realms. Both Satan and sin need to be overcome. **Matthew 18:18** states:

Assuredly, I say to you, whatever you bind on earth will be bound in heaven, and whatever you loose on earth will be loosed in heaven.

The agreement of two together has unlimited power. The very name of Jesus is in the midst of two or three gathered together. Jesus is manifest where two or three are gathered together as a congregation under the authority of the name of Jesus. All the supernatural power of agreement and binding and loosing are related to the authority within the congregation to exercise discipline. Spiritual authority refers both to the binding and loosing of invisible demons as well as to the authority to exercise covenantal confrontation and discipline within the body of believers.

15

CONGREGATIONAL MEMBERSHIP

Such clearly defined principles for removing someone from the ranks of members in a congregation must be preceded by the fact that there is such a thing as an official membership. There could not be such clear definitions in I Corinthians 5 as to who was inside the church and who was outside the church if there was not at least some sort of reckoning of what membership was. In New Testament times there was a strong identification and unity when the people immersed the new believer in water. The congregants who witnessed the immersion or the pastoral figure who officiated at the immersion were the recipient of that person's loyalty. The new believer's membership was in the universal Body of Christ, but also in the local community of faith.

In I Corinthians 1:12-16, Paul notes that certain believers were saying that they were personally identified with a specific minister (though with a wrong attitude in this case). That minister was the one who baptized them. **I Corinthians 10:2** describes the people who passed through the Red Sea with Moses as having been baptized. This symbolic baptism was not only unto God, but was also an identification with Moses:

All were baptized into Moses in the cloud and in the sea.

One way of sealing someone into the covenant of the congregation is through the time of immersion in water as a uniting with and commitment to the congregation's membership.

Formal Membership

I used to believe that it would be unspiritual to have a formal roster of the members of the congregation. It seemed more organizational to me than organic. It seemed to lack a certain spontaneity of identification with the group. However, we can compare membership to the model of marriage to understand what a commitment to covenant is. Two people may live together, enjoy one another's companionship, and intend one day to get married. They may even consider themselves in an unspoken way to be married. But, until they come together in a formal and public declaration of their commitment, there has been no covenant made. The commitment to the relationship is only an assumed one. If we do not see a clearly stated commitment unto membership, then the congregants may drop back to a non-covenantal form of relating to one another.

Even if a couple was living together before they got married, there is a distinction in their same co-habitation after they have made their marriage covenant. Physically, their relationship may be the same, but the wedding vows add a depth and permanence in their commitment to one another. People may worship and participate in the activities of the congregation, but a clear distinction occurs in their attitude once they make a statement of commitment to membership.

Congregational membership is not the formulating of a roster but a calling forth of a commitment to covenantal integrity. One aspect of covenantal relationships is that the parties involved make an effort to communicate and define what their relationship is. What, then, does membership in a congregation mean? What comprises a congregational covenant?

Let us define membership by the following five elements: attendance, service, tithing, vision, and eldership.

Attendance

Attendance is the commitment to attend the worship services and any other scheduled meeting set up by the congregation. The attendance of each member at an event is not only edifying for himself, but is also an encouragement to the other congregants. There is a sense of greater anointing and strength when more of us are gathered together. The presence of each individual is greatly missed when he is not there. **Hebrews 10:25** reminds us about:

not forsaking the assembling of ourselves together, as is the manner of some, but exhorting one another.

Commitment to attendance particularly has to do with how one schedules his free time and appointments. Usually a congregation will have a few occasions a year where it schedules a major time to be together. Perhaps there is a retreat or a series of evangelistic meetings. It is important for the members to look ahead on their schedule and make room for those dates. If there is an important conference lasting several days, then the members should be willing to schedule some vacation time toward it.

For example, if a congregation has a particular meeting on Wednesday evening and none of the other evenings of the week, if a member schedules a business or medical appointment on that day instead of a different day of the week, it is an indication that he is not thinking ahead about adjusting his schedule around congregational commitments. Our commitment to attendance means that we set those dates on our calendar first and try to schedule other items around the congregational events.

A person grows spiritually by making a firm commitment to one congregation. Some people hop from one church or meeting to another. They think that by their exposure to different types of ministers they will grow more in the Lord. This attitude shows a lack of understanding of covenant. Real spiritual strength will come when one finds his God-given placement and grows in commitment and covenant with the people there. Exposure of different ministers can still come through books, tapes, conferences and so on.

Service

Every member of the congregation should have an area of practical service. Everyone helps out with the family chores of the community. The important thing is not the quantity of work but rather that the person embraces a clearly designated area of responsibility. The seizing hold of responsibility for service lends itself toward covenantal strength.

Some have the image that serving should only be done by those who have been in the congregation a long period of time. This is not true. Serving is for everyone. Serving is a helpful way to draw someone into closer relationships. When a person has an area to serve in, he feels as if he belongs. By guarding a new attendee from having to do any service, we are not doing him a favor but forcing him to feel alienated. People want to be part of the group. People are happier when they feel that they have something to do. They want to be able to participate in the work of the congregation. People need to be needed.

If all the members are helping and serving, the pastor will be freed for more time for prayer and evangelism. Widespread delegation of service also has the benefit that the congregation will run smoother and be more attractive to new people. A person visiting a congregation can quickly sense that there is a spirit of cooperation. The practical chores and details of the congregation should not be burdened and entangled among a few people.

Practical service is an important area of spiritual growth for each individual. Jesus taught us that as He washed His disciples' feet, each one of us was to go forth and serve one another. Practical service increases the fruit of unselfishness, love and humility in our lives.

Tithing

Each person should be committed to major, regular, undesignated giving of finances into the budget of the congregation. We worship God with our substance (Proverbs 3:9). There are many different modes of giving.

One type of giving is that of the widow's mite. Someone who is very poor can exercise great faith by giving a small quantity since it represents a large part of that person's need. Giving out of need releases a powerful spiritual force.

The second area of giving is that of tithing itself. Tithing means giving 10% of one's income to the congregation. One should recognize the difference between alms, offerings and tithes. Jesus said in **Matthew 6:3**:

When you do a charitable deed (or give alms), do not let your left hand know what your right hand is doing.

Alms is giving a relatively small amount in secret directly to a poor person. It is done in secret in order not to demean the honor of the poor person. The alm is not related to the substantial support of the on-going work of the congregation.

The offering, on the other hand, is a free-will gift. An offering is given above the tithe commitment. The offering is not required, but given as one's choice to be generous. The offering may go to an outside ministry or to a private cause or to a special project announced by the congregation.

Tithing is not something necessarily secretive. No one's honor is to be demeaned as in the case of alms. Certainly, one should not give tithes in a public way to try to impress people. On the other hand, the tithe is an open step of congregational commitment. Unlike the free-will offering, the tithe should generally not be a separately designated gift.

The tithe is the expression of the belief that money belongs to God and is willingly yielded to the general purposes of His kingdom. A designated gift implies that it is a free-will offering above the tithe. The purpose of the tithe is to support the normal functions and budgetary needs of the local worship and teaching center. In the Law of Moses, the tithe was given to support the local Levites. The Levites were spread out around the country and performed the task of teaching and worship leading.

The giving of the tithe regularly demands discipline. The giving of the tithe in an undesignated manner demands humility. The giving of the tithe toward the regular budget shows a covenantal responsibility for financial support.

Major Donations

In addition to the giving of alms, the widow's mite, the tithe and the free-will offering, there is the extraordinary step of faith of making major capital donations. This might be called "new covenant giving" in the sense that it is not required in the Law but is a faith response to the grace of God. **Acts 4:34** states:

Nor was there anyone among them that lacked; for all who were possessors of lands or houses sold them, and brought the proceeds of the things that were sold and laid them at the apostles' feet; and they distributed to each as anyone had need.

It is a great testimony of God to see people take major possessions, liquidate their capital, and turn the proceeds over to the ministry. In the revival of Acts 4, wealthy people gave almost all they owned into the ministry. They took the money and laid it at the apostles' feet. Not only did they give, but they yielded to the apostles the complete authority to do with the money as they saw fit. They were not trying to manipulate or influence the ministry by the size of their gift. Many times in the Old Testament, such as in the building of the temple, wealthy people gave vast portions of what they had. At a time of great outpouring of the Holy Spirit, we should believe that men and women of wealth will be moved even to sell what they have to make the money available for the ministry.

We have here discussed five types of giving: the widow's mite, alms, the free-will offering, the tithe, and major capital donations. **Luke 8:3** records that certain wealthy women followed the ministry of Jesus and supported him out of their personal finances:

Joanna the wife of Chuza, Herod's steward, and Susanna, and many others who provided for Him from their substance.

Giving money is related to one's heart commitment. If one is committed to a cause, he will give to it. The reverse is also true: if one gives to a cause, his commitment will then grow in it. Jesus said in **Matthew 6:21**:

"For where your treasure is, there your heart will be also."

Giving money into the kingdom of God is an expression of heart commitment. It is also a means to exercise dominion over the attacks of greed or fear of financial insecurity. When one gives money, his potential to believe to receive more money increases. Jesus said in **Luke 6:38**:

Give and it shall be given unto you.

Believing to Receive

People need not only be obedient to give, but also to exercise the faith to receive. There are two parts to giving: the first is to give; the second is to believe to receive. My wife and I realized that we had spent years tithing and giving but had never exercised the prayer of faith to receive a multiplied provision for what we had given. Now when we send in tithes or gifts, we pronounce over them the covenantal blessings of prosperity. **Deuteronomy 8:18** states that it is God:

Who gives you the power to get wealth that He may establish His covenant.

We receive by faith a one hundredfold return to be able to be more generous.

In Mark 10, Peter says that he has given everything he has toward the sake of the gospel. Jesus' response is that once one gives, he should also believe to receive a one hundredfold return. Jesus also indicates that there will be a spiritual battle connected with receiving finances by faith. **Mark 10:29-30** states:

Assuredly, I say to you, there is no one who has left house or brothers or sisters or father or mother or wife or children or lands, for My sake and the gospel's, who shall not receive a hundredfold now in this time—houses and brothers and sisters and mothers and children and lands, with persecutions— and in the age to come, eternal life.

As we move toward the distressing times seen in the book of Revelation, it is important to be developing in the hearts of our congregants the faith in God's provision. Our people need to know how to give; our people need to know how to receive a hundredfold provision in return; and they need to know how to fight spiritual warfare. Persecutions will come along to hinder the flow of finances into the work of the ministry.

Much of the end-times anti-christ system will have to do with finances (Revelation 13). Even though believers may use some of the world systems of finances, they must be dependent on God alone. They must not let the power of the world's credit systems gain control over their lives. God desires to grant us all faith for financial provision.

Vision

Another aspect of membership in the congregation is vision. There are many things that congregations of faith around the world have in common. On the other hand, each community of faith has a certain identity and calling and destiny in God. The vision for the congregation should be adequately expressed by the leadership. The member is coming on purpose to support the vision of the congregation. When a congregation grows in size, many people start to attend because they enjoy the music or the teaching. Attendees, who enjoy what they receive, may not necessarily be committed to seeing the congregation fulfill its destiny. These attendees are not moving the congregation forward. The member should be sure that he understands the vision of the congregation and that he is called by God to help support that vision.

In ancient Israel, the people gathered around the banner of their particular tribe. The banner was a symbol that represented the calling and identity of that particular tribe. Key aspects of a congregational vision can be communicated through slogans and phrases that are caught easily by the memory.

In any congregation there must be a set of shared values that are commonly written on the hearts of the people. For example, in our Messianic congregations, we have the shared values that the congregations are built on the three foundations of word-of-faith teaching, covenantal relationships, and a Jewish calling. If a person disagrees with a major area of the vision of a congregation, he should probably seek somewhere else to be a member. Becoming a covenanted member of a congregation is tantamount to signing your name to a confirmation of the primary vision of that community.

Receptivity to Elders

The fifth area of congregational membership is a receptivity to the authority, anointing, and counsel of that congregation's local body of elders. The elders are the primary governing body of the congregation. The head or lead elder is called the pastor. From the pastor and through the elders there should be a flow of spiritual unity through the congregation. When one joins a congregation, he is saying that he affirms by faith the calling of the men presently in the position of eldership. He has faith that he will receive edification from their leadership. His act of commitment to the congregational family is also an act of submission to the spiritual authority of that congregation.

Receptivity to pastoral input is an act of faith on the part of the congregant. It makes no sense for a person to be coming to a congregation and then report that he is not receiving any feeding from the teaching. The same faith unto commitment for the congregation is also to the anointing and authority of the pastoral leaders.

The more the congregants have faith in the elders, the more the elders will relax, feel confident, hear from the Lord, and pass it back on to the congregants. If the congregants are unreceptive, it is all the more difficult for the leadership to act in faith and flow in the anointing of God.

Obey those who rule over you, and be submissive, for they watch out for your souls, as those who must give account. Let them do so with joy and not with grief, for that would be unprofitable for you (Hebrews 13:17).

A cooperative submission radiates a confident spirit of joy upward toward the elders, which then, in turn, will profit the members as well. This will produce a positive cycle in which everyone will grow in joy and faith and authority.

The congregation is a training center, and the new congregant is one who has come to enlist in the program to be trained for the kingdom of God. **Ephesians 4:12** states that the work of the different types of ministers is for:

equipping the saints for the work of ministry, for the edifying of the Body of Christ.

The role of leadership is to do the equipping of the members. If the leaders' work is to do training, then the congregant is someone who is being trained. This training is to do the work of the ministry. A congregant must be one who desires to serve the kingdom of God.

Participation in the work of the ministry is not a full-time job in a ministry position. There is no distinction between the clergy and the laity. Every believer is seen to be working for the ministry. Joining the membership of the congregation is a statement that one wants to enter the work of the ministry. Ephesians 4:12 states that this ministry is for the building up of the community of believers. The community is built up by its individuals separately and by the group corporately.

The person who joins a congregation is like someone who enlists in the army or registers in a school where he says, "Take me, train me, get me going for the goal." The purpose of membership is to present oneself to be built up in every way to go forth as a soldier for the kingdom of God. If this is the attitude of the members of the congregation, there will be minimal internal problems.

Participation

Each member must see himself as a specific joint or ligament in the general body. The parts of the body need for one another to function. **Ephesians 4:16** says:

from whom the whole body, joined and knit together by what every joint supplies, according to the effective working by which every part does its share, causing the growth of the body, the edifying of itself in love.

The Body is joined and knit together. There must be a linking of each one of the members between themselves. A commitment to membership is a commitment to be joined; it is a commitment to be knit, linked, bound together. Verse 16 says, *"what every joint supplies."* Being a member means supplying and giving helpful input. Membership means a commitment to supply that which one has. Verse 16 says that *"every part does its share."* Membership is not passive. It is a taking up of active participation where the whole group can benefit.

This participation will cause the *"growth of the Body."* Membership is a commitment to cause the growth of the congregation. One helps with evangelism to see the numbers of the congregation grow. One participates in prayer and worship to see the spiritual qualilty of the community grow. Lastly, verse 16 says that the Body is *"for the edifying of itself in love."* Membership is a commitment to see oneself built up to one's highest capacity to love others. We are all growing strong together. We contribute to the peace and unity of the spiritual community.

Calling not Comfort

Congregational membership must be seen as a calling of God. It is not the same thing as picking out a restaurant. The question is not, "Where do I want to go to church?" It is rather, "What has God called me to do? Where has God called me to make a commitment?" We do not pick out the place where we might feel most comfortable. We pick out the place that God has ordained for our participation.

16

COVENANTAL CHARACTERISTICS
Teamwork

God sees us together as a body, with each of us a joint or ligament within that body. There are spiritual connections between us. The body as a whole can do nothing unless each one of its part does its share. An individual part of a body can do nothing unless it is connected to the body.

In **John 5:19**, Jesus said that He could do nothing outside His connection to His Father.

The Son can do nothing of Himself, but what He sees the Father do; for whatever He does, the Son does in like manner.

All spiritual action comes out of relationship. Our most important relationship is that with God Himself. Each one of us must be fully dependent on God. We also have relationships with others. As Jesus was absolutely linked with His Father, so are we linked with Him and with one another.

Jesus denounces an independent spirit. He said, *"the Son can do nothing of Himself."* He was not striving to do something particularly unique or original for its own sake, but to cooperate with his Father's pattern. As a son, Jesus only acted "in like manner." A man who understands covenant will see himself as a team player.

Each person is fully motivated for his own actions. He should step out to preach the gospel to the entire world, even if no one else were a believer. Since there are other believers, we incorporate the attitude of a team player. There is a certain spirit that one gains in seeing himself as a team player. Anyone who has played in a competitive team sport will understand that spirit.

Team Sports

When I was in college, I competed in a sport called "crew" in an eight-man shell with coxswain. The hull of the boat was very sharp. The boat could tip over with the slightest movement to the side. When we first learned to row together it was extremely awkward, with the oars slapping from side to side and the boat rocking. After months of practice, the men were able to move and row with perfect balance, the keel of the boat would even out, and the boat would move with great speed through the water.

Even though each of the individual men was rowing with extremely violent force, the timing and cooperation was so perfect that there would be no side movement in the boat. When the rowing reached racing speed, the hull would begin to rise slightly up out of the water. There would be moments of poetic beauty that were experienced through the strength, speed, balance, timing, and rhythm.

Part of the beauty was an intuitive sense of teamwork and unity among the men. The slightest wrong move by any of the eight oarsmen could have ruined the race. We had spent months in grueling preparation for the few minutes of the race. We were all interdependent on one another. Not only was it a joy to win the race and compete well, but the privilege to experience that perfection of teamwork was an asthetic and spiritual reward in itself.

The same could be said for any team sport or team activity. Serving in the kingdom of God should have the sweet spiritual reward of being a member of a team. There is a joy of fraternity and kinship in working together.

In a team spirit one is looking not so much for his own separate fulfillment, but for the good of the whole group together. Those who have played basketball remember times when a certain friend would desire to shoot the ball every time he got his hands on it. His desire was to build up his own score. While he may have achieved a higher score for himself, the team suffered overall.

When a basketball team spends time practicing for its competitive season, it works on team play. Much of the time of practice is not so much learning individual basketball skills, as it is learning how to play-interact with the other members of the team. As each one has control over his own body, they are learning in practice to gain coordination of the corporate body of the team.

In the body of believers, there are also different types of players. In a basketball team one might have forwards, guards, centers, coaches, managers, water boys, and members of the business part of the club. Even the owner and the fans themselves may be considered as part of the identity of the team. In the body of believers, we have deacons, elders, worship leaders, administrators, janitors, Sunday school workers, nursery attendants, sound equipment helpers, hospitality coordinators, and so on.

Ephesians 4:11 describes five different types of ministers:

Some to be apostles, some prophets, some evangelists, and some pastors and teachers.

These five should be taken as members of a team. They might be likened to five players on a basketball team. The ministers should operate in a spirit of teamwork. There is a growing awareness today of the interrelationship among these five ministries.

Members One of Another

All the members of a team have unique talents, gifts, anointings and motivations. Romans 12:6-8 lists the gifts of prophecy, service, teaching, exhortation, generosity, administration and mercy. These gifts are to be exercised in that spirit of teamwork.

All spiritual gifts are given for the sake of the whole. Every gift is a help in the general functioning of the group. The gifts in **Romans 12** are introduced by these statements in **verses 4** and **5:**

> **For as we have many members in one body, but all the members do not have the same function, so we, being many, are one body in Christ, and individually members of one another.**

The three aspects of teamwork are the following: First, we must adopt the inner spirit of being a team player. We breath the same air of the team spirit. We are motivated with an attitude of teamwork.

Secondly, we direct our goal for the good of the overall team. We do not see a separate achievement; our eyes are on the greater good of the victory of all of us together. Our goal is for the group, not individual success.

Thirdly, we are committed to learning how to interact with one another. We need to develop the ability to pass the ball back and forth. We must spend time training in interrelationship, communication and team play. It is not enough to have a team spirit; one must develop the techniques of team play.

The three aspects of teamwork are team spirit, team goal and team play. A covenant-oriented man is a team player.

The Agreement Principle

Related to teamwork is the principle of agreement. In arithmetic, one plus one equals two; but in the world of the spirit, one plus one may equal ten. In the agreement principle there is a greater power when we work together than there is in the sum of the separate parts added up by themselves. Not only is there an exponential spiritual power, but there is also the added authority of the agreement of the second or third person.

Matthew 18:16 states that if one does not bear enough authority in his witness by himself, he should go with a companion.

> **If he will not hear you, take with you one or two more that, "by the mouth of two or three witnesses every word may be established."**

In this case, there was not enough spiritual weight or authority behind the words of the one person. One person's viewpoint may be merely his subjective opinion. When a second or third witness is brought in, there is an authority that makes the situation a valid and legally-warranted fact. In a courtroom, one person's testimony may be dismissed; but if two separate witnesses are found independently to be in agreement, that testimony has become established.

A single human eye can only convey images in a two-dimensional plane. The double perspective of the second eye creates a three-dimensional image in the mind. Depth perception only comes when both eyes are acting in tandem.

In prayer there is an added dimension of authority when a second person comes into agreement. **Matthew 18:19** states:

I say to you that if two of you agree on earth concerning anything that they ask, it will be done for them by My Father in heaven.

If two believers can come into unity of mind and spirit concerning the will of God, they can exercise great authority to establish their prayers.

Matthew 18:20 adds to that authority the dynamic power of the Spirit of God.

For where two or three are gathered together in My name, I am there in the midst of them.

There is an added dimension of anointing, prayer and worship when two or more come into spiritual agreement. The Spirit of Jesus is present in power in their midst.

Two by Two

When Jesus sent forth the seventy disciples, he sent them forth in groups of two:

After these things, the Lord appointed seventy others also and sent them two by two before His face into every city and place where He Himself was about to go (Luke 10:1).

There is a special spiritual presence of the Lord when two or three are in agreement. Jesus sent them by twos so they could use the principle of agreement in their ministry.

Agreement in faith increases effectiveness in spiritual warfare. **Deuteronomy 32:30** asks:

How could one chase a thousand and two put ten thousand to flight?

The agreement principle works by exponential power. If one man chases a thousand and another man chases another thousand, they have been effective in routing an enemy of two thousand. If they fight together, the two of them may put ten thousand to flight. If we work together, we can accomplish more than working separately. Putting ten thousand to flight is by faith. When one commits to working with another person, it does not necessarily seem to be more effective according to natural circumstances. It takes faith to know that in the realm of the Spirit, the two working together are accomplishing exponentially more than they could alone.

Mutual Protection

Similar to teamwork spirit and the agreement principle is mutual covenant protection. When two or more work together, they can watch out for one another. We use the expression "to cover one another's backs." In old Western movies, one cowboy would cover his partner as he moved forward under gunfire. Both of our eyes are on the front side of our head; we have no way to perceive directly what is behind us. Perhaps we were designed to work together.

There is an example of mutual military protection in **I Chronicles 19**. Joab, the leader of David's army, goes out with his men to fight the Ammonites, who have hired the Syrians to help them. The Ammonites and the Syrians have positioned themselves on two opposite sides of the army of Israel. Seeing that he was surrounded, Joab divides the army in two and places one half under the command of his brother Abishai. The two halves of the army take their stand back-to-back and face their opponents. Joab says to Abishai:

If the Syrians are too strong for me, then you shall help me; but if the people of Ammon are too strong for you, then I will help you (verse 12).

Each party is primarily committed to working on his half of the problem, but there is an alliance to look out for and help the covenant partner. In the same way, two nations can become allies. An ally is a nation which has entered into covenant with another. In World War II, the various nations that covenanted together to defeat the Nazis were called "the Allies."

Mutual protection was also the reason Jesus sent out His disciples two by two. Not only were they to agree in prayer, but they would be fighting together and protecting one another as covenant brothers. They would be like a pair of mighty men from David's army, standing alone in a field back-to-back and fighting off an entire brigade of Philistine troops (II Samuel 23).

Cooperation

Another aspect of teamwork is covenantal cooperation. There is a beautiful passage describing this cooperation in **Ecclesiastes 4:9-12:**

Two are better than one, because they have a good reward for their labor. For if they fall, one will lift up his companion. But woe to him who is alone when he falls, for he has no one to help him up. Again, if two lie down together, they will keep warm; but how can one be warm alone? Though one may be overpowered by another, two can withstand him. And a threefold cord is not quickly broken.

The threefold cord and its strength should be a common theme among covenant brothers.

Verse 9 states that if two are together, they will have a *"good reward for their labor."* This good reward is the added effectiveness of teamwork. More can be accomplished if two are cooperating.

If one person has a problem, the other one can help him. The ability to rely on a covenant friend in a moment of weakness is a blessing of cooperation. Helping one another is what is intended for us in **verse 10:**

If they fall, one will lift up his companion.

In this passage again is the indictment against an independent or loner spirit.

Woe to him that is alone if he falls (verse 10).

We are not called to be "Lone Rangers" in the ministry. Pride eventually leads to a fall. In pride, someone may try to do things all alone, but eventually he may find himself unprotected from the enemy. If, after years of independence, a man should fall, he will not have developed the trust with anyone to be able to help him.

Part of cooperation is mutual comfort and encouragement. **Verse 11** states:

If two lie down together, they will keep warm.

This is speaking of more than physical warmth of two people on a cold night. How many husbands and wives have experienced that special reassurance after a difficult day to be hugged by a comforting companion? If a person has a comforting companion that he can rely on, there seems to be no task too difficult to overcome. No area of discouragement can defeat him.

Between two people, there can be a warmth of love and affection that brings a rekindling of spiritual enthusiasm. We encourage one another not to be defeated by the devil. We encourage one another by the dependability of our companionship to go forward in the grace of God. While this passage may be applicable to a husband and wife, it also pertains to any set of covenant friends. Any two people committed to a supportive companionship can be a source of encouragement and comfort to one another.

Ecclesiastes 4:12 promises us victory in spiritual warfare:

Though one may be overpowered by another, two can withstand him.

As believers, we fight satanic forces. The Devil is referred to by Jesus as a strong man who must be overpowered. When we work together in covenant, we can conquer demonic forces. We can withstand any evil day. We can resist any attack of the forces of darkness as we stand in unity.

Three-Fold Cord

Verse 12 states:

A three-fold cord is not quickly broken.

What is so graphic in this description is the image of the cord. As a cord is braided, the three strands are alternately laced together. This intertwining produces great strength. A thick three-corded rope that one might use on the deck of a ship is a good image of the trust of covenantal relationships.

I was once mountain climbing with a friend. Over a particularly difficult spot, my foot slipped, my hands lost their grip, and I began to fall away from the rock's face. My companion, who was above me, had the cord around his waist. By a difficult and strenuous maneuver, he managed to guide me back on to a ledge where I could get a footing. It was the faithfulness of my companion, along with the security of the cord, that saved my life.

Some cords are made of light stranded material, and other cords are made of thick gutsy fiber. The stronger the rope, the more weight it can hold. We need to develop our covenantal relationships from being a weak strand to a full-bodied rope that can handle any amount of strain and wrestling.

Heart-to-Heart

Sometimes people have doubts and misgivings about being committed to one another. We must first know who we are ourselves and what it is that God has called us to do. Then we can deal straightforwardly with someone else. Too many people do not really intend to fulfill what they say they are going to do. The issue of making covenant is to bring our hearts to the point that we can be firm in the commitments we make.

There is a beautiful passage in **II Kings 10** in which two mighty men of God, Jehu and Jehonadab, meet together. Jehu is on his way to bring judgment against evil King Ahab's family; it is a crisis which required great courage and determination. Jehu needs to know man to man, heart to heart, if Jehonadab will stand with him. When he meets him, Jehu asks Jehonadab:

> **"Is your heart right, as my heart is right toward your heart?" And Jehonadab answered, "It is." Jehu said, "If it is, give me your hand." So he gave him his hand, and he took him up to him in the chariot. Then he said, "Come with me and see my zeal for the Lord." So they had him ride in his chariot (verse 15-16).**

What a stirring interchange! It grips me to the core of my being. I desire to serve God and to stand in covenant with courageous brothers.

It takes courage to make covenant. It takes courage to be determined not to be unfaithful. Too many people's hearts are wavering so that they could never bring themselves to make a firm commitment. It takes courage to forge your heart to be perfect toward another person. The word perfect does not mean flawless in performance. Perfect means being faithful to a covenant.

David was described as being perfect in his heart toward the Lord. He was not flawless in his performance. He was, however, tenaciously faithful toward his covenant with God. We need to be perfect in our hearts toward God. We need to be perfect in our hearts toward one another. Flawless conduct is not an issue. We must make the effort to purge every unfaithful quality out of our hearts. We must be men and women of tempered steel in our character to keep covenant.

Eye-to-Eye

There is something about looking another person directly in the eye that reveals his attitude of heart. If a person's attitude is wrong, he will usually not be able to look the other person in the eye. Guilt, embarrassment or bitterness will cause him to turn his eyes away. Fear of rejection and a poor self-image can also keep someone from being able to lift his eyes to another. The eye is a window to the soul. What manifests in someone's eyes often shows what is in his heart. Someone who is dissipated through drugs or drunkenness will have discoloration in the whites of his eyes. Much discernment can be gained by looking someone in the eyes to perceive what is happening on the inside.

Matthew 6:22-23 states:

The lamp of the body is the eye. If therefore your eye is good, your whole body will be full of light. But if your eye is bad, your whole body will be full of darkness.

Other translations describe the good eye as being clear, healthy or single. Through the eyes, the soul of a person rises up to touch the soul of another. We should train ourselves to look another person in the eye. I am not talking about a stare-down contest. That would be a grotesque perversion of eye-to-eye integrity. The ability to look someone else in the eye, if it is done in a right attitude, can reflect simplicity, caring and openness. We should be personal and direct with one another. The inability of a generation to look one another in the eye indicates widespread lack of covenant-keeping.

If my motives are upright toward you, I can look you in the eye. Turning one's eyes away while being addressed in conversation is a sign of disrespect. If my words toward my children are important, I need them to look me in the eye so that I can make an impression upon their soul. I like to look other people in the eye to generate respect and support toward them.

If someone is talking, we need to look him in the eye to communicate that we are giving his words full attention. Diverted eyes can mean one is thinking about something else. We need to make our relationships with other people a priority, so that our thoughts are not elsewhere when we have the opportunity to spend precious time with them. Looking someone else in the eye with a spirit of loving encouragement and positive affirmation communicates to him that he is important enough to warrant one's undivided attention.

Elisha and Hazael

In **II Kings 8**, the prophet Elisha confronts Hazael, a high official under King Ben-Hadad of Syria. Elisha discerns in the spirit that Hazael is planning to murder Ben-Hadad and usurp the throne. There is a confrontation between the two men and they lock eyes.

Then he [Elisha] fixed his gaze in a stare until he was ashamed; and the man of God wept. And Hazael said, "Why is my lord weeping?" And he answered, "Because I know the evil that you will do" (verses 11-12).

Through his stare, the prophet is challenging the character and motives of this evil man. It was the outright brazenness of Hazael that, not only was he planning to do evil, but he was willing to stare back at the prophet.

.Pushy, manipulative people will stare into another's eyes. That is wrong. A defeated, double-minded or guilty person will not be able to lift eyes to another.

This is also wrong. What is correct is to look one another in the eye with a wholesome, attentive and relationship-affirming attitude. The light of our eyes will project love into the soul of another.

Eye Contact

In the high school classroom, an important teaching technique is to command the obedience and attention of students through one's eyes. As the teacher deals with the class, he must clearly, firmly, and gently grip the souls of the students by holding them in contact with his eyes.

A king who sits on the throne of judgment scatters all evil with his eyes (Proverbs 20:8).

As a high school principal, I have found that in dealing with a disciplinary matter, one must command the eye contact of the student to communicate authority and reproof. The eyes communicate through their light what the mouth communicates through its words.

Young preachers and teachers should be trained to look people in the eye as they are sharing a message. It is a boring experience to listen to someone lecture without making eye contact. Home-group leaders should draw out the people through the light of personal interest in one's eyes. Looking at people in the audience with one's eyes is part of the body language of effective public speaking.

17

THE DEFINITION OF CHARACTER

Character

Central to an understanding of covenant is the development of character within an individual. We can only have covenant between us to the degree that we have character within us. The root of the word character means to engrave or cut into, such as branding with a mark of ownership. When referring to personality, it is the sum of all of one's inner qualities. Webster's Dictionary defines character as "the stamp of individuality impressed by nature, education, and habit; moral vigor and firmness acquired through self-discipline."

As believers in Jesus, we ought to be noted for our high moral character. In describing his ministry to the Thessalonians, Paul said that he delivered the Word of God not only with spiritual power, but also:

in much assurance, as you know what kind of men we were among you for your sake (I Thessalonians 1:5).

Part of the evidence of the gospel is the display of character in the one who is preaching. The testimony of our moral standards should confirm the testimony of the Word. **I Thessalonians 2:10** continues:

You are my witnesses, and God also, how devoutly and justly and blamelessly we behaved ourselves among you who believe.

Character is not formed overnight. It is acquired through time, by self-discipline and habit. Character is equivalent to the fruit of the Spirit. Character also implies nobility and conscience. **II Corinthians 1:12** speaks about:

the testimony of our conscience that we conducted ourselves in the world in simplicity and godly sincerity.

Character joins our inner conscience to our behavior in the world. It is a wrong understanding of grace to think that the free forgiveness of God does not elicit the development of character and integrity in our lives.

There is a Greek legend about an elderly philosopher who traveled the world seeking to find one honest man.

Many a man claims to have unfailing love, but a faithful man who can find? (Proverbs 20:6).

A faithful man is one in whom moral character has been developed. Our nation has been struggling with a vacuum of trusted moral leadership. The populace of the country thinks that nationally known religious leaders and politicians are smudged with adultery, dishonesty and greed. Too many of our leaders seem to be hucksters and hustlers, shysters and swindlers.

Integrity

A related quality to character is integrity. Integrity comes from a word meaning whole or complete. In mathematics, an integer is a whole number that has not been broken into fractions. Webster's defines integrity as "an unimpaired state, moral soundness, uprightness, and purity." One of the reasons there has been a breakdown of character and integrity is that public education has centered on technical proficiency without equivalent morality. If the Bible and prayer are taken out of school, education will produce leaders with complex intellects but hollow moral foundations.

In prophesying over the young child Jesus, the prophet Simeon said to Jesus' mother:

This child is destined for the fall and rising of many in Israel and for a sign which will be spoken against (Luke 2:34).

If a young person is trained in character and integrity, he will be able to stand in the face of disapproval from others. Integrity is to stick with one's conscience without being swayed by popular opinion. We need a generation to stand up for what is right, even if they are criticized and spoken against by the media.

Discipline

The only way one can develop character is through self-discipline. When a child is young, he is disciplined externally by his parents. As the child develops into maturity, the external discipline of his parents is internalized. By a mechanism of conscience and will-power, he imposes discipline on himself. This internal mechanism is called self-discipline.

The word discipline is related to the word disciple. How can we be a disciple if we are not going to be disciplined by Jesus? How can we be a disciple if we are not going to exercise the self-discipline needed to follow Him? Self-discipline involves an effort to control the will to do what one knows is right. Self-discipline is not allowing the lazy and lustful tendencies of our flesh to guide us. Without self-discipline, our conscience is incapable of taking command over our beings. Self-discipline is the demand of the will for our bodies and minds to obey the leading of the Spirit.

Self-discipline will lead toward a productive life-style. **Proverbs 21:5** states:

The plans of the diligent surely lead to plenty, but those of everyone who is hasty surely to poverty.

A self-disciplined mind can begin to plan and dream of positive solutions. Self-discipline produces diligence and patience. One who is not self-disciplined will sink into laziness. He will not be able to exercise the self-control to be patient. An undisciplined person will be over-hasty and make mistakes. Diligence, patience and self-discipline work together.

An example in Scripture of self-discipline was the prophet Daniel. Daniel demonstrated discipline in his study habits while he was at school in Babylon. He demonstrated discipline in his decision to maintain a diet of simple food, even though he was being offered the rich menu of the king. He demonstrated discipline in his prayer life in that he prayed three times everyday. Daniel demonstrated discipline in his work in the government such that no one could find any fault with what he had done.

Excellence

The exercise of self-discipline should yield the fruit of excellence. Excellence should be part of every believer's vocabulary. We are not called to do a second-rate job at anything. The old adage that "anything worth doing is worth doing well" is certainly a biblical concept. Too often believers have used a phony form of spirituality to excuse second-rate effort and shoddy workmanship. We are the workmanship of God; therefore, everything that we do should reflect a workmanship of excellence. We are motivated to do everything in a first-class manner.

The prophet Daniel had this heart for excellence. His self-discipline produced the excellence. Everything he did was ten times better than anyone else around him. **Daniel 2:20** states:

and in all matters of wisdom and understanding about which the king examined them, he found them ten times better than all the magicians and astrologers that were in his realm.

The magicians and astrologers here are the professional advisers of the king. They might be the equivalent of modern scientists and government leaders. We should operate according to the Daniel standard. Our standard should be an excellence ten times better than the best of the standards the world has to offer.

Excellence is demonstrated in every aspect of life. We should have excellence in our school curriculums, musical performances, manner of dress, use of grammar and vocabulary, posture and demeanor, upkeep of lawns and houses, clarity of thinking, marital relations, courtesy in driving, business records, work for our employer, ability to handle stress, promptness, cheerfulness and so on. We should manifest first-rate quality in everything.

In the parable of the unjust steward, Jesus commended him for dealing shrewdly. **Luke 16:8** states:

The master commended the unjust steward because he had dealt shrewdly. For the sons of this world are shrewder in their generation than the sons of light.

Even in the matters of worldly affairs, we should demonstrate a sharp quality of excellence. We are not to be dull-witted, but clear-minded. Everything we do should have a "class" about it that reflects nobility of character. Style should not put emphasis on externals, but our quality of style should manifest the importance of what we do. In **II Corinthians 5:20**, Paul states:

We are ambassadors for Christ.

If we are ambassadors, then everything we do should represent an ambassadorial quality and excellence.

Self-Control

If we are to have character, we must also develop self-control. Self-control is one of the fruits of the Spirit (Galatians 5:22). The fruits of the Spirit are a symbolic way of defining godly character. Fruit of the Spirit means the traits of the Holy Spirit. The traits of godliness are revealed through our own spirits. The fruit of the Spirit is the evidence of God's character reflected through our own character. Self-control is one of the most important fruits of the Spirit.

Proverbs 16:32 states:

He who is slow to anger is better than the mighty, and he who rules his spirit than he who takes a city.

The image here is that of a leader of an army who conquers a fortified city and becomes its ruler. He is obviously a man of great strength. However, it takes more strength to govern one's inner being than to perform such an heroic military feat. Being able to control one's own emotions is a key to spiritual success. We are to govern our anger. We are to govern our tongues. We are to govern our thoughts. To exercise self-government over our feelings, words, and thoughts is to walk in victory in the Spirit of God.

The entire universe is to be brought under the authority of the name of Jesus. The first priority of the authority of the kingdom of God is to cause someone's spirit to be recreated. The second priority is for a person to be filled with the Spirit of God. After these two great priorities, the primary goal is to gain government over our soul. The extension of the authority of the name of Jesus must be in the area of self-control. Self-control is the lordship of Jesus over our feelings, words and thoughts. The extension of the kingdom of God then moves outward to health in our bodies, harmony in our relationships, and prosperity in our finances. The kingdom of God encompasses every area of life.

Self-control is the lordship of Jesus over our souls. We exercise self-government under the overall government of Jesus. Paul tells us in **II Corinthians 10:5** that we are to exercise self-control in our intellect by:

bringing every thought into captivity to the obedience of Christ.

James tells us in chapter 3 that we are to bridle our tongues, even as we might put a bit in a horse's mouth or use a rudder to direct a boat.

Self-Control and Leadership

Through the fruit of self-control God's government in our lives will begin to extend outward to others. Self-control is the expression of God's government in our lives individually. All authority over other people is an extension of one's own self-government under Jesus. One can only lead and govern others to the degree that there is self-control in his own life. All spiritual authority is an extension of the government of Jesus in our lives through the fruit of self-control. The greater degree there is of self-government, the greater degree there can be of outward governance.

Meekness is a type of self-control. Moses was a man who had as great an authority as anyone who ever lived. He was a paramount leader and a classic example of governing authority. Moses was granted such great authority because he had learned self-control and meekness.

The man Moses was very meek, more than all men who were on the face of the earth (Numbers 12:3).

This meekness and self-control was the secret of his ability to govern others.

Moses did not always have this self-control. He started out as a brash and quick-tempered man. God had Moses spend forty years in the wilderness of Midian to teach him meekness. In the one instance in his life when Moses did not exercise self-control, he was disqualified from entering the Promised Land. In **Numbers 20**, Moses lost his self-control and struck the rock twice to bring water out for the people at Kadesh. The Lord's response to this in **verse 12** was:

Because you did not believe Me, to hallow Me in the eyes of Israel, therefore you shall not bring this congregation into the land which I have given them.

The limitation of outward governance is determined by the degree of inward self-control.

When one is in leadership, he will find many pressures and attacks upon him as a person. These attacks from the enemy would attempt to make him lose control. The people look up to a leader and need him not to lose his temper or to become "unglued." A flock of sheep cannot afford to have the shepherd lose control. An explosive loss of temper by one in leadership can damage many members of the group. Leadership is guidance; one cannot guide others if he has lost his personal bearings. Self-control in a leader communicates stability, security and safety to his flock.

The Fool

The opposite of having self-control is being a fool. **Proverbs 25:28** states:

Whoever has no rule over his spirit is like a city broken down without walls.

A person who is out of control is a fool. The fool of Proverbs 25:28 is contrasted with the strong, self-controlled man of Proverbs 16:32. A person who has no rule over his own spirit is like one who has no fortified walls of defense. He is a weak person who is easily defeated. Any attack or temptation overcomes him.

In dealing with teenagers, I have found that some will end up getting into trouble even though they have done nothing malicious. They act foolishly but almost do not know why they did such a foolish act. They look back on what they did wrong and say, "I don't know why I did it. I just couldn't help myself." They could not resist the peer-group pressure or the need to gain attention from others. Their foolishness was a cheap tactic to get some momentary approval through the laughter of their peers. Someone who has no self-control has no ability to resist wrongdoing or foolishness when tempted.

If a young woman has no walls of spiritual self-control, she may not be able to resist the sexual and romantic accostings of a young man. The walls of self-control inside a young woman were built there through the affection of her father and mother. If a young girl was well-loved and disciplined while growing up, she will have the wholesome spiritual strength to say "No." If not, her need for affection will open gaps in her defense and make her prey to immoral sensual affection.

In the **Song of Solomon 8:9**, the Shulamite maiden's brothers question her:

If she is a wall, we will build upon her a battlement of silver; if she is a door we will enclose her with the cedar.

The judgment of her brothers is that if she has had enough walls of self-control to stay out of immorality, she will be worthy of much honor. If she has let down her walls to indiscretion, she will be forced to live in disgrace. The blessings of grace, honor and favor will be heaped upon someone who has been wise enough to develop the fruit of self-control.

Respect

Respect is treating every person with dignity. Respect for others is born out of the fear of God. We treat other people with respect because we have a reverence for God. Since other people are made in the image of God, we treat them with respect as well. If we disrespect another, we have shown disrespect to God.

We are not to show disrespect for a poor person. **Proverbs 14:31, 17:5,** and **22:2** state:

He who oppresses the poor reproaches his Maker, but he who honors Him has mercy on the needy. He who mocks the poor reproaches his Maker. The rich and the poor have this in common, the Lord is Maker of them all.

The rich and the poor here refers to more than finances alone. An emotionally wounded or unlovely person can be considered poor. We should respect them even if they are in the lowest status in society. If there is someone you feel is not worthy of respect, you are still commanded to respect him because he is a creation of God.

All human beings were made by God. We treat every other person with respect, because God deserves respect. Our attitude of respect toward others is not contingent on their relative human worth. Demonstrating respect is an act of covenant character coming out of our faith in God.

In our high school, I call our students by their last name with the prefix Miss or Mister. They realize that I have a commitment to treat them with respect at all times. I treat them with dignity even if they are not acting dignified. What we sow is what we will reap. They understand the intuitive demand that if I will treat them with respect, they need to return the favor.

Respect for others and polite speech are inherent to a covenantal attitude. We always act with dignity. We treat ourselves and others with the same respect and dignity. I am not talking about putting on superficial social graces. By faith we are to live up to the self-image that we are created in the image of Jesus. By faith we should treat others as divine beings.

The prophet Jeremiah described disrespect for elders as an indication of the destruction of a nation. **Lamentations 5:12** says:

Princes were hung up by their hands, and elders were not respected.

Disrespect of young people toward elders and among adults is an indication of a breakdown of covenant. Respect for parents is an act of covenant keeping. Children should call their mothers blessed (Proverbs 31:28). Great honor should be given in the presence of elderly men and women (Leviticus 19:32). One should never say a negative word about his father or mother (Exodus 21:17).

We use polite speech and courtesy because we act out of a heart that desires to keep covenant. If we are reverent, the blessings of God's covenant fall upon us. **Proverbs 28:14** states:

Blessed is the man who is always reverent.

Godly character is expressed through integrity, self-discipline, patience, diligence, excellence, self-control, self-government, respect and dignity. Politeness of speech and courtesy are expressions of the divine self-image within us.

18

TO CONFRONT
OR NOT TO CONFRONT

While we must confront one another in love, it is equally important to learn when not to confront. If covenant brothers feel they have to confront one another at all times, they may soon get worn out and lose the joy of their relationships. We are not out to manufacture a product but to learn how to love one another. Confrontation is only done to the extent that it enhances the relationship. Much of the time we can extend the grace to one another to overlook a problem.

Improving

In counseling, as long as a person is moving forward in some area of his life, the counselor should take the posture of encouraging and affirming him. If a person is improving in one area of life, he will be in a better position to deal with the others. It is not necessary to confront all areas at the same time. As long as the person is making progress, it is not necessary to correct him. We may think that a person is moving ahead so slowly that he is making almost no progress at all. However, the degree of improvement is relative to how the obstacle appears to the one involved.

What may seem like a minor challenge to one person could be a major one to another. Any progress is an indication that the person's eyes are facing forward and that his heart is moving in the right direction. When I was learning how to sing, I had very little confidence in that area. To some, this may have seemed a relatively minor affair; however, to me it seemed insurmountable. I would feel sick, nervous, and unsure of myself. I was asked why my singing was not improving more. Learning to carry a tune was a painstaking affair for me. Playing music and singing has since become a central joy in my life. We must not underestimate the effort that someone else is making to improve. It will always seem small to us and large to him.

Overlooking

Proverbs 19:11 states a very significant principle:

The discretion of a man makes him slow to anger, and it is to his glory to overlook a transgression.

An act of love is to overlook a transgression rather than confront it. Sometimes it is more effective to turn the other cheek than to deal with a wrongdoing. It takes character to put up with someone's irritating behavior. Living a godly example backed by the power of prayer can be an effective way to change a person's attitude. **Romans 12:20** quotes from Proverbs 25 saying:

If your enemy hungers, feed him; if he thirsts, give him a drink; for in doing so you will heap coals of fire on his head.

If someone has offended me, I have the option of directing toward him little blessings and practical favors. We can exercise love, and love can never fail. By loving someone who is offended against me, I can exert a positive spiritual force to his conscience. Action can speak louder than words, particularly if it is reinforced by prayer. One method of loving confrontation is serving someone's practical needs in love.

Giving

A second method of bringing about reconciliation is to send someone money for a gift. If money is given with love and a humble heart it can be spiritually very effective. **Proverbs 21:14** states:

A gift in secret pacifies anger.

This can have the positive connotation of using money as an expression of love for someone. If someone has become offended, you can pray that God will raise up an opportunity to bless that person with a gift or with money. An easy way to bless someone is to buy a certificate at an expensive restaurant for him to share a meal there with his spouse. This kind of gift blesses the couple with a lovely evening that they might not have spent on themselves otherwise.

Take note of the commendation that Jesus gave to the unjust steward in **Luke 16:9**:

And I say to you, make friends for yourselves by unrighteous mammon, that when it fails you, they may receive you into everlasting habitations.

Everlasting habitations are part of the positive relationships we have with other people. We can use money, though it is nothing of itself, to promote a good spirit between friends. Covenant friendship is high in value. Sometimes we can exchange money, which means little, to promote reconciliation, which means everything.

Praying

Loving confrontation without verbal correction can be done through submissive conduct backed by prayer. Peter advised women with stubborn husbands to use this method. If we can be submissive, demonstrate good conduct and pray intensively, a person is likely to be won over by such godly influence. **I Peter 3:1** states:

Wives, be submissive to your own husbands, that even if some do not obey

the word, they, without a word, may be won by the conduct of their wives, when they observe your chaste conduct.

If a friend is disobeying Scriptures, we can win him over through a silent example. This is particularly appropriate when dealing with someone who is in authority over us. It may be a husband, employer, pastor, or older person. When someone's ears are not ready to hear a corrective word, his conscience can be spoken to with a living example. Loving confrontation is always to bring about personal reconciliation.

How to Make the Choice

When is it more appropriate to overlook a transgression than to confront it (Proverbs 19:11)? Sometimes we need to change another person; other times we need to put up with his problems. We have two choices. If a person sins against me, I have the choice of correcting him. I also have the choice of overlooking the matter. If a person's sin is not likely to be repeated in the future and has not broken our relationship, I can choose to forgive and forget. If an act of forgiveness will eliminate the problem, there is no reason for confrontation and correction.

Some people say it is proper to tell the other person for the sake of being honest that he has hurt you. I disagree. If there is a pattern in the other person's life whereby the hurt may reoccur, then there must be dialogue to work out the problem. If it is just a case of having been wounded once, we should be strong enough in the Lord to forgive the other person, receive healing and proceed as if nothing has happened. The question to ask is which of the two routes will better promote our relationship. Our relationship is not promoted if I am going to continue being hurt. We can use the power of healing and forgiveness that can be gleaned directly from God.

Galatians 6:1-2 presents these options very clearly:

Brothers, if any man is overtaken in any trespass, you who are spiritual restore such a one in a spirit of gentleness, considering yourself lest you also be tempted. Bear one another's burdens, and so fulfill the law of Christ.

The process of covenantal confrontation must be done in an attitude of gentleness. Covenant confrontation can fall into a trap of judgmentalism, pride and temptation.

We can bear or carry another person's burden in order to fulfill the law of love. Love can cover a multitude of sins. Our concern is for the growth of the other person. Confrontation is for the sake of helping and protecting the body of believers. Our primary motivation is not to feel more comfortable. In worldly psychology, people discuss their problems for the mere sake of bringing them into the open. We have no sense of fascination for our sins or for someone else's. We are not playing a psychological game of opening each other's can of worms. If dealing with someone else's problems can help set things right, we should do so. If not, we should skip the confrontation, overlook the problem and move on in faith. To overlook a transgression can be an act of character, faith and love.

No Over Sensitivity

Covenant is both costly and delicate. Covenant is costly because people's trust for one another is extremely sensitive. It is all too easy for a person to become offended. Jesus' disciples were at times offended by one another's actions or statements. If one of them did something prideful, the others were offended. It is pride that inflates the ego and makes it overly sensitive. If people were not so prideful, they would not be so easily offended.

It is important to purge oneself of the tendency to be easily offended. We should not be offended if someone else insults us. We should not be offended if someone else corrects us. **I Corinthians 13:4** states:

Love suffers long and is kind; love does not envy; love does not parade itself, is not puffed up; love does not behave rudely, does not seek its own, is not provoked, thinks no evil.

We can paraphrase this verse by saying that love is not easily offended. A person cannot get anywhere spiritually if he allows himself to be offended.

If a person says that he is easily hurt and very sensitive, he may seem to be humble. In reality, his pride is putting off other people by saying, "I do not give anyone permission to speak correction into my life."

Recently, some loving but corrective input was given to a certain brother. Afterwards, he came back and replied that he had been hurt by what was said to him. He said this with an air that he was being open and receptive by sharing the fact that he had been hurt. This however was an unacceptable response. While it seemed so humble and sensitive it was really quite the opposite.

Not Getting Offended

Instead of opening up the relationships, this false sensitivity cut off future dialogue. We had come to an impasse. An emotional reaction to loving correction is a denial of covenantal relationship. To say one was hurt by past input is to say one does not want to receive future input. By faith we will not be people who react emotionally; by faith we will not be people who get offended easily; by faith we will not say that we are hurt by people who are trying to help us.

A brother offended is harder to win than a strong city, and contentions are like the bars of a castle (Proverbs 18:19).

If we do not get offended, we make covenantal dialogue easy. If we do get offended, we make covenantal dialogue difficult. We must be attentive not to offend one another. Once a person is offended, it is difficult to love him out of that offense. An old proverb says, "An ounce of prevention is worth a pound of cure." An ounce of preventing someone from being offended will be worth more than a pound of cure to get him out of that offense. When someone is offended, it takes much spiritual application to restore him. An offended brother must be approached in dialogue and prayer. We tend to underestimate how much others are offended.

In nursing the offended brother back into reconciliation, it is sometimes necessary to deal strongly with the reasons why he allowed himself to get offended. **Proverbs 21:22** states:

A wise man scales the city of the mighty and brings down the trusted stronghold.

If an offended brother is like a walled city, sometimes the only way to help him is to tear down the sources of wrong attitudes that have allowed him to be offended. This takes delicateness and strength. An offended brother is trusting some stronghold of carnality or selfishness. With wisdom, those areas can be torn down and removed. If they are not removed, he may be likely to get offended again. Once a person has become offended, it is difficult to draw him back into reconciliation.

Communication Breakdown

One of the most energy-demanding duties a person can be engaged in is to communicate. Communicating takes tremendous effort. The process of covenant takes communication and more communication. Therefore, covenant demands effort. Communication is worthwhile because it keeps people from being hurt, confused and misunderstood. We must make the effort to communicate at all times.

The human race is in a state of widespread communication breakdown. We do not even speak the same language. The human race used to speak one language, but it was divided when the privilege was misused at the Tower of Babel. Since that time, language has been fractured. We are in a state of linguistic entropy. Every time we try to communicate something, we need to overcome the breakdown of language skills.

If a pack of cards is scattered over a room, the cards are not going to come back into the deck by themselves. Communication does not just happen by itself. Due to the effects of the Tower of Babel, every act of communication takes energy to unify the two minds involved. Communicating is similar to cleaning a messy room. Communicating is a messy chore; it will not happen by itself; it requires energy; and it must be repeated over and over again.

In **Ephesians 4:3**, Paul says that believers should be:

endeavoring to keep the unity of the Spirit in the bond of peace.

Effort must be expended in maintaining the harmony of our relationships. Covenant is costly. Covenant demands vigilance to guard the bonds of our interrelationships. We must make the effort to keep unity. We must put forth energy to ensure the bonds of covenant. Covenant keeping may be costly, but it is the central issue of redemption.

Each evening, when I come home from work, my wife and I purposely take the time to communicate what has happened during our day. This is often the last thing I feel like doing. Husbands and wives face the difficulty that their prime time for good communication comes after the children have been put to bed and the chores taken care of. They are already quite tired. The smallest amount of communication under these circumstances seems exhausting. A husband and wife cannot allow themselves to become alienated from one another. The only way to prevent alienation is to communicate. A good marriage is maintained by putting the effort and time into covenantal communication.

Among Pastors

Pastors of different congregations must build good relationships. Pastors are usually quite busy; for them to find the time to build quality relationships is difficult. To draw a group of pastors together to relate to one another seems like a miracle. Such a meeting has to be scheduled in advance, and people have to be persuaded to come. Previous divisions must be overcome. Communication between ministers is costly.

In our local congregations, we schedule regular meetings for the pastors and heads of outreach ministries to get together. These meetings primarily involve prayer and fellowship. Building trust is a major investment in the kingdom of God. Each minister must pull away from his own area of involvement. He must convince himself of the priority of investing quality time with the other ministers.

Patient Persuasion

Now we exhort you, brethren, warn those who are unruly, comfort the fainthearted, uphold the weak, be patient with all (1 Thessalonians 5:14).

Confrontation must be done in a spirit of affirming love. We must confront, but we must be gentle. Paul is encouraging us to continue covenantal communication. We are to warn those who are unruly, hardhearted or lazy. We are to comfort, cheer up and support anyone who has become faint-hearted. We must have patience to continue working with people even though it takes time for them to improve.

Patience is a key in being able to counsel people in authority. It takes patience to continue persuading someone toward covenantal attitudes. **Proverbs 25:15** says:

By much patience a prince is persuaded.

Every believer can be seen as a prince in his own right. Every believer is worth the patience to persuade him toward what is right. Persuasion is a beautiful concept of Scripture. Persuasion is the art of continued dialogue over a period of time where a person's spirit is brought into unity with another's. Persuasion does not want the other just to accept one's view unthinkingly. It desires to minister sufficient perspective and vision that the other person sees it for himself.

The prince or ruler can also be seen as a leader in a congregation. Since there are many factors pulling on a leader's life, it often takes repeated appeals to get him to change directions. At times someone will have suggested to me a good idea, but through all the influences going on around my life, I did not get the opportunity to act on it. The person who made the suggestion may have felt that I ignored him or rejected his advice. This is not so. We need to draw to a leader's attention a new perspective over a period of time.

Time for Discipline

Covenant requires patience because we want to give a person every opportunity to change. Sometimes people are frustrated if they feel a leader is not moving quickly enough to correct someone. However, if they were the one being disciplined, they might think the process too abrupt. Discipline needs time because we desire only the best for the other person.

In **Luke 13**, Jesus told a parable about a tree that was not giving fruit. It was thought that the tree should be cut down since it was not producing. As the keeper of the vineyard wanted to give the tree every chance to grow, he appealed for a little more time. In **verses 8-9**, the keeper of the vineyard states:

Sir, let it alone this year also, until I dig around it and fertilize it. And if it bears fruit, well. But if not, after that you shall cut it down.

In a process of discipline, sufficient time must be given for the person to change. When sufficient opportunity has been given, the bad tree must be dealt with decisively.

There is a dynamic tension between the desire to give the person another chance and the need to discipline quickly to protect the rest of the flock. **Ecclesiastes 8:11** states:

Because the sentence against an evil work is not executed speedily, the heart of the sons of men is fully set in them to do evil.

Discipline must be carried through without delay. If it is not, the force of evil will begin to drag down others. A carnal person will influence other people to be carnal. On the other hand, the process of discipline does take time. People must not be frustrated at the length of time it takes to administer justice. In American courtrooms, a case can last for years in order to bring in all the evidence. A leader desires to see every bit of evidence come in and not to act too hastily. Even though we must execute justice, there is always the fervent hope that the person will improve.

Changed by Others

When we enter into covenantal relationships, we are going to be changed by those relationships. Other people affect us. Many times people do not want to undergo change. When we enter into relationship with someone, we are going to be influenced by him. The area in which I am irritated by another person may be the very area in which that person is being used by God to change some aspect of my life.

Change feels uncomfortable. A covenantally challenging relationship can also be uncomfortable. Discomfort is often the evidence of change in our lives. **Proverbs 27:17** states:

As iron sharpens iron, so a man sharpens the countenance of his friend.

The friction we experience in relationship building sharpens us. We challenge one another; we rub against each other; we soften one another; we build one another up; and we tear down one another's carnal areas. Both sides of the relationship should mature and become more godly.

A person who does not want to be involved in relationships is too caught up in his own perspective. A minister who does not want to relate to other ministers is too caught up in his own ambitions. Self-seeking or striving for achievement will cause a person to isolate himself and avoid relationships.

A man who isolates himself seeks his own desire (Proverbs 18:1).

If we desire the common good, there is no need to be isolated. If we are trying to accomplish a goal that involves only ourselves, working with others will seem to be a diversion.

Covenantal character desires to be morally accountable. A man of integrity wants to have others around him to hold him accountable to do what is right. We should look forward to accountability, not avoid it. We should esteem those who have the courage to hold us accountable.

No One Exempt

Some people believe that once a person attains a certain level of spiritual maturity, he no longer needs to be held accountable. This could not be farther from the truth. The higher someone rises in ministry leadership, the more he needs accountability. As the options for success are greater, so are the temptations. A major figure, who is doing much effective ministry is not above accountability. The leaders are especially under attack from Satan. Because of that attack, they need the protection of being surrounded by others who will directly hold them accountable.

Strong Friends

When one is in the leadership of a ministry, there is a subtle temptation to justify slight wrongdoings for the sake of the greater good of the ministry. The temptation that the end will justify the means is intensified the more successful the ministry becomes. We must put to rest the lie that any man outgrows accountability. The higher the position of spiritual leadership, the more accountability is needed. A spiritually mature person will embrace and appreciate accountability.

He who rebukes a man will find more favor afterward, than he who flatters with the tongue (Proverbs 28:23).

Recently I was invited to be part of the board of directors of a certain ministry. Being a new member of the board, I was hesitant to address the difficulties for fear of offending the others. However, I found that the men involved were appreciative of being able to deal with issues in frank and open fashion. A wise person will appreciate a friend who will hold him accountable. The fear that others will reject us for honest correction is unwarranted. Loving correction will gain more favor with others. Let us rid ourselves of the fear of dealing with one another in a straightforward manner. If we behave with strength, others will become strong. If we all become strong, we will be able to love one another with refreshing freedom and honesty.

Covenant keepers desire the friendship of strong people. We should not shy away from strong people but welcome their companionship. Having spiritual strength is not, in any sense, being stubborn or willful. People with enough strength of character and courage will challenge us to rise to a greater level of capacity. Believing in Jesus is not a sign of weakness but of strength. We are strong people by faith and enjoy strong faith in others.

Faithful are the wounds of a friend, but the kisses of an enemy are deceitful (Psalm 27:6).

It takes no courage to be a flatterer. People who hold us accountable are the ones who are truly faithful. The person who is willing to correct you is the one who really loves you. A person who will not bring to your attention what you are doing wrong is not deeply committed to the relationship. Covenant keeping takes courage. Accountability takes strength. Let us be faithful enough to one another to hold each other accountable to covenantal standards.

19

THE EXTENT
OF COVENANT KEEPING

Love is the cardinal rule of God's universe. Were we in a perfect state of harmony, love would lead us to enjoy and explore relationships with one another. Seeing that we live in a world in which perfect harmony has been broken, love must seek to restore potential relationships. Love restores harmonious relationships by means of establishing covenant. Love confronts the one we are seeking to establish covenant with by communicating to that person the areas that are hindering the relationship. Love attempts to reestablish a more perfect relationship.

Ephesians 4:15 describes this action as:

speaking the truth in love.

What a far reaching statement this is! If we love someone, we must speak the truth to him about whatever may be hurting him or hurting our relationship. Truth not spoken from love is not legitimate.

Love must speak the truth. Love must speak. Truth is spoken for the purpose of restoring relationships. Truth must be spoken in a loving manner. Truth promotes covenant. Speaking and listening promote covenant. Love operates through covenant.

Evangelism as Covenant

Evangelism is an act of love in the sense that it seeks to restore a relationship that is broken. An unsaved person is alienated from his relationship with God. Evangelism confronts a person with the blood covenant offered by Jesus. He is invited by this loving confrontation to reenter a relationship with God and the other believers in the world.

All of God's actions on earth are redemptive. God's method of redemption and restoring relationships is to make covenant. God's operations in the earth are done through covenant. God's posture toward us is one of offering and keeping covenant. **Deuteronomy 7:9** describes God as:

the faithful God who keeps covenant and mercy for a thousand generations with those who love Him and keep His commandments.

God is faithful to keep covenant with those who are faithful to keep covenant with Him. His love for us responds to our love for Him.

There is no reason for God to perform any action outside of covenant. A non-covenantal action would not serve to reestablish a committed relationship. If God operates outside of covenant, He nullifies His own purpose. A non-covenantal action would be self-defeating and lack integrity. God never does so.

Not only does God refuse to act outside of covenant, but in a certain sense He is legally not allowed to. Covenant bears with it a restriction on outside activity. **Ezekiel 20:37** states that God's desire toward Israel was to:

make you pass under the rod and bring you into the bond of the covenant.

In a covenant one binds himself not to act outside of the boundaries of that relationship. In a marriage, a man and a woman bind themselves not to have relations with others. Restriction of activity outside the covenant ensures freedom for activity within the covenant.

Prophecy as Covenant

God will not act outside His covenant with a human being. **Amos 3:7** states:

Surely the Lord God does nothing, unless He reveals His secret to His servants the prophets.

This is not a sneak preview where a movie is shown to a select group of critics before it is released to the general public. The prophets in this passage are representative partners of God's covenant. God will not act unless He comes into agreement with His covenant partner on the earth. In **Amos 3:3**, the question is asked:

Can two walk together unless they are agreed?

The rhetorical answer is, "No."

God cannot walk on this earth unless He does so in cooperation with an earth citizen. To walk together, they must come into covenant agreement. An understanding of the fact that God restricts Himself to acting within the boundaries of covenant will help to explain many questions as to why God did not seemingly intervene to prevent some evil occurrence. The purpose of prayer is to establish an action in the earth based upon a covenant agreement between God and His human partner. Prayer itself is an act of exercising covenant.

David states in **Psalm 25:14:**

The secret of the Lord is with those who fear Him, and He will show them His covenant.

God extends revelation to a group of human beings in response to and in formation of a covenant with them.

If everything that God does is wrapped up in covenant keeping, so should be the life of a believer in Jesus. We are in kinship with any fellow human being since we are part of the same race. We are obliged to confront him that he is breaking covenant with us and with Almighty God. We seek to restore that covenant. We are ambassadors from God. We are brokers of the new covenant. We are legal witnesses in evangelism, bringing an official testimony to the other person, which influences his standing before the courtroom of heaven. I witness to another human being because of a commitment to relationship with him. As I might go to a fellow believer in order that we might be reconciled, so I go to a fellow human being in the hope that he will be reconciled to God.

Hear now in the light of covenant restoration this classic passage on evangelism from **II Corinthians 5:18:**

> **And all things are of God, who has reconciled us to Himself through Jesus Christ, and has given us the ministry of reconciliation, that is, that God was in Christ reconciling the world to Himself, not imputing their trespasses to them, and has committed to us the word of reconciliation. Therefore we are ambassadors for Christ, as though God were pleading through us: we implore you in Christ's behalf, be reconciled to God.**

Since *"God was in Christ reconciling the world to Himself,"* God's way of salvation through Jesus may be seen as an act of covenant. The cross confronts us with our need for reconciliation. Evangelism is a call for covenantal reconciliation to a second party, namely God.

Prayer as Covenant

Prayers offered to God in faith are done on the basis of covenantal agreement. In **Matthew 18:19,** Jesus states:

> **If two of you agree on earth concerning anything they ask, it will be done for them by My Father in heaven.**

If two earth citizens come into covenantal agreement, it will be established through God as their covenant partner in heaven. Prayer is an agreement with a partner on earth with his Partner in heaven.

Prosperity as Covenant

The ebb and tide of the flow of finances upon the earth are based upon God's covenants with mankind. **Deuteronomy 8:18** states:

> **For it is God who gives you the power to get wealth, that He may establish the covenant that He swore to your fathers, as it is this day.**

Certain men become wealthy. Their wealth goes on to their sons. Their sons may use the money productively and benevolently, or they may waste it. A nation's economy grows and falters. While it may not seem apparent, all of the trends in economics can be traced back to some aspect of God's covenant. All wealth originally comes from God, and only those who are in covenant with Him have a right to have it.

How far does the responsibility for covenant keeping with fellow human beings affect us? As he was fleeing from God's justice after having murdered his brother

Abel, Cain claimed that he was not his brother's keeper. To what extent are we to be our brother's keeper?

An underlying theme of Scriptures is that of the kinsman-redeemer. The picture of the kinsman-redeemer is symbolic of Jesus. It also has applications for human interaction. **Leviticus 25:25** states:

If one of your brothers becomes poor and has sold some of his possession, and if his kinsman-redeemer comes to redeem it, then he may redeem what his brother sold.

If a man fell into debt and was unable to extricate himself, his next-of-kin had the duty of conscience to redeem him out of his financial bondage. God wants us to grow in our commitment and trust to the point that our possessions and finances will be available to serve one another. In the book of Acts some of the wealthy believers sold their lands to make available enough money that the poorer covenant brothers would not go without. We are not to establish some new policy about communal possessions, but we should take our commitment to one another seriously enough that we would be ready to "bail one another out" in times of need. We are kinsmen of one another, co-heirs and covenant partners in the kingdom of God.

The image of covenant encompasses our entire view of Scriptures. Scriptures themselves are a testament, a document of covenant testimony. In the ancient temple, animals were slain, and the blood was poured out as the covenant was cut. Scriptures speak of the blood and the salt of the covenant, the signs and the ark of the covenant, the curses, blessings, and promises of the covenant, the people and the God of the covenant. The Bible is a book of covenant.

Stages of Love

Love, in its ideal state, is one of perfect harmony. This is the paradise stage. If that harmony is broken, love must go into restorative action. This is the redemptive stage in which relationships are sought to be established by a guaranteed commitment; we can call this the covenant stage. The covenant stage is working back toward the paradise stage. Where sin abounds, love must move to a protective state in which personal interactions are enforced by punitive sanctions. This is the law stage. Harmony is love's ideal. Covenant seeks to reestablish that harmony. Law punishes violations against that harmony.

Depth of intimacy must be matched by corresponding depth of commitment. In the case of marriage, there is complete human intimacy, and there must also be absolute commitment. As marriage is the only form of covenant that is familiar to our culture, it serves as a model from which to view salvation and the law.

In the Garden of Eden before the fall, man and woman were designed to come into perfect unity, with no suspicion or mistrust. Later, when the possibility of mistrust entered their hearts, their intimacy was brought under commitment to an oath. Later still, through the hardness of men's hearts, specific legislation for a process of divorce and sanctions against adultery were required to be formulated.

Matthew 19:5-9 reads:

"For this reason a man should leave his father and mother and be joined to

his wife, and the two shall become one flesh." So then they are no longer two but one flesh. Therefore what God has joined together, let not man divide. They said to Him, "Why then did Moses command to give a certificate of divorce, and to put her away?" He said to them, "Moses, because of the hardness of your hearts, permitted you to divorce your wives, but from the beginning it was not so."

Being joined together is the intimacy shared between a man and a woman. Becoming one flesh is the command: if they have been joined together, they must commit to being one. The idea that they are one flesh is a moral imperative from God. Since they have been joined in intimacy, they must have the covenantal commitment to stay unified and not betray their covenant. The marriage covenant is the way that God made them one; it should not be broken.

Law Stage of Love

The stage of law was forced to be enacted when the people could not maintain the heart attitude of faithfulness to their marriages. Since people were not being faithful to their marriages, the only loving and covenantal option was to adopt the legal process of divorce. Divorce was an act of God in response to man's hardness of heart. Jesus is not saying that there is no longer a process of legal divorce.

Personal marital harmony is stage "A" (paradise love). An oath of marriage commitment is stage "B" (covenant love). Just procedures of certified divorce is stage "C" (legal love). Jesus is teaching that the ideal in God's mind is the perfect trust between a man and a woman. One can break the spirit of a marriage covenant through one's heart-adultery even if one has not outwardly broken the law. The legal procedures of divorce are not God's ideal. Jesus is describing the necessity of God's having gone to stage C of legal enforcement protecting marital intimacy. If stage A and stage B love cannot work, the only moral thing to do is to operate through stage C.

When covenant has broken down, the only loving thing to do is to enact legal procedures. If one does not enact legal procedures, he is promoting both immorality and illegality. Divorce was created by God in reaction to man's hardness of heart. Divorce is a step of love relative to that hardness. Divorce is the equivalent to marriage as disfellowshipping is to congregational membership. God does not want divorce, just as He does not want to disfellowship a member of a congregation. If the situation demands, legal action is the only proper, covenantal and loving thing to do. If a person commits a crime without repentance, the only loving thing to do is to enforce punishment against him.

Divorce should be seen as a legally punitive measure against the man for having broken the covenant of marriage with his wife. Divorce procedures protect the innocent party from cruel and unjust treatment. Divorce is the final step of covenantal confrontation against the offending spouse. The certification process prevents a state of confusion and abandonment. To say that there is no such thing as divorce is to pretend that one is in a stage B relationship when the reality is that it needs the legal protection of a stage C action.

Jesus does not contradict Moses' teaching on divorce. Jesus is describing the difference between legal sanctions, covenantal commitment, and heart faithfulness. Jesus would not break previously given, God-ordained Scriptures. Divorce should be seen as the just legal procedure when covenant breakdown has occurred. If not, one is leaving the innocent party, usually the wife, virtually helpless at the impropriety from the renegade spouse.

Reconciliation Better than Law

We should try to act in perfect heart unity with every believer. To do so, we should act under the guidelines of covenantal relationships. Personal reconciliation is more advantageous to both parties than procedures of law. Covenant deals with the dynamics of personal relationships. Law deals with a contract that is written down on paper. The mechanics of law operate according to exact detail even if it is to the disadvantage of both parties. Once one starts the mechanism of law, it must be carried out to the end. **Luke 12:58-59** states:

When you go with your adversary to the magistrate, as you are on the way, make every effort to settle with him, lest he drag you to the judge, the judge deliver you to the officer, and the officer throw you into prison. I tell you, you will not depart from there until you have paid the very last mite.

Making every effort along the way to settle with someone with whom we are in disagreement is the process of covenantal dialogue. We communicate and draw one another toward reconciliation. If we cannot be reconciled, we may have to fall upon the impersonal machinery of law. The law says that when its judgment is made, every last penny must be paid according to the letter. The law is a mechanism of letter. The law is not dealing with the heart of personal reconciliation. When two people turn themselves over to the mechanism of the law, they have conceded that they cannot operate on a basis of heart reconciliation. It is always better to deal with disagreements on a personal covenantal level rather than having to go to the legal system.

Recently, a group of neighbors appealed to a local governmental agency to bring legal measures against one of our ministries. As they did not inform us ahead of time, we had no opportunity to meet with them in dialogue to reconcile the matter. Once the machinery of law was put in motion, neither group could get it to stop. The authorities examined the papers and came down with certain decisions. These decisions did not grant what the neighbors wanted because there was no legal basis for their complaints. On the other hand, the authorities did enforce some restrictions upon us that did not help the neighbors but cost us a great deal of money and time. Had we been able to meet and discuss the matter, we would have been able to come to a solution that would have helped both of us.

As it happened, the law was enforced, and neither party got what it was looking for. The decision of the law was perfectly just according to the letter of the code. However, the real issue of concern behind the matter had not been dealt with.

We should make the effort ahead of time to reconcile an issue on a personal basis with a brother before it degenerates to enforcing the law. Most congregations have some type of legal codes or bylaws. If a division between the brothers gets to a point that the different sides are demanding the enforcement of their interpretation of those documents, they have already passed out of the realm of covenantal dialogue. That should be a time to stop the discussion and turn to the Lord in prayer and repentance until everyone's heart is restored to a covenantal attitude. To pursue the written code at that point will probably destroy the group. The purpose of law is enforcement; the purpose of covenant is reconciliation.

20

KEEPING OUR WORD

Covenant brings commitment to our personal relationships. That commitment is formulated into words. The words are the covenant proper. The words of the covenant describe the commitment to the relationship. Any understanding of covenant must be based on the commitment to keep the words that one says. The words of commitment to a relationship are only as good as one's capacity to keep those words. In Matthew 21, Jesus tells the story of a man who had two sons: one who said he would do what his father asked but did not, and the other who said he would not obey but did. Words of commitment without the keeping of those words are not effective. Jesus said that the second son was the righteous one.

One of the keys, therefore, to covenant is doing what one said one would do. Keeping our words is essential in (1) maintaining covenantal relationships, (2) being a person of integrity, and (3) operating by faith confession. Our integrity is only as good as the degree to which we can be trusted to do what we said we would do. The expressions "He is as good as his word," "His word is good," and "He is a man of his word" show a covenantal perspective.

Contract versus Covenant

The law of the land is that an agreement between two people is only valid if it has been written down and signed. This is known as a contract. A contract is not the same thing as a covenant, but it is the legal parallel to a covenant.

In the early years of our nation, a verbal agreement between two people was considered as binding. Usually this agreement was witnessed and reported to others. If it was between two individuals privately, it was called a gentleman's agreement. Between two gentlemen, a man's word was his bond, more sacred than law. Verbal agreements were accepted in 17th and 18th century English and American common law. So many people in this country are now literate that written documents can always be used. Putting an agreement in writing has a more formal nature to it and a greater legal and spiritual authority. People can be more single-minded when the issue in question is more definite.

On the other hand, this development in law also reflects a trend that people in our society do not consider one another's word as valid or trustworthy. We operate only by legal contract and not by covenantal trust. Writing down a covenant based on character trust is different from initiating a legal contract depending on the law for its enforcement.

Standing behind our Words

The power of words is central to spiritual understanding. The Scriptures themselves are a body of words. Faith teachers point out that not only did God create
the world through the use of words, but also that our words are imbued with power
and authority. From a faith viewpoint, a man is only as good as his word. If one
were to break his word, his entire sense of identity and integrity would be
destroyed. **Psalm 15:4** describes a righteous man as:

He who swears to his own hurt, and does not change.

If a man swore to do something, he would always see that these words were
fulfilled. Even if these words meant harm to himself, it would be better to suffer
some outward harm than to have his entire worth as a person negated. When a
person sees his very being standing behind his words, he becomes a man of
covenant. We ought to place our lives behind every word we speak.

**They overcame him (the accuser) by the blood of the Lamb and by the word
of their testimony, and they did not love their lives to the death (Revelation
12:11).**

These believers placed their lives behind the word of their testimony. This gave
their words full faith power and authority to overcome the devil. They stood firm
with the name of Jesus. They preferred to lose their lives rather than break the
word of their testimony. They understood that their lives were more wrapped up in
the words of their testimony than in their physical existence. The name of Jesus is
a word. Had they broken the word of their testimony, only to remain physically in
the body a little longer, they would have lost their real lives. They kept their lives
in full integrity even though their physical bodies were killed.

We should be people of this kind of integrity. Because our society has become
so lax in accepting people's words, we will need to discipline ourselves to say only
the words that we are committed to keeping. The ease with which the modern
person says, "Oh, I didn't really mean that," is outright shocking from a biblical
point of view. A person who could make a statement and pass it off lightly that he
did not mean what he said, is spiritually almost a non-existent person. His person-
hood in God is so shallow as to bear practically no weight at all.

The Little Words that Count

A person who wants to become a covenant man and a faith man must train
himself to be faithful in the little words that come out of his mouth. There are not
spiritual words at certain times and mundane, "not counting" words at the other
times. The same faithfulness that backs one's words on the most insignificant point
will be the same faith that backs a prayer of mighty dimension and authority. If a
person believes that he can operate great faith through the words of his prayers,
and yet not be faithful in the everyday words of his everyday life and conversation,
he is self-deceived. He is a cloud without water carried about by the wind.

We have to undergo a complete reorientation in how we speak and how we back up what we have said.

But I say to you that for every idle word men speak, they will give account of it in the day of judgment. For by your words you will be justified, and by your words you will be condemned (Matthew 12:36-37).

Idle words are words that someone did not really mean or that he did not intend to fulfill. Idle words are any words that are not covenantal words. Covenantal words are backed by one's integrity and commitment to fulfill them. Any word that is not spoken out of a covenantal heart negates the purpose for which words were created.

We start by training ourselves in the little things. If we commit ourselves to being at a place at a particular time, we should be prompt in arriving there. If we say we are going to help out with a certain administrative chore, we should make sure that we complete it. If someone asks us to go somewhere, and we are not sure if we really want to go, then we should refrain from giving a phony positive answer. Silence is a good technique. One will not be judged for silence. If a word is about to come out of your mouth and you do not know if you are committed to it, then wait for another opportunity before speaking. One can always say that he needs more time to think before giving a definite answer.

The power of words cannot be overestimated. Whenever we say, "I am..." or "I will...," we must make sure that the words that follow are exactly correct according to Scriptures.

In **Mark 11:23** in describing the prayer of faith, Jesus says that one must not doubt but:

believe that those things which he says will come to pass.

The words of our prayers will be fulfilled when we realize and believe that our words outside of prayer time will also be fulfilled. Every word that we say is significant and important. Covenant brothers need to be extremely serious about the use of words in everyday life. One is not likely to say unscriptural words in the middle of a prayer of faith. Faith will be destroyed in allowing our words to become contradictory in what seems to be the insignificant details of life. The detail may be insignificant, but the word uttered out of our mouth is not.

God is vigilant that whatever words come out of His mouth, He will fulfill. As God is the ultimate covenant keeper, He believes that the formulating of every word is an act of making covenant. God does not have some words that are covenantal and other words that are not. Every word that comes out of His mouth is cutting a covenant. God stands behind every word He speaks.

In **Jeremiah 1**, the Lord shows Jeremiah a vision of an almond tree. The root of the word almond in Hebrew, "shakad," is the same as the root for the word vigilant. In **verse 12**, the Lord gives Jeremiah the interpretation of the vision saying:

You have seen well for I am vigilant to perform My word.

God is vigilant to watch over the words that He speaks. God is standing on guard, ready and expectant. He is insistent that any word He has spoken will come to pass. We should have the same character about us. When a word leaves our mouth, we should follow that word and wait upon it until it comes to pass. God said that He did not let the words of His prophets fall to the ground. He does not let His word return void. We must be the same in our own commitment to fulfill the words that come out of our mouth.

Adjusting our Vocabulary

We should adjust our vocabulary to remove references to fear and death. We can use the word "due date" instead of "deadline," as the time limit has nothing to do with anyone dying. We can say "where the street ends" instead of "dead end," as again there is no reason to mention death. We have learned to tell our children to "watch out" or "be attentive" instead of saying "be careful," for we do not want to inculcate anxiety into an impressionable child. The Bible tells us to be anxious and careful for nothing.

We should avoid overusing the word "feel." The spiritual realm is quite different from the emotional realm. Feelings deal with the emotions. Believers often say, "I feel this" or "I felt that." Better expressions to use would be "I perceive" or "I sense in the Spirit."

When someone would say to me, "Please remember so-and-so in your prayers," my response used to be "Sure, I will." Although my response was sincere, I did not know if I could fulfill the promise. If I have a long range commitment to pray for a certain person, then I will be glad to do it. In other cases, it is better to turn to the person immediately, grab him by the hand, and say, "Let's pray for this right now." A decisive faith prayer at that timely moment is better than a vague commitment to follow up on it sometime in the future.

Being There on Time

Many of our interactions with other believers have to do with agreeing to meet together at certain places and times. Here are three suggestions for adjusting our attitudes concerning going to meetings:

(1) When going to a meeting at a scheduled time, plan to arrive long before the starting time. If one does arrive early, he can use the time to prepare himself for the meeting. If one plans to arrive exactly on time, there is the anxiety of possibly being delayed. If one is running a little late, there is frustration and rushing to try to force the time. The Bible says that to be in haste is to sin. I found those times of frustration and rushing to be unhealthy enough for my spirit, that I would rather invest the time to go early and allow my soul to be well-watered and on top of the situation.

(2) So many people tend to be late that one can fall into frustration when he shows up on time for a meeting, and no one else does. The issue of promptness

and punctuality has nothing to do with the other person. It is a matter of integrity of one's own words and his character before God. Punctuality is done as an offering to God and is acceptable to Him regardless of how anyone else acts.

(3) People often ask you to do little things and go places that are not appropriate for your particular schedule of priorities. There is social sway to say that you will go in order to give a positive response to the friend. A better response is to indicate that you will have to give it some consideration. Do not make a flippant commitment that you may be unable to fulfill.

These examples show the types of details that one has to deal with to keep every word that comes out of his mouth. Although these details may seem petty, exactness of speech and a concern for integrity are matters of conscience and godliness.

A Wrong Covenant

Covenant making is not always done for godly reasons. Sometimes men take oaths and end up swearing to their own hurt when they have evil intentions. Acts 23 describes a conspiracy by a group of men to kill the Apostle Paul. **Acts 23: 12-13** states:

And when it was day, some of the Jews gathered together and bound themselves under an oath, saying that they would neither eat nor drink until they had killed Paul. Now there were more than forty who had formed this conspiracy.

There was antagonism in the first century between the leaders of the Jewish religious structure and the leaders of the Jewish movement of believers in Jesus. People in all ages who have an investment in their religious position are often antagonistic against those who represent a spontaneous revival movement.

These men did make covenant together. They had a stated purpose. They made an oath together which had blessings and curses. There were more than two or three involved in this covenant, in fact more than forty people. Although this particular covenant was made for evil intentions, it is still reflective of a culture that was familiar with the concept of covenant keeping. Their radical view of oath is taken out of the same context from which the entire Bible was written. The understanding that keeping words of covenant is a matter of life-or-death seriousness is a foundation for understanding Scriptures. Men and women would stake their lives on words spoken in covenant.

Backed by our Integrity

If men do not fulfill the words of a covenant, God calls them to account for it. If one does not make a covenant commitment toward doing something, there is no moral responsibility to fulfill it. Once words are spoken, we do have a responsibility to be faithful to them. Covenant men and women believe that every word that comes out of their mouths is a statement of integrity. What comes out of our mouths is sourced from what is in our hearts. Our hearts should be filled with a godliness that makes us want to fulfill the words we speak. Every word that comes out of our mouths should be an expression of our covenant-keeping God who lives in our heart.

A godly expression is, "Say what you mean, and mean what you say." We should have a commitment that backs every word we speak. If we offer those words in the form of a promise, we should be even more committed to fulfill them. If a promise is ever backed by an oath, there should be an absolute commitment of the soul behind it. We must learn as people of covenantal character to limit our speech and refrain from making superficial promises. In **Matthew 5:37**, Jesus said:

> **Let your "Yes" be "Yes," and your "No," "No." For whatever is more than these is from the evil one.**

We should not be quick to make promises lightly. We take our words seriously. We resist the temptation to make exaggerations when reporting on an event that has happened. It is a challenging task to bring our spoken words to a state of simplicity, exactness and honesty. Training and controlling the tongue is a major part of the self-discipline toward godliness.

21

SOCIAL COMPACTS

There are many different types of covenants that men can make with one another. Often these covenants involve a larger group of people. When this covenant embraces an entire society, it is called a national covenant, a constitution, or a social compact. A social compact is a compact or covenant made with an entire society. It is a contract between groups of men as they operate in the realms of society, business and government.

The best kind of social compact takes place when an entire society bands together to serve God. Enacting a covenant that affects an entire society is done through its representative leadership. Investing leadership with the authority to make covenant is necessary if one is to see such a covenant encompass an extremely large group of people. As a woman can yield herself into a covenant of marriage with a man, so can an entire society yield itself into a covenant with God. If an entire society does this, it has become a godly nation. The times that whole societies have been able to make a covenantal commitment with God are the high points of the span of history.

Jehoiada's Covenant

We find in Scripture a special commitment from God toward the people of Israel because throughout their history, they often came before God to make covenant with Him as a whole nation. When they failed to keep these covenants, they were subject to judgment. But the other nations of the world were generally unconcerned toward making covenant with God at all. In Exodus 19:5-8, Moses and the elders of Israel come forward to make covenant with God before receiving the Ten Commandments at Mt. Sinai. In Joshua 24, Joshua brings all the families of the nation before God to call them to witness that they have committed themselves under oath to be faithful to Him.

In **II Chronicles 23:16-21**, a covenant is made with the high priest, the general population, and the king:

> **Then Jehoiada made a covenant between himself, the people, and the king that they should be the Lord's people.**

In this covenant, Jehoiada represents the priesthood, the religious authority of the day. The young king represents secular government and authority. The people gathered together were represented by their elders. In this covenant, the people are not only reforming the society and the government, but they are making a consecration to God. God is a partner to their national constitution. God is a partner and a part of the very nation itself.

Josiah's Covenant

Another national covenant was made under King Josiah; it is recorded in **II Chronicles 34:29-33**. All the elements of making a national covenant are here:

> **Then the king sent and gathered all the elders of Judah and Jerusalem. And the king went up to the house of the Lord, with all the men of Judah and the inhabitants of Jerusalem: the priests and the Levites, and all the people, great and small; and he read in their hearing all the words of the book of the covenant which had been found in the house of the Lord. Then the king stood in his place and made a covenant before the Lord, to follow the Lord, and keep His commandments and His testimonies and His statutes with all his heart and all his soul, to perform the words of the covenant that were written in this book. And he made all who were present in Jerusalem and Benjamin take their stand for it. So the inhabitants of Jerusalem did according to the covenant of God, the God of their fathers. Thus Josiah removed all the abominations from all the country that belonged to the children of Israel, and made all who were present in Israel diligently serve the Lord their God. All his days they did not depart from following the Lord God of their fathers.**

It is important to examine such passages as these to understand biblical principles of government and national covenant. They can guide our attitudes concerning government, economics, current events, moral standards, legislation, history, military force, educational standards, and politics. To what degree should we be involved? In what way should we be an influence for godliness on the society around us?

As Josiah's covenant was made late in the history of the first commonwealth of Israel, it gives us an opportunity to see how the earlier principles of blood covenant from the patriarchs had come to be applied to a constitution of a nation. In ancient Israel, religion and government were completely intertwined. The purpose of examining Josiah's covenant is to show us how the principles of covenant can be applied to a nation's society.

There are several groups of people involved in making this national covenant. First there is the king, who is the single leader of the executive power of the government. The king's role is roughly equivalent to that of a modern president. Secondly, there are the elders of the people. These men are the representative leaders of the major sections of the nation. In a modern representative republic, these men would be somewhat similar to state governors or members of a parliament, congress or senate. The third group is the general populace, described in verse 30 as *"all the people great and small."* They have an egalitarian standing before the law. There is no bias whether or not they have a high social or financial status. While this is not a democracy, each person does have a participatory role in the forming of the covenant.

Another group of people described in verse 30 is *"the priests and Levites."* The priests and Levites are a unique tribe, ordained to be ministers, caretakers and worship leaders in the central religious sanctuary. These men are not exactly equivalent to the ordained religious leaders of our nation because of the unique tribal arrangement that supported the ancient temple. On the other hand, religious leaders are clearly involved as an influential and authoritative group in establishing this national covenant.

In this covenant under King Josiah, the people are looking back to the original document of covenant law that was formulated during the time of Moses. They were not composing a new philosophy of government, but reconfirming the principles on which the nation had been founded. The documents of Scripture were both their Bible and their constitution. We should look back to the original documents upon which this nation was based, as well as to the Scriptures, when we try to determine right principles of government to be applied today. A biblical understanding of government involves our turning back to such documents as the Constitution and the Declaration of Independence to use as a source and guidebook.

In **II Chronicles 34:31**, the king:

read in their hearing all the words of the book of the covenant.

All the citizens of a nation should be well-read in the constitutional statutes which originally defined the purposes of their government. As it is a step of covenant to have our children trained in the study of Scripture, so is it also a step of covenant to have them educated in the national documents of our founding fathers. A constitution should be based on the Bible, and a government should be based on a constitution.

Constitutional Government

We should seek to have our modern government conform to the functions and purposes outlined in the founding constitution. King Josiah called the people to *"perform the words of the covenant that were written in this book."* The government is not an evolving series of legislative actions; it is an authority that functions subject to the primary national constitution or covenant which ordained the government into being. A covenantal government is subject to an original document of agreement by the people who founded it. A biblical government is essentially a constitutional government.

A government and legislature is based on a founding constitution. The founding constitution is based on the principles of Scripture. A constitution is a delineation of the scriptural principles that best apply to the nation at hand. If the constitution is based on biblical principles and the government adheres to its constitution, then the system of government is closest to a biblical standard. In the United States of America, we are blessed to have a constitution written by men who were highly knowledgeable of Scriptures and well-studied as to how to apply the principles of Scripture toward government.

We as believers should be aware of the biblical principles that apply to government and the extent to which our constitution is based on biblical principles. We should be well-versed in the articles of our constitution, studying them in context of the times in which they were written. Understanding the constitution and its context will help us to know what functions our government is actually designed to perform. For instance, the Constitution of the United States states that government is "to promote the general welfare." This phrase has been taken out of context to justify the modern multi-billion dollar welfare system. Promoting general welfare did not mean establishing a welfare system. This welfare system would not have been acceptable to the function of government as outlined by the Founding Fathers.

Another phrase in the Preamble to the Constitution is that the government is to "provide for the common defense." Providing for the common defense is the funding of enough military forces to keep the nation well-protected from external enemies. There were many spheres that the framers of the Constitution did not want the government to get involved with. They saw that the individual states should unite their finances into a common means of defense. They did not want the government to tell individuals what to do nor to take authority away from the states. The federal government was to help the states cooperate in the forming and funding of a military to protect them from foreign enemies. The pooling of resources for a national militia was one of the reasons the states originally formed an alliance together.

In examining the priorities for the national budget today, we have to turn back to the question of what is the function and purpose of the government. The issue is not whether we would prefer to spend money on armaments versus welfare to the poor. The question is that of identifying the ordained spheres in which the government was designed to function. A covenantal view of government sees each legislative choice in light of the constitutionally defined functions.

The first sentence of the Preamble to the Constitution is the foundation in defining the limitations of governmental functions in the United States.

We the people of the United States, in order to form a more perfect union, establish justice, ensure domestic tranquility, provide for the common defense, promote the general welfare, and secure the blessings of liberty to ourselves and our posterity, do ordain and establish this Constitution of the United States of America.

The Preamble states the overall covenantal direction and purpose of our government. The Constitution with its Preamble is an excellent example of applying scriptural principles to form a modern government. As a biblical view of male-female relationship is defined by the covenant of marriage, so a biblical view of government is defined by the covenant of a national constitution. The constitution of the states of America is the covenant that united them in the same way that a marriage is the covenant that unites a man and a woman.

Pledging Support

In II Chronicles 34:32, the leaders and the people read the covenant and come forward to "take their stand for it." This taking of a stance was an act of ratifying the covenant under Josiah. It was their pledge to support it. This stance of support was not a vote but a pledge of loyalty to the covenant. The signing of the Declaration of Independence was likewise a pledge of loyalty by the signers to support the establishment of their independent government. Signing that declaration was a dangerous and risky action to take. These American patriots had a deep sense of national covenant. Their commitment to a covenant was more than most modern people, even believers in Jesus, would imagine. When the signers of the declaration affixed their names to the document, they were pledging themselves unto death to be loyal to the new nation.

Notice the covenantal language and understanding revealed in the last sentence of the Declaration of Independence:

And, for the support of this declaration, with a firm reliance on the protection of Divine Providence, we mutually pledge to each other our lives, our fortunes, and our sacred honor.

Few congregations have this level of covenantal commitment. The signers' covenant was based on a clear set of words written in the declaration. It was based on a trust and faith in the miraculous power of God to intervene in their lives. It involved a mutual pledge between the parties of the covenant. It staked behind that covenant the commitment of their lives, their financial possessions, and even their reputations as men of honor. What a beautiful statement! As in the case of Josiah, so it was in the case of the signers of the Declaration of Independence. Men came forward and took a stance of covenant commitment. They pledged themselves to one another to establish a godly nation.

Revival Causes Reform

II Chronicles 34:33 states:

Josiah removed all of the abominations from all of the country.

Josiah led a sweeping reform of the social, moral and spiritual values of the nation. In ancient Israel, civil standards and religious standards were linked together. The covenant under Josiah resulted in sweeping moral reforms across the nation. Decadence, injustice and occult practices were purged out of the society.

The social reforms did not result in the making of the covenant; the making of the covenant resulted in the social reforms. Spiritual revival will produce covenantal attitudes, which will in turn produce social justice. Revival produces reform; reform does not produce revival. Anytime in history that there has been a sweeping reform of social justice, it must have been preceded by a widespread spiritual revival.

The great historical events connected with the United States were preceded by a wave of repentance, evangelism, Bible reading and prayer. Historical events would be understood in a different light if their relationship to spiritual movements were considered. Behind the events of the Revolutionary War was the widespread repentance and revival known as the "Great Awakening." The emancipation of the black people in the United States, gained during the Civil War, was fostered by the preaching and evangelism under men such as Charles Finney. Intense intercession in the United States and Great Britain involved spiritual warfare while the Allied military forces were fighting in World War II. Revival produces reform, and prayer changes the course of historical events. A covenantal view of faith will cause believers in Jesus to influence the course of history and society around them.

Freedom of Religion

Some believers think it is unspiritual to be a force of influence in the secular world. To pull back from influencing the world around us is a form of pietistic mysticism. True spirituality leads to covenantal attitudes, which in turn lead to social justice. Out of a heart of prayer and meditation, believers should be a force of godly influence and moral light to the society around us.

Separation of church and state was intended to promote the free exercise of religious beliefs, not to limit them by an ungodly secular government. The freedom of faith of the people was to be protected from the interference of government. Secular government should be seen as a benevolent patron and protector of the free exercise of biblical faith. The more biblical values there are among the people, the more the foundations of society will be healthy and prosper. Moral and spiritual strength among the people will foster strength and stabliity in the government. The **Proverbs** say:

a throne is established in righteousness (16:12, 25:5 and 29:4).

II Chronicles 34:33 states that King Josiah:

made all who were present in Israel diligently serve the Lord their God.

Not only was government restricted from hindering the free spread of biblical faith; it was designed to foster and facilitate that faith. The original pioneers in America were men of intense devotion and commitment to an evangelistic Christian faith. They saw the discovery and colonizing of America as an effort to establish a purely Christian nation.

The Mayflower Compact

One of the most godly documents ever written was the Mayflower Compact of 1620. The compact was a covenant that the people on the Mayflower made to establish government for their community. The central portion on the Mayflower Compact reads as follows:

> **Having undertaken for the glory of God and advancement of the Christian faith and honor of our King and country a voyage to plant the first colony in the northern parts of Virginia, do by these present solemnly and mutually in the presence of God and of one another covenant and combine ourselves together into a civil body politic for our better ordering and preservation and furtherance of the ends aforesaid; and by virtue hereof to enact, constitute and frame such just and equal laws, ordinances, acts, constitutions, and offices from time to time, as shall be thought most meet and convenient for the general good of the colony unto which we promise all due submission and obedience. In witness whereof we have hereunder ascribed our names.**

They saw government as an extension of their faith and desire for evangelism. The pioneers in America saw themselves as a new Israel, a nation wholly covenanted with God.

The Mayflower Compact states that the purpose of planting a colony in America was to glorify God and advance Christianity. The compact then states that in order to accomplish the advancement of Christianity, the people pledged themselves into a mutual covenant. The government, or body of civil politics, was considered to be the outward organization and manifestation of that pledged covenant. All future laws and ordinances were to be seen as further extensions of their original covenant. Each person promised to be in complete submission and obedience to the constitutional covenant. In order to ratify the compact, they wrote their names on the document by way of witness and oath. They were participants in the covenant. What an astonishingly beautiful spiritual view of government this is! There is a parallel of form and purpose between the Mayflower compact and the covenant of Israel under Josiah.

God's Government

We must recover a spiritual view of government and of our roles in taking dominion over the earth. The kingdom of God is the authority of God expressed in every area of life. The kingdom of God is the kingship or government of God. The kingdom of God starts within the spirit of a man and flows outward to his body, his possessions, his relationships, and to all areas of society. We must train our congregations to have an attitude of dominion toward the world around us. We reject pietism and mysticism. Our spiritual values include influencing society toward a more godly form. We see Jesus as the head and authority over every form of principality, power and government. He is a King over all other kings. He is the ultimate Governor and President over all other governors and presidents.

22

PATRIOTISM AND PROPHETIC POLITICAL IMPACT

We should not allow the necessity of being a prophetic influence upon society to sap the spiritual life of the congregation. Social impact should not keep people away from the priorities of Bible study, prayer and evangelism. On the other hand, we should not avoid the issues of social morality. The condition of the world around us affects our ability to spread the gospel. Prophetic impact into social action can create an intense desire for prayer among the believers. Exercising a spiritual influence on the world around us will promote a greater degree of effectiveness in evangelism.

Prayer, Politics and Evangelism

There is a triangular relationship between social impact, devotional community life and effective evangelism. These three go together and complement one another. With evangelism and social impact, our devotional life will be healthy and realistic. If social impact becomes separated from devotional community life or evangelism, it will be unbalanced and unspiritual. We demonstrate our faith by our works. We are spiritual people whose moral standards become manifest in an influence toward society.

The relationship between prayer, politics and evangelism is outlined in **I Timothy 2:1,2 and 4:**

> **Therefore I exhort first of all that supplications, prayers, intercessions, and giving of thanks be made for all men, for kings and all who are in authority, that we may lead a quiet and peaceable life in all godliness and reverence... (God) desires all men to be saved and to come to the knowledge of the truth.**

Our prayers and intercessions have a strategic order. One of the first priorities in prayer is to intercede for those in authority. This intercession will promote a social order with minimal disturbances and upheavals. This peaceful social condition is the most ideal setting for the spread of the gospel so that all men within that society might be saved. When there are political upheavals and revolutions in a nation, there are hindrances to evangelism. Prayers for government leaders will cause favorable social conditions to maximize the number of people saved. Devotional life affects social order, which affects evangelism.

Patriotism

The issue of patriotism has caused some double-mindedness among believers. Are we to be patriotic or not? Is there a contradiction between being loyal to God and being loyal to an earthly nation?

Our citizenship is in heaven (Philippians 3:20).

We have more loyalty to heaven and its spiritual government than we do to any earthly nation. If an earthly government turns in direct opposition to the gospel, we may be forced to disobey its authority. When it comes to our right to preach the gospel, we must stand up for our heavenly citizenship.

On the other hand, Peter tells us that it is God's will for us to cooperate with government institutions:

Therefore, submit yourselves to every ordinance of man for the Lord's sake, whether to the king as supreme, or to governors... Honor all people. Love the brotherhood. Fear God. Honor the king (I Peter 2:13 and 17).

Our primary allegiance is to heaven. Our innermost identification is not with a temporal nation, but with heaven itself. We have a secondary allegiance to the nation in which we live.

Patriotism is godly to the extent-that it is an expression of a covenant heart submitted to God's authority. I am more loyal to God than I am to my family. However, in God's priorities, I am directed to be loyal to them as part of the kingdom of God. God is my primary father in heaven, yet at the same time I am called to respect and obey my earthly parents.

The Pledge of Allegiance

Patriotism is a positive attitude for believers. The Pledge of Allegiance reads:

I pledge allegiance to the flag of the United States of America and to the Republic for which it stands, one nation under God, indivisible, with liberty and justice for all.

Patriotism to our nation is a secondary allegiance under the general umbrella of covenant loyalty to God. We are submitted to God's authority, and are therefore submitted to every authority that He allows on earth (Romans 13:1-7).

In the allegiance to the country in which we dwell, we have a covenantal obligation to seek its welfare. In Jeremiah 29, the prophet writes to the Israelites who have been taken captive and are living in Babylon. They thought that perhaps they should rebel against the king of Babylon and try to return to Israel immediately. Jeremiah tells them that for the time being they should live in prosperity and seek the good of that foreign nation. Although Babylon was not their primary allegiance, they were to show loyalty, cooperation and a certain degree of patriotism. They realized that Babylon was not the kingdom of God; yet because they were a covenant people, they acted in integrity and showed loyalty to the country in which they dwelled.

Build houses and dwell in them. Plant gardens and eat their fruit... Seek the peace of the city where I have caused you to be carried away and pray to the Lord for it; for in its peace you will have peace (Jeremiah 29:5-7).

In the long run, the Israelites would be regathered out of that pagan nation. In the meantime, they had to cooperate with the authorities in their historical setting and physical location.

When we pledge allegiance to the flag of the United States, we are not doing so in a blind loyalty which says, "My country—right or wrong." We recognize the flag as a symbol of the nation in which we are living temporarily. As we show commitment and submission to every human organization, we also demonstrate our integrity by showing patriotism to our country.

Allegiance to National Israel

As the believer shows secondary allegiance to his nation, so does every Jew and Christian bear a certain loyalty to the nation of Israel. Neither Jew nor Christian confuses the state of Israel with the actual kingdom of God itself. Yet we have a historical identification with the nation of Israel. All believers are spiritually grafted into the olive tree of Israel. A believer in Jesus sees his primary citizenship in heaven and a secondary citizenship in the commonwealth of Israel.

Remember that you, once Gentiles in the flesh—who are called Uncircumcision by what is called the Circumcision made in the flesh by hands—that at that time you were without Christ, being aliens from the commonwealth of Israel and strangers from the covenants of promise, having no hope and without God in the world. But now in Christ Jesus you who once were far off have been made near by the blood of Christ (Ephesians 2:11-13).

Although this passage is referring to a believer's universal spiritual citizenship, it also indicates that a covenant is not separated from its specific historical development. God is a god of history, and God is a god of people. The covenants of promise offered in the world had historical placements and involvements. Although our citizenship is in heaven, we have a loyalty to the historical covenants made with the nation of Israel.

When one becomes a believer in Jesus, he is spiritually initiated into the covenants of the commonwealth of Israel. A Christian should not see himself as a foreigner from the nation of Israel. He is a spiritual citizen of that nation. Through our reconciliation with God, Jesus has also made every Christian reconciled to the historical people of natural Israel. Although many Jews are enemies of the gospel, they are beloved because of their forefathers (Romans 11). As Christians are loyal to America for the religious freedom it has fostered, so should Christians be loyal to Israel for being the commonwealth that fostered the biblical covenants of faith. The blood of the Messiah brings any individual not only into covenant with God but also into covenant with the people of God.

Zechariah 14:2 states:

I will gather all the nations to battle against Jerusalem.

Zechariah is prophesying of a time in the future when all the governments of the world will turn in enmity against the nation of Israel. Their attack against Jerusalem is seen as an attack against God. For a nation to become a direct military enemy of Israel is a step of betrayal by that nation of God's historical covenants on the earth. A believer should pray that his nation will maintain itself as an ally to the nation of Israel.

We do not believe that the nation of Israel is in spiritual perfection. We do have a covenantal allegiance to the Jewish people that God has miraculously regathered in our times. A priority for our nation's foreign policy is to be a strong military ally to Israel. Let us pray that the United States, as a Christian nation, will be an exception to the prophecy in Zechariah 14.

Respecting Government Officials

In I Peter 2, we are instructed to honor and respect the person who holds the highest office in our nation. Reporters and political commentators sometimes display disrespect, sarcasm and condescension when speaking about the President. At times they will even be discourteous when directing a question to him during a press conference. Disrespect toward the President of the United States on the part of a newscaster shows a horrible lack of understanding of the nature of authority and covenant. The issue is not whether one agrees with all the policies of a president. One should give deference to a person who bears such a weight of responsibility for so many others.

One also shows deference to a president because God's authority is above and behind any such office. A reporter flaunting his disrespect for the President on national television displays reprehensible covenant breaking and treachery before the eyes of millions. Peter said of such people that they:

walk according to the flesh in the lust of uncleanness and despise authority.

They are presumptuous, self-willed; they are not afraid to speak evil of dignitaries (II Peter 2:10).

Jude also spoke of this type of people as those who:

defile the flesh, reject authority, and speak evil of dignitaries (Jude 8).

Loyal Opposition

It is within the bounds of covenantal character to set forth an opposing position before the governing authorities. Covenant allows for confrontation and opposition; it does not allow for disrespect and disloyalty. Some countries even refer to the opposing political party as the "loyal opposition." Proposals for change and differences of opinion are welcomed by covenantal government. Opposition that is loyal is to be accepted. Despising of authority, however, is in itself despicable. The apostle Paul in Acts 23, for example, voices severe opposition to the Sanhedrin, but refrains from speaking disrespectfully.

Opposing ideas can be brought without any rebellious intentions of undermining the authority of the government. Speaking prophetic truth against social injustice should be considered an act of moral responsibility. There is a spiritual obligation on the community of believers to speak as a prophetic voice into society. Confronting wrongdoing in the government is parallel to speaking the truth in love on an individual level. We are called to be a prophetic community, speaking with the voice of God to the corporate conscience of the nation. We challenge society as a whole to keep the values of covenant. We are the salt of the earth.

Prophets and Kings

Moses confronted Pharaoh not only on religious freedom but also on justice for an enslaved people. All of the prophets spoke to their respective governmental leaders to adhere to moral and ethical principles. John the Baptist challenged King Herod not to commit adultery. The prophet Nathan challenged King David; the prophet Elijah challenged King Ahab. The prophet Jeremiah was ordained to tear down and set up nations and kingdoms (Jeremiah 1:10).

The community of believers speaks with a prophetic voice that represents a higher authority than the government. The prophetic community should respect the functions of government to conduct civil business. The government should, in turn, respect the voice of the Church, calling its society to spiritual and moral standards. Spheres of authority work in balance to one another. In ancient Israel, the king had the priest on one side and the prophet on the other.

King Saul stepped out of his authority as civil executive and moved to usurp the authority of the priest and prophet. Even though Saul may not have had conscious rebellious intentions, he violated a primary principle of the spheres of spiritual authority. Samuel challenged him as a prophet to a king. Saul had acted in disobedience to the God who had placed him there as a king. He was acting out of self-serving motivations, ignoring the lines of covenantal authority.

Samuel confronted Saul publicly for his impropriety. **I Samuel 13:13** states:

And Samuel said to Saul, "You have done foolishly. You have not kept the commandment of the Lord your God, which He commanded you. For now the Lord would have established your kingdom over Israel forever. But now your kingdom shall not continue. The Lord has sought for Himself a man after His own heart."

I Samuel 15:28 reads:

So Samuel said to him, "The Lord has torn the kingdom of Israel from you today, and has given it to a neighbor of yours who is better than you."

Believers should respect their government leaders because God has placed them there. God also challenges the government leaders that, since He has placed them in office, He can also remove them if they act unjustly.

National Conscience

There are many moral issues in society today that believers are called to speak about to the nation's conscience. Freedom for the unborn from abortion; freedom for private religious education; traditional family and marital values; freedom from drugs, crime, and pornography; limitations of government spending; secular humanism; strength and security in our military forces; and many more are topics of immediate concern. These issues take discernment, prayer and a wise application of scriptural principles.

God is calling certain believers to attain higher offices of government. Joseph, Moses, David, Daniel, Ezra, and Nehemiah are biblical examples of those whose divine calling included that of being government leaders. **Revelation 11:15** says:

The kingdoms of this world have become the kingdoms of our Lord.

The ultimate destiny of mankind is that every sphere of life will come under the personal government of Jesus as our Messianic King.

Freedom from Social Injustice

When a nation and its leaders make a covenant before God to perform a certain action, God will hold them accountable. Jeremiah 34 records that the Lord instructed the prophet to challenge the king and the people not to have slaves any more. Slavery is a classic example of mankind's injustice to man. Enslaving men and acting tyrannically over them is a byproduct of sin. The law of Moses called for moral restrictions to the abuses of slavery. The law of Moses called for the release of slaves after a period of seven years. The prophets spoke forth visions of equality and brotherhood of men under the rule of God. Jeremiah prophesies to the leaders of the nation:

You recently turned and did what was right in My sight—every man proclaiming liberty to his neighbor; and you made a covenant before Me in the house which is called by My name. Then you turned around and profaned My name, and every one of you brought back his male and female slaves, whom he had set at liberty (Jeremiah 34:15-16).

Setting the slaves at liberty was an act of covenant keeping. This social reform was the result of a spiritual repentance among the people. Spiritual repentance always precedes true social reform. Revival leads to covenantal standards, which lead to social justice and legal order. The concept of freedom from slavery originates from the prophetic mandates of Scripture, not from modern liberal humanism.

Social injustice is seen as a profaning of the Lord's name. Since slavery was an act of covenant breaking, the just punishment was that the curses of the covenant fall upon the nation and its leaders. Since an animal was slain in ratification of the covenant, the breaking of that covenant brought upon them the same slaughter and pouring out of blood that was done to the animal.

I will give the men who have transgressed My covenant, who have not performed the words of the covenant [to set the slaves at liberty], which they made before Me when they cut the calf in two and passed between the parts of it, into the hand of their enemies, into the hand of those who seek their life (Jeremiah 34:18 and 20).

In many of the modern nations, particularly Britain, America and Israel, covenants were made with God when these nations were formed. We the people are now under obligation to maintain the national covenants originally made before God. If we do not, judgment will fall upon our nations. As the patriarchs slaughtered an animal to ratify their covenants, so will our enemies slaughter us if we do not remain faithful to our national covenants.

An Everlasting Covenant

God holds before us the promise of everlasting covenant as individuals and as nations. In Jeremiah 42, after the destruction of Israel by Babylon and the insurrection against King Gedaliah, the people present themselves before the prophet Jeremiah. They come to make a renewed national covenant to obey the Lord. Jeremiah knows that they do not have the character to keep covenant with God and accuses them of being unable to do so.

Finally, at their insistence, he allows them to enter into a fully-witnessed covenant. They immediately proceed to break the covenant, and Jeremiah is faced with the prophetic challenge to confront them with their wrongdoing. He says to them:

> **You used deceit before your own souls when you sent me to the Lord your God, saying, "Pray for us to the Lord our God, and according to all the Lord your God says, so declare to us and we will do it" (Jeremiah 42:20).**

Jeremiah calls them hypocrites and covenant breakers. Now the judgment of God is sure to fall upon them.

On the other hand, Jeremiah later prophesies a vision of restoration and beauty. He foresees a day when people will come before God and renew an everlasting covenant that will never be broken. He says there will be a godly people who:

> **shall ask the way to Zion with their faces toward it, saying, "Come, let us join ourselves to the Lord in a perpetual covenant that will not be forgotten" (Jeremiah 50:5).**

Our nation stands at an important crossroad. If it continues to break its national covenants with God, judgment shall fall upon it, and the nation shall be destroyed. If we turn our hearts to God and receive the restoration of covenantal standards as a nation, God will receive our nation back and cause it to fulfill all of the glorious destinies that God intends for it. May we pray and seek to be an influence toward such a goal.

23

THE EXPANDING KINGDOM

The kingdom of God within each person's heart expands outwardly to cover the entire earth. The kingdom of God may be seen as a series of concentric circles or ever-widening spheres of authority. The innermost sphere is that of an individual person's spirit, and the outermost sphere is the entire world. The kingdom of God is a continually expanding kingdom.

What is the Kingdom?

There are different angles from which to view the kingdom of God. There are differing opinions as to what the kingdom of God is. Some see the kingdom as a heavenly reality that has little to do with activity here on earth. Others see the kingdom of God as a spiritual presence within a person's heart. Some see the kingdom of God as a manifestation of the power and authority of God in healing and miracles. Others see the kingdom of God through the restoration of the Church in its glorious fullness. Some see the kingdom of God as a commonwealth extending out of the nation of Israel. The kingdom of God can also be seen in its last stage as the kingdom of heaven descending down to earth.

All of these views have grasped a certain aspect of the truth. They can be brought into a coherent whole by understanding that the nature of the kingdom is that it starts in one form as a seed and then grows to a fuller expansion in its later stages. The expanding nature of the kingdom of God forms a framework for understanding the varying aspects of the kingdom as outlined in Scriptures.

Strategy Sessions

In **Acts 1,** Jesus spends forty days with His disciples after His resurrection. He is preparing them for the ministry that they would start. He is setting in the right direction the future of the Church that would come through their ministry. **Verse 3** describes Jesus as:

being seen by them forty days and speaking of the things pertaining to the kingdom of God.

He spent these last forty days teaching and explaining to the disciples about the nature of the kingdom of God. There is much to know about the kingdom of God. There is much to understand about how it works. Jesus has already won the primary battle against the powers of death and Satan. He is here instructing His emissaries on the nature of the new kingdom they were about to instill within the hearts of men and install upon the earth.

How wonderful it would have been to have been party to those strategy sessions! The most important points of those discussions are laid out for us in Scriptures. The Scriptures are our strategy manual for fostering the kingdom of God.

After those forty days of instructions, as Jesus was about to leave, His disciples said to Him:

Lord will you at this time restore the kingdom to Israel (Acts 1:6)?

After those forty days of instruction, the disciples still saw the kingdom of God as something that was future, something that was related to Israel, and something that had an outward manifestation. They were not wrong in these three aspects. The kingdom of God is future, it does relate to the commonwealth of Israel and it does have an outward manifestation.

What the disciples did not see was the aspects of the kingdom of God in regard to its spiritual origin, its empowerment through the Holy Spirit, its process of development, and its scope of including all races of people. Jesus answered them saying:

It is not for you to know the times or the seasons which the Father has put in His own authority. But you shall receive power when the Holy Spirit has come upon you; and you shall be witnesses to Me in Jerusalem, and in all Judea and Samaria, and to the end of the earth (Acts 2:7-8).

The times and the seasons indicate the length of time that is needed for developing the kingdom of God. The Holy Spirit coming upon them indicates the heavenly origin and spiritual nature of the kingdom. The power they would receive has to do with manifestation of the kingdom in faith and miracles. Their starting in Jerusalem has to do with the Israelite focus of the kingdom of God. The ends of the earth indicates the universal scope of the kingdom.

Taking the Earth

While many believers today see the universal and spiritual nature of the kingdom of God, they may in turn miss some of the earthly manifestations and present fulfillments that the disciples did grasp. The earth is important to God. He predicts that the meek will inherit and take over the earth (Psalm 37). When He created the earth, He said that it was good (Genesis 1). He tells us to pray that His kingdom would be manifest here on this earth (Matthew 6). The ultimate goal of the kingdom is not for us to go to heaven, but for heavenly Jerusalem to come down to earth (Revelation 21).

There is a real place called heaven, and the kingdom of God is fully manifest there now. Jesus rules as a king beside His Father in the kingdom of saints and angelic beings located in heaven. When Pilate questioned Jesus as to whether He was a king in the natural, political and military sense that Pilate was familiar with, Jesus gave this reply:

> **My kingdom is not of this world. If My kingdom were of this world, My servants would fight, so that I should not be delivered to the Jews; but now My kingdom is not from here (John 18:36).**

The purpose of Jesus' making this statement is to draw a sharp contrast between the worldly political empires and His spiritual Messianic kingdom. Jesus was not to be just another Alexander the Great or Julius Caesar. There is a great difference between Jesus and worldly emperors. The Greeks and Romans had in their minds a king as a military and political emperor; the Jews had in their minds a Messianic king along the lines of David and Solomon.

The fact that Jesus is drawing a contrast between His kingdom and these other kingdoms is not to say that His kingdom has no outward political or governmental manifestations at all. Jesus states that His *"kingdom is not from here."* The kingdom of God does not start from earthly origins. Its source of power is not from the earth. It does not operate according to worldly tactics. It will, however, in the end take over this planet.

Within the Heart

The vision for the kingdom of heaven is birthed in the hearts of individuals who have been born again. **John 3:3** states:

> **Unless a man is born again, he cannot see the kingdom of God.**

When a person is born again, he can see the kingdom of God. The kingdom of God is in his heart.

> **For the kingdom of God is not food and drink, but righteousness and peace and joy in the Holy Spirit (Romans 14:17).**

The presence of the kingdom of God inside one's heart produces the blessed results of righteousness and peace and joy within him. It causes our hearts to be as the Psalmist said, "like a cup that overflows." There is no doubt that the kingdom of God is an innerspiritual presence. That innerspiritual presence can also flow out onto other people. The kingdom of God is not only the power to have peace and joy; that same power can reach out in miraculous strength to heal others.

Manifest in Miracles

A miracle should be understood as a manifestation of the authority of the kingdom of God. A miracle is not an accidental breaking-through, or splash of God's power. It is a moment of victory in which the authority of God wrests a person's life from the opposing kingdom of darkness. A miracle is a purposeful conquest by God's government. It is a manifestation of the kingdom of God's love. In **Matthew 12:28**, Jesus said:

> **If I cast out demons by the Spirit of God, surely the kingdom of God has come upon you.**

The demons used to live inside this person. Jesus cast the demons out and rescued the person from the kingdom of the demons. He brought the person back into the kingdom of God.

> **He has delivered us from the power of darkness and translated us into the kingdom of the Son of His love (Colossians 1:1).**

The kingdom of God is the authority of God. A miracle is the manifestation of the power of God to change physical nature, heal a person's body, or cast out a demonic entity.

Manifest in the Church

If the kingdom of God is manifested in the power of miracles, how much more is it manifest in the corporate life of the Body of believers. The kingdom of God is manifest upon the earth today by the presence of the Church. The Church here is not any particular denomination or any institutional structure, but rather the aggregate lives of those who are truly walking in the Spirit and believing in Jesus. The kingdom of God is manifest now on this planet through the assembly of those individuals who are themselves subject to that kingdom.

Abraham and his household, though few in number, represented the early stage of the kingdom of Israel. They were not the fullness of the kingdom to be manifest many centuries later. Yet they were the reality and presence of that kingdom while they lived. The believers here upon earth are the reality of the kingdom of God, even though they are not the full manifestation of the kingdom, which will occur later on. They are the reality, not the totality.

The nature of the government of God should be manifest through the governmental leadership within the Church. The victory, vigor and vitality of kingdom life should be manifest in our times through the lives of believers. Our worship should be a taste of the heavenly worship itself. Everything we do as a body of believers should be conquering an ever-expanding sphere of authority for the kingdom of God. Our lives individually and corporately should manifest more and more of the lifestyle of heaven.   -

As the Church comes to the fullness of its own restoration, the kingdom of God will be manifest upon earth. The restoration of the Church, or the community of faith, is one of the most exciting revelations touching the lives of believers today.

Unity and Restoration

The ministries of apostles, prophets, evangelists, pastors and teachers are part of the blossoming of the restored Church. The restoration of the Church is a stage in the expansion of the kingdom of God. As an individual miracle manifests God's glory by defeating an evil power, so does the corporate miracle of the Body of believers manifest God's glory by defeating vast realms of evil principalities.

Now the manifold wisdom of God might be made known by the Church to the principalities and powers in heavenly places (Ephesians 3:10).

It is through the community of faith that the manifold wisdom of God is made manifest. The Church on earth is the outworking of God's plan from heaven. It is through a fully restored Church that the world will know about the glory of God's kingdom. God is not in the business of sky-writing His messages with vapor trails on the Fourth of July. His method is to make His glorious kingdom manifest through the lives of His people here on earth whom He calls the Church.

Jesus said that as we come into unity and a more fully perfected and restored condition, the world would know of God's glory. Unity is a central aspect of restoration. **John 17:21** states:

That they all may be one, as You, Father, are in Me, and I in You; that they also may be one in Us, that the world may believe that You have sent Me.

It is through the unity and restoration of the Church that the world will know and believe. As the Body of believers expresses its full glory and authority, the world will be evangelized.

Parallel Restoration with Israel

The restoration of the Church will include the restoration of a remnant of Jewish people who will believe in Jesus. This remnant of Jewish believers in Jesus will be instrumental in fostering an end-times revival in the land of Israel. That Israelite revival will be the last stage before the full ushering in of the kingdom of God and the second coming of Jesus.

The parallel restoration between the Church and Israel is outlined in Romans 11. The restoration of the Church will bring about a remnant of Messianic Jewish believers. This Messianic Jewish remnant will bring about a full revival in Israel. This revival will usher in the kingdom of God.

The fact that a restored Church will bring about a remnant of Jewish believers in Jesus is indicated by Paul in **Romans 11:13-14:**

As I am an apostle to the Gentiles, I magnify my ministry, if by any means I may provoke to jealousy those who are my flesh and save some of them.

At first not a majority of Jewish people will be saved but only "some of them." As

Paul's ministry to the Gentiles is magnified, the world-wide Gentile Church is brought to its fullness.

The restored Gentile Church and the Messianic Jewish catalyst will eventuate in a widespread revival in Israel. **Romans 11:25-26** state:

> **until the fullness of the Gentiles has come in. And so all Israel will be saved.**

The fullness of the Gentiles includes the full restoration of the Gentile Church. This fullness is to be followed by a massive revival in which all Israel will be saved. The end-times pattern is Church restoration, then Messianic remnant, then Israeli revival.

This widespread revival in Israel will be a catalyst for the kingdom of God. **Romans 11:15** states:

> **If their being cast away is the reconciling of the world, what will their acceptance be but life from the dead?**

The reconciling of the world is the preaching of the gospel to all the ends of the earth. The acceptance of the Jews is the receiving of salvation by the general body of Jewish people. Life from the dead is the resurrection that accompanies the coming of the kingdom of God.

The Expanding Seed

The parable that describes the kingdom of God as a seed expanding in size is given in Matthew 13, Mark 4 and Luke 13. **Mark 4:30-32** reads:

> **To what shall we liken the kingdom of God or with what parable shall we picture it? It is like a mustard seed which, when it is sown on the ground, is smaller than all the other seeds of the earth; but when it is sown, it grows up and becomes greater than all herbs, and shoots out large branches, so that the birds of the air might nest under its shade.**

Jesus uses this parable as the model by which He portrays all of the kingdom of God.

The kingdom of God is first very small and is planted like a seed. It is planted in the earth and then goes through a process of growth which is steady and prolonged. This growth has different stages of shoot, branch, leaf and so on. Eventually, the plant extends outward with larger and larger branches. At the end, animals are able to find a home under the umbrella-like protection of such a large plant. All the parables about the kingdom of God can be fitted into some aspect of the growth of this mustard seed plant. The plant has fruit in one stage, branches in another and seed in another; yet it is a single unit.

The Church is a manifestation of God's presence and authority on earth, yet the kingdom of God does not originate in the earth. The kingdom of God is a government connected with the commonwealth of Israel, yet it is expressed in the miraculous power of a healing or deliverance.

The Expanding Stone

The revelation that the kingdom of God is continually expanding is also found in Daniel's interpretation of King Nebuchadnezzar's dream. Daniel's interpretation encompasses vast epochs of time. In the dream, the king sees a giant image made out of gold, silver, bronze, iron and clay. Daniel tells the king:

You watched while a stone was cut out without hands, which struck the image on its feet of iron and clay, and broke them in pieces (Daniel 2:34).

The stone that was made without human hands is figurative of the kingdom of God. The fact that it was made without human hands is parallel to Jesus' statement that His kingdom was not from this world. The power of this new kingdom comes and destroys the other kingdoms.

Daniel gives his conclusion about this dream in **verse 44:**

And in the days of these kings, the God of heaven will set up a kingdom which shall never be destroyed; the kingdom shall not be left to other people; it shall break in pieces and consume all these kingdoms, and it shall stand forever.

The kingdom of God is of different and unique origin. It breaks through into the course of human history and politics. The kingdom has an essentially spiritual nature, but it will move in to displace and replace the other kingdoms.

In **verse 35, Daniel** states:

The stone that struck the image became a great mountain and filled the whole earth.

The kingdom of God starts out as a stone and ends up as a large mountain. The kingdom of God starts out as a small seed and becomes a full-sized tree. God's kingdom is continually growing and expanding. The kingdom of Israel was first a single promise between God and Abraham, stored up in Abraham's heart. This promise grew through various stages over almost a thousand years until the kingdom of Solomon extended over much of the known world.

The kingdom of God is marked by its spiritual origin, its differing stages, its continual growth and its eventual takeover of the world. The beautiful Messianic prophecy of **Isaiah 9:7** says of the miracle child that:

Of the increase of His government and peace there will be no end.

Increase means continuous growth and expansion. Government is the ruling authority of the kingdom. No end encompasses the ultimate vision of world take-over.

In summary, evidence for the expanding nature of the kingdom includes:

(1) The varying and contrasting aspects of the kingdom of God

(2) The Romans 11 passage describing the relationship between the Church and Israel

(3) The parable of the mustard seed's growth

(4) Daniel's vision of a rock expanding into a great mountain

(5) The Messianic prophecy about the increase of the Messiah's government

(6) The history of the expansion of the kingdom of Israel from Abraham to Solomon

(7) The strategy sessions that Jesus had with his disciples about ministering the kingdom of God

(8) The Ephesians revelation of restoration in the Church and the kingdom now manifest in it

(9) The many national covenants that were made with the commonwealth of Israel

(10) The proclamation of Revelation 11 that the kingdoms of this world will become the kingdom of the Messiah.

24

SPHERES OF KINGDOM AUTHORITY

The kingdom of God has ten spheres of expanding influence and authority.

1. Spirit

The first sphere is within the spirit of an individual person. The authority of God on an individual's spirit causes that person to be born again. The person who is born again in his own spirit can be indwelt by the Holy Spirit. As he is filled to a point of overwhelming power and immersed in the Spirit of God, the kingdom has reached its full extent in that person's spirit.

2. Soul

Sphere number two is the soul of an individual person. The soul includes the intellect, will and emotions. Under the government of God, a person's intellect or mind will become renewed. All its faculties will function perfectly. His will power will be restored to be single-minded instead of double-minded. He will become active instead of passive. His emotions will reflect the fruits of the Spirit in peace, joy and self-control.

3. Body

The third sphere of influence is an individual's physical body. The kingdom reflects the order of God, and the order of God reflects the design of God. A person's body is under the kingdom of God when it is functioning as God designed it to function. When a physical body comes under the authority of the kingdom, it must be brought to perfect health. Sickness is by definition a change in the original design of the created physical body. Sickness is an aberration; it is a contradiction of the kingdom's order. Health and healing are the manifestations of the kingdom of God in a physical body.

4. Finances

The fourth sphere of authority is an individual's finances and possessions. God's very nature is to be a provider. When a person comes under the kingdom of God, his finances will manifest the nature of God as a provider. Kingdom order in any individual's finances is prosperity, provision and freedom from debt. Debt is a lack of provision; a lack of provision is a break from the source of provision. Debt is a lack of connection between the debtor and his God-provider. Debt by definition is a breakdown in the order of the kingdom of God in a believer's life. The order and authority of God reflected in an individual's finances is that there will be enough provision to meet each need at the appropriate time.

5. Family

Sphere five of the kingdom includes the relationships among members of a family. The marriage between the husband and wife should reflect the harmony and order that is in God's paradise. There should be love, affection, discipline and respect between the parents and the children. Respect and honor should be generated toward the grandparents. The family is a mini-church, a subsection of the Body of believers at large. The family is a unit within the greater kingdom of God.

The family is part of the kingdom of God and a subdivision of the congregation. A congregation is made up of cell groups. A cell group is made up of families. A cell group is a family of families. A congregation is a family of home cell groups.

If the family is seen as a separate category unit outside of God's kingdom, it has no priority whatsoever. If the family is seen as one of the spheres within the kingdom of God, time with the family is time spent in ministry. Time with the family is time spent in church activity, because the family is part of the Church. The family is a manifestation of the kingdom of God. Time invested in more harmonious family relationships is time spent in ministry. If the family were a separate category from the kingdom of God, then we should ignore it altogether. As an expression of the kingdom of God, it becomes a high priority.

In **Matthew 10:37**, Jesus stated:

He who loves father or mother more than Me is not worthy of Me. And he who loves son or daughter more than Me is not worthy of Me.

Jesus also stated in **Luke 14:26** that:

If anyone comes to Me and does not hate his father and mother, wife and children, brothers and sisters, yes, and his own life also, he cannot be My disciple.

All of our love is directed toward God and His kingdom. If it so happened that within the priorities of God's kingdom the family was not important, we should reject it. A family in and of itself has no value; a family as an expression of God's will has very high value. After we give up everything in the world, and after we give up all desires other than the kingdom of God, we find out what that kingdom is like. God places emphasis on covenantal relationships, and a central area of covenant is the family.

Our family becomes a primary target of our motivation to serve God. One who gives up everything in this life, including his family relationships, in order to serve the kingdom, will soon find that God has placed his family before him as one of his uppermost priorities. There is no double-mindedness; there are no split loyalties. As the kingdom of God has different spheres within its realm, so do we have different spheres of influence and ministry.

6. Congregation

The sixth sphere of kingdom authority is that of the local congregation or pastorate. The community of faith is a central manifestation of God's presence in the earth. The local congregation is our center of worship, covenantal relationships, teaching, children's ministry and evangelistic planning. The pastorate is an extension of the heart of the pastor. The heart of the pastor is an extension of God's heart to shepherd the congregation.

A functioning eldership and deaconate is necessary to the order of the kingdom of God within a congregation. To the degree that the elders and deacons are not functioning in full anointing, the congregation will fall short of reflecting the fullness of God's kingdom. To the degree that a congregation is fully restored in all of its biblically-designed roles, it manifests here on earth the glory and authority of the kingdom of God.

7. Apostolic Movement

The seventh sphere of kingdom of God order is a flow of cooperation between congregations in an apostolic movement. The trans-local flow of congregations is an expression of the ministry of an apostle. The apostle is a pastor among pastors, as a pastor is an elder among elders. The cooperation of different congregations under the direction of an apostle constitutes a broader base of cooperation and unity.

Members covenant together to form a congregation; congregations covenant together to form an apostolic flow. The ministry of an apostle, together with the prophets, evangelists, pastors and teachers, reflects a restored trans-local church. An apostolic movement is a manifestation of the kingdom of God as is the local congregation or a single family. Much glory and corporate anointing will blossom in our congregations as the apostolic teams gain more and more a degree of maturity.

8. Society

Sphere number eight is the dominion of the kingdom of God in a whole sector of society, such as a county or state. When an area of society is fully evangelized, its educational system is brought to godly values and its streets are cleaned of crime. When a whole area is affected by a widespread revival, the kingdom of God is manifested. Large revivals have happened many times in history. If one lives in an area where most of the people are unbelievers, such a possibility might seem difficult. A revival can sweep a whole sector of society and change it radically from top to bottom.

9. Nation

The ninth sphere of the expansion of the kingdom of God is an entire nation, its government and economy. If a national population were to be fully evangelized, the kingdom of God would be manifest in that country. This happened in ancient Israel in times of its greatest revivals.

What could be more precious in God's sight than an entire nation turning to him? Several countries in modern history have come close to doing so. Although secular history books avoid speaking of national revivals, they have occurred. England and America have each had two or three such periods. Recently in the revival in Guatemala, a pentecostal preacher named Efraim Rios Mont actually became president of the country. It would not be hard to imagine with the current spread of evangelism in South Korea that the entire nation could turn to the Lord.

II Chronicles 7:14 states:

If My people who are called by My name will humble themselves, and pray and seek My face, and turn from their wicked ways, then I will hear from heaven, and will forgive their sin and heal their land.

A whole land can be healed and restored to God. A full saturation of evangelism would cause success in the nation's economy, prosperity in agriculture, and reconstruction of the nation's government. In the 1970's in the United States, President Carter openly professed himself to be a born-again Christian. In the 1980's, President Reagan has been outspoken to stand up for biblical values and prayer in the government. High educational standards, a strengthened military, use of the media for evangelism, a prospering economy and freedom from organized crime would be some of the evidences of a nation yielding itself to the dominion of the kingdom of God.

10. International Scene

The tenth sphere of influence for the kingdom of God is the international scene. Each sphere of authority has an outward form that most reflects the order and spiritual health of the kingdom of God. In a physical body, the authority of the kingdom of God is reflected in the form of freedom from sickness and disease. Prosperity in finances, harmony in the family and revival in a nation are all expressions of God's design. The community of nations also has an order and pattern that best reflects God's plan.

There are seventy Gentile nations, and the nation of Israel is at their center. Each nation has been designated a geographical place upon the earth to dwell (Acts 17:26). The nation of Israel was designed to be the head among the nations and a center of evangelism and worship. If kingdom of God order is to be brought to the international scene, Israel will have to emerge as a world leader. As the United Nations is so often a forum to denounce Israel, its agenda is not outwardly reflective of kingdom-of-God order.

Kingdom-of-God order on the international scene would mean a defeat of the forces of Gog and Magog and of spiritual Babylon. Continents would be free of widespread famine. A period of military peace and security would reign.

Solomon's Reign

The early years of King Solomon were close to the format of God's order in the international scene. **I Kings 4:21 & 24** state:

So Solomon reigned over all kingdoms from the River to the land of the Philistines, as far as the border of Egypt. They brought tribute and served Solomon all of the days of his life. He had dominion over all the region on this side of the River from Tiphsah even to Gaza, namely over all the kings on this side of the River; and he had peace on every side all around him.

The Queen of Sheba said of Solomon:

Blessed be the Lord your God, who delighted in you, setting you on the throne of Israel. Because the Lord has loved Israel forever, therefore He made you king, to do justice and righteousness (I Kings 10:9).

I Kings 4:34 also states:

And men from all nations, from all the kings of the earth who had heard of his wisdom, came to hear the wisdom of Solomon.

Joseph ruled over most of the known world in the time of Egypt's empire. Daniel ruled over most of the known world during the Persian empire.

We need to stretch our faith to see a revival of international proportions. At the height of Great Britain's dominion, they were sending missionaries all over the world. World-wide evangelism is not beyond the realm of possibility. In 313 A.D., the Edict of Milan issued by Constantine I made Christianity legal in the Roman Empire; in 392 A.D., Theodosius made Christianity the official religion of the Roman Empire. In the years when Spain was a ruler among nations, it also promoted worldwide missionary activity. While these events were fraught with many worldly attitudes and negative ramifications, they do at least highlight the possibility that an international empire could in some form or another be Christianized. Massive revivals in Third-World countries could soon see whole continents turn to the Lord.

International Order

Under international biblical order, Israel would be the head of the nations. This does not mean that the Jewish people are better than other people. God is not prejudiced toward one group of people. The fact that men are the heads of the home does not mean that God is a male chauvinist. International order is an outworking of God's plan to demonstrate His sovereignty over the flow of history. Bringing Israel back into headship among the nations will be the great end-times sign of God's all-powerful ability to control the course of human events.

Israel does not have a righteousness of its own, but God uses Israel as a sign among the nations. The fact that people identify the nation of Israel with the ancient biblical promises will allow God to draw the forces of history towards a pattern that will give glory to His name.

The Messianic Age

The forces of communism and Islam will eventually be defeated. As there was a Pax Romana that covered the globe for two centuries, so will there be in the end of days a Pax Messianica to bring a period of peace to the world. As America and Britain have been centers for evangelism and revival, so will Israel be a spiritual center in the end times. As the tiny nation of Japan has become a leader in computer technology and business management, so it would not be inconceivable to see Israel a leader among the nations in the near future. **Micah 4:1-3** states:

> **Now it shall come to pass in the latter days that the mountain of the Lord's house shall be established on the top of the mountains and shall be exalted above the hills; and peoples shall flow to it. Many nations shall come and say, "Come and let us go up to the mountain of the Lord, to the house of the God of Jacob; He will teach us His ways and we shall walk in His paths." For out of Zion the law shall go forth, and the word of the Lord from Jerusalem. He shall judge between many peoples and rebuke strong nations afar off. They shall beat their swords into plowshares and their spears into pruning hooks. Nation shall not lift up sword against nation, neither shall they learn war any more.**

The mountain refers to a nation and a government. The fact that the law will go forth from Zion indicates that Jerusalem will be a world center for revival and biblical teaching. People in the Catholic Church have looked toward Rome as their spiritual center. Many in the "word-of-faith" movement have looked to the ministries coming out of Tulsa as their spiritual center. At other times, different locations have been spiritual centers for a religious movement. The right order on the international scene is that Jerusalem should once again emerge as a spiritual center on this earth. The prophet Micah also speaks of an extended period of peace where there would not be any more war between the nations.

God's Authority

The kingdom of God can be expressed in different spheres of life. These spheres start from the inner spirit of a man and move outward to cover the entire earth. A kingdom is the sphere of government of a king. Today we would use the word authority for the word kingdom. The kingdom of God is the authority of God expressed in every different area of life. Inwardly and outwardly, the kingdom of God manifests God's loving and powerful authority in every conceivable way. Every nook and cranny of every created area will be filled by God's Spirit. God's rule and order will be reflected in every situation. God's peace and love shall fill the entire earth as the waters cover the sea.

All the earth shall be filled with the glory of the Lord (Numbers 14:21).

25

THE DOCTRINE OF WORK

The kingdom of God starts within a man's inner being and grows to affect every area of life. Covenantal principles can be applied to any area of endeavor. One of the most important yet neglected areas of biblical application is that of a man's workplace. The average man spends most of his time and certainly most of his productive energy toward his occupation. If this area of vocation cannot be brought in line with the purposes of the kingdom of God, a believer will find himself to have wasted the greater part of his life. Even if a man is fairly disciplined in devotional times and participates in ministerial activities, he can in no way match the effort he puts into his job.

For many believers, and particularly for young men who are at the beginning of their work career, the attitude toward a job is crucial. A man's self-image and sense of self-worth is to a large degree wrapped up in what he does for a living. It is in the workplace that a man learns most of the practical aspects of life. His character is forged by the realities of the job situation. No matter how lofty a man's biblical ideals are, if he cannot make them succeed in the job field, he has failed with his life. It is important in discipleship that one know the meaning of work and be able to approach work with a sense of biblical conviction.

I want to thank my friend Bill Woodrow, who has taught both in precept and example in this area for years. Bill pastors a thriving community of believers and leads a secular business at the same time. Part of Bill's discipleship program is to bring young men in to work for his company for a year or two. There they receive a type of apprenticeship where they can work together on the practical areas of life as well as pray and study the Bible. If a man is off center in the area of his job, he must, as well, be off center in the will of God for his life in general.

God's Work Schedule

The biblical concept of work starts with the personality of God. **Genesis 2:2** says:

And on the seventh day God ended His work which He had done, and He rested on the seventh day from all His work.

There is a balance between productive labor and restorative rest. This balance of work and rest runs as a theme throughout Scriptures, particularly in the law of Moses. The rabbis have laid much emphasis on understanding this principle in the classical teachings of the Jewish faith. Because of the theological confusion over the relationship between law and grace, the biblical attitude on what is normal in work loads has often fallen to one side or the other.

Because the balance of work and rest is inherent in God's own personality, the rhythm of work and rest is therefore reflected throughout all that He has created. There is a pattern of work and rest in the bio-rhythms of nature. Man, having been made in the image of God, finds within himself an inherent inclination toward the pattern of labor and leisure. Indulgent, complacent laziness on the one hand, and fretful, stressful workaholism on the other hand, are both aberrations from God's plan.

As it takes faith to work, it also takes faith to rest. Many ministers of the gospel have become less effective in the long run because they over-extended themselves in their work pattern during the early years. The "burn-out" syndrome was not supposed to be a form of Christian martyrdom. It takes faith to believe that one can rest from his work during certain periods and that the work will still be productive. **Mark 4:27** states that, after a man of faith has worked to scatter his seed in the ground, he should then:

sleep by night and rise by day, and the seed should sprout and grow, he himself does not know how.

The Sabbath Principle

Part of the covenant that God has made with mankind is certain provisions for periods of rest. There are many types of sabbaths in the Bible besides the one day in seven. There are new moons, annual feasts and years of jubilee. God was the inventor of the principle of weekends and vacations. It is an act of faith to put away one's work and concentrate on worship and the Word of God. The origin of the word holiday is holy day, or a day set apart for God.

In addition to designated periods of rest, the sabbath principle also includes the concept that one can work while being continually refreshed by the Spirit of God. We enter into a spirit of restfulness as we work, because we have trust in God. God's guarantees of success remove from us all fears and stress. Because we are ensured of God's working with us, we can face any situation with an ease and graciousness that can overcome the problem. The fruitfulness of our spirit during times of difficulty is an important aspect of our witness and testimony to those around us.

Isaiah 40:31 states:

Those who wait on the Lord shall renew their strength.

The Spirit of God refreshes us during our labor to help us have victory over weariness and fatigue. **Hebrews 4:9-10** states:

There remains therefore a rest for the people of God. He who has entered His rest has himself also ceased from his works as God did from His.

For the born-again believer there is an attitude of restfulness and inner sabbath that should be with us at all times.

When Jesus was questioned for having supposedly broken the sabbath, He answered:

My Father has been working until now, and I also have been working (John 5:17).

It is the physical body that needs rest. The Spirit of God and the spirit of man indwelt by the Spirit of God have no need for rest. God himself continues to work and uphold all creation at all times. When we are under the anointing of God, we are given life and energy from God's Spirit so that we never have to become tired at all.

Burn-Out

Fear of burnout can be a dangerous thing. It is helpful to realize that pure fatigue is rarely the actual problem. Burnout is more caused by the stress brought on by fear and frustration than it is by fatigue itself. I can remember as a child going out to play strenuous football and basketball games for hours on end. Although the physical fatigue would seem almost overwhelming, I was so happy on the inside that my spirit was completely refreshed. The more we played the more happy we became.

Fear and frustration are means for the devil to attack a person with stress by making him think that fatigue is the problem. Fear of fatigue is more the problem than fatigue. If one can see the source of his stress as fear and frustration, he may be able to direct spiritual attention in that direction and gain victory over the problem. If ministers could find out what subtle areas are causing them fear and what are causing them frustration, they would be free to serve the Lord with more vigor and cheerfulness.

Productive Labor

In contrast to the principle of sabbath rest, we are called to exert ourselves in work. Productive labor, even long and strenuous at times, is a positive quality in the kingdom of God. A distinction must be made between productive labor on the one hand and vain toil on the other. Work is the positive experience of a man being actively involved in the function for which he was designed to do. Toil is the perverted counterfeit of work; it is purposeless and frustrating, and occurs when a man is separated from the designs of God.

Work is to a man as flying is to a bird. A man should be content and fulfilled through the expression of what he does. **Genesis 2:15** states:

Then the Lord God took the man [Adam] and put him in the garden of Eden to tend and keep it.

Man's role is tending and being a steward over God's creation. Before the fall, during the ideal state of Eden, Adam was found working happily in cooperation with God. Man was made to be active. Man desires to be involved and to participate. Work is not a product of the fall of man. Work is not a way for man to try to earn his way back to God. Work was changed to toil at the fall of man. When we are saved, the frustrating aspects of the curse of toil are removed. We are returned to a positive work experience.

Our ultimate state of paradise is not one in which we will all become passive, inactive and lazy, doing nothing as it were but watching heaven's activities on a television set. Enjoyable, productive activity is part of the pre-fall and post-restoration design of God. The work and rest patterns of man should be seen as part of the gracious symphony of the cycles and seasons of the universe. **Psalm 104:21-24** states:

> **The young lions roar after their prey and seek their food from God. When the sun arises, they gather together and lie down in their dens. Man goes out to his work and to his labor until the evening. O Lord, how manifold are Your works! In wisdom You have made them all.**

We come into harmony with God as our pattern and style of labor are drawn into line with His plan.

There are two ways to pervert the balanced activity of fruitful labor. One way is lazy inactivity; the other way is toilsome overactivity. God's plan for us in work is an expression of His grace. We are to be diligent, to take dominion, and to have great success.

Dominion

God's overall plan for mankind may be expressed in the word "dominion." Man's dominion mandate was originally expressed in **Genesis 1:28:**

> **Then God blessed them, and God said to them, "Be fruitful and multiply; fill the earth and subdue it; have dominion over the fish of the sea, over the birds of the air, and over every living thing that moves on the earth."**

This dominion is the purpose that we rejected when we fell from God's grace in sin. Our purpose in life is to be an extension of God's benevolent authority. We were to be the delegated image of God's kingship throughout creation. The great commission in which we are called to preach the gospel to every nation on earth should be seen as part of this original dominion mandate. We had, as a human race, fallen away from God's gracious dominion; now, through the message of the lordship of the new Messianic king, we are calling everyone everywhere to return to God's authority.

Work is part of God's original intention for us to tend His garden and to take dominion over the earth. We must be able to reconcile each of our individual jobs to fit into this overall design of dominion and stewardship. When a farmer works his property, he is both tending the ground and taking dominion over it. When a man works in a position of government, he is both tending the flock of the people in his nation and exercising God's governing authority through his position. If a man works in education, he should see his job as training young people to return to their ultimate role as wise and knowledgeable stewards.

Fields of Endeavor

David's kingdom in Israel was a foreshadowing of the Messianic kingdom of Jesus. Within David's kingdom, men were assigned to different areas of work and responsibility. **I Chronicles 27:25-34** gives a sampling of the range of activities that can be an expression of God's dominion:

> **And Azmaveth was over the king's treasury; Jonathan was over the storehouses in the field, in the cities, in the villages, and in the fortresses. Ezri was over those who did the work of the field for tilling the ground. Shimei was over the vineyards.... Joash was over the store of oil.... Obil the Ishmaelite was over the camels, Jehdeiah was over the donkeys...also Jonathan was a scribe; and Jehiel was with the king's sons. Ahithophel was the king's counselor, and Hushai was the king's companion ... the general of the king's army was Joab.**

Many different areas of endeavor were included. Business, agriculture, education, industry, government and military were all part of David's kingdom.

I have a friend who is a genius at the piano. He knows how to construct, repair, tune and play the piano with an intense concern for quality in every area. He has absorbed into his spirit the essence of the piano. We have talked together about the role of pianos in the kingdom of God. The Lord will assign people to have responsibility for the care and production of quality musical instruments.

I have another friend who has a deep concern for the oceans. He has a master's degree in oceanography, with an emphasis in policy making. He works with the Coast Guard and has a broad sense of the philosophical and creative importance of the seas. If David could assign a man to be in charge of the stewardship for his fields, would not Jesus assign someone for stewardship over the oceans. In the kingdom of God, there will still be real life. God is using the experiences of our present life to train us for our future greater stewardship.

The parable of the ten talents explains that what we do in this lifetime is preparation for the extension of our authority in the kingdom of God. In **Luke 19:17** Jesus addresses the one who had been productive in his labor by saying:

> **Well done, good servant; because you were faithful in very little, have authority over ten cities.**

This passage can be seen as referring to ministry, faith and evangelism, but it is also referring to our faithfulness in the practical tasks of our jobs.

Jesus looks at our jobs to determine what kind of spiritual people we are. **Verse 15** states:

> **He then commanded these servants to whom He had given the money to be called to Him that He might know how much every man had gained by trading.**

As we are called to go out into the world and take dominion, our jobs are part of that calling. We are to gain positions of authority and influence in the world. We are to be occupying forces in the real areas of life as we await the coming king. **Verse 13** states Jesus' directive to us:

Occupy until I come.

We are to do business and exercise godly dominion through our jobs.

Success and Promotion

Believers should expect to rise toward the top of whatever field of endeavor their vocation is in. We should be the best workers on the job in any situation. When we have a covenant with God, we have not only the promise of eternal life later on, but also the assurance of victory in this life now. Rising to the top in one's job field is a central promise of the covenant we have with God.

Deuteronomy 28:13 says that the Lord will make us:

the head and not the tail.

This is not some vague ethereal promise, but a contractual covenant in which God promises to help us be on top of the practical areas of business and life. The passage of Deuteronomy 28 is talking about such things as our work in the city, our work in the fields, our work in our household and our work in the military. A man of covenant will expect to excel in his job.

Promotion comes from the Lord (Psalms 75:6). If a man is walking in covenant, God will cause him to excel in his work. This excellence will bring him success. **Proverbs 22:29** states:

See a man that excels in his work, he will stand before kings; he will not stand before unknown men.

Both Psalm 1 and Joshua 1 promise that if we will meditate continually on God's Word, He will cause us to prosper and have success in everything we do. A noncovenantal view of Scriptures will say that this success is only in a mystical realm. An understanding of covenant brings the blessings of God into a man's character and life, and thereby into his work and the world around him.

Believers should grasp the relationship between work and faith. A covenantal attitude in the heart will produce an excellent quality in the workplace. Quality will cause promotion and blessing. We need to develop our faith that we will be promoted in the workplace. An example of this grace and favor is given us by the patriarch Joseph. **Genesis 39:2-4** states:

The Lord was with Joseph, and he was a successful man...and his master saw that the Lord made all he did to prosper in his hand. So Joseph found favor in his sight and served him. Then he made him overseer of his house, and put all that he had in his hand.

The witness of the fact that Joseph was walking in covenant with God was that he was successful in what he did on his job. The quality of work at our job is the primary testimony that most people will see about our faith in God.

Real Life Faith

There is an important relationship between how we grow in using authority in the natural affairs of life and how we are able to handle spiritual authority in the heavenly principalities. It is in learning to direct people and submit to others in the flow of authority of the workplace that we grow in the real substance of understanding how faith works. Jesus said of the centurion that he had such great faith that Jesus had not found anyone else equal to him. When the centurion described how he acquired such faith, he simply said that it was the same as the authority he had learned to use in his job in the military. **Luke 7:8** states:

For I also am a man under authority, having soldiers under me. And I say to one, "Go," and he goes; and to another, "Come," and he comes; and to my servant, "Do this," and he does it.

Sometimes young men claim to have spiritual zeal and faith, but they show fear, avoidance and irresponsibility in their work. If one's character has not been trained through the apprenticeship of the workplace, his spiritual faith may be an exaggerated bravado to compensate for a sense of failure. Faith is real and work is real. One of the prerequisites to full-time ministry should be to demonstrate competence in at least one area of vocational endeavor.

One of the key characteristics of being able to succeed in the workplace is the quality of diligence. Diligence is the ability to maintain effort and concentration toward a certain goal. Diligence is the opposite of laziness. Diligence is an application of the human will. Proverbs 10:4 and 13:4 both say that the characteristic of diligence will cause a person to become wealthy. Proverbs 12:24 says that diligence will cause a person to become a leader or ruler. Proverbs 21:5 says that diligence will cause a person's thoughts to be aligned in a productive direction. His thoughts will tend toward increase.

Toil

The opposite of work is toil. Toil is labor that is unproductive, inefficient and frustrating. Toil is the sinful version of work. Toil is a product of the separation of Adam from God. Toil is an indication that one's work is not flowing in blessed harmony with God. Toil is a result of the curse of Eden. **Genesis 3:17-18** states:

Cursed is the ground for your sake; in toil you shall eat of it all the days of your life. Both thorns and thistles it shall bring forth for you.

Before the fall there was no toil; there was only productive labor. After the fall and outside of any covenant, there was no blessed labor, but only cursed toil. After one is redeemed by Jesus and comes under a covenantal arrangement with God, his toil should be transformed back to a state of positive labor. Sin-ridden toil is evidenced by working much and reaping little. Covenant-protected work is evidenced by planting seed and having it return one-hundredfold.

In toil, man strives to achieve something but never achieves it.

I saw that for all toil and every skillful work a man is envied by his neighbor. This also is vanity and a grasping for the wind (Ecclesiastes 4:4).

When a man works under the covenant, he is brought into promotion and leadership. When one is striving under toil, he slips further down into lower states of degrading activity. **Ecclesiastes 2:26** states:

For God gives wisdom and knowledge and joy to the man who is good in His sight; but to the sinner He gives the work of gathering and collecting, that he may give it to him who is good before God. This also is vanity and a grasping for the wind.

Leftist political philosophy tends to glorify low level work positions and demean those of management responsibility. Many times a person's lack of cooperation with his employer will initiate a downward cycle of increasing frustration. A person who is willing to take on responsibility will usually be given more and more opportunity.

Enjoying One's Work

A great victory of faith is to walk in a spirit of joy while on one's job. While this is challenging, the rewards are meaningful. Solomon said in Ecclesiastes that a sign of wisdom was for a man to be able to enjoy his work. **Ecclesiastes 2:24, 3:13** and **3:22** all state that there is no greater accomplishment then to be able to enjoy ones work.

So I perceive that there is nothing better than that a man should rejoice in his own works for that is his heritage (3:22).

One must reconcile his life to God's plan to be able to enjoy his day-to-day job. It may seem easy to be spiritual in the midst of a praise and worship service. The more difficult test is whether one can bring this joy and peace into the Monday through Friday workplace.

Working full time in a ministry requires a great deal of effort. If one thinks ministry does not require much effort, he will soon find himself resisting the very things he has to do to make the ministry succeed. The Apostle Paul put enormous effort into his work. Grace and work complement each other.

God's grace towards me was not in vain; but I labored more abundantly than they all, yet not I, but the grace of God which was with me (I Corinthians 15:10).

Grace inspires hard work. Grace is laboring inside a man as he works for the ministry. If one realizes that the ministry requires great effort and work, he can prepare his heart and faith to meet that challenge. A man should not make the mistake of dividing work and ministry in his mind between spiritual activity and unspiritual activity. We must believe that whatever effort we invest into the ministry will reap a great reward. As believers, we hold fast to our covenant which says that nothing we do will be in vain. **I Corinthians 15:58** states:

Be steadfast, immovable, always abounding in the work of the Lord, knowing that your labor is not in vain in the Lord.

Sometimes when I have worked hard and am being attacked by doubts that the work was not fruitful, I use this verse to confess success over the work. None of our effort can be done in vain. All that we do is, by faith, producing worthwhile results.

Ministry Salaries

Full-time ministry must be recognized by the congregants as hard work worthy of high salary. We should support our ministers well, as we would anyone else who is in a professional and well-trained vocation. **I Timothy 5:17-18** state:

Let the elders who rule well be counted worthy of double honor, especially those who labor in the word and doctrine...the laborer is worthy of his wages....

The congregants should have a heart of generosity to bless their pastor and to free him from financial burdens so that he can better focus his spiritual energy on the kingdom of God. The more the congregants give to him materially, the more they will receive from him spiritually.

Another viable option for a pastor, evangelist or elder is to maintain work in a secular job field while developing his ministy of preaching and teaching. This has the benefit of setting an example to the rest of the congregants of how to work a job and participate in the ministry of the congregation at the same time. This model-creates an atmosphere within the members that each one is required to do his own share of the work as much as the minister. It also creates a freedom for financial flow to be put into the projects of the ministry. Pastor and congregants can see themselves in the healthy relationship of being on the same team. They share the responsibilities to see the ministry succeed. There is less room for complaining, and all the members can be called to definite service. **I Thessalonians 2:9** states:

You remember, brethren, our labor and toil; for laboring night and day that we might not be a burden to any of you, we preached to you the gospel of God.

II Thessalonians 3:8-9 states similarly:

We did not eat anyone's bread free of charge but worked, labored, and toiled night and day that we might not be a burden to any of you, not because we do not have authority, but to make ourselves an example of how you should follow us.

Setting a pattern for right order in the job field is a central aspect of discipleship.

Faith Prosperity

When we are outside God's will for our lives, our jobs can be unproductive. When we are walking with God, our work should be blessed. **Haggai 2:18-19** contains a challenge to examine the effectiveness of our work as a test to see if we are walking in the will of God. The Lord points out that without His blessing, all the works of our hands will fail to accomplish anything. When we turn to Him, we should be able to note an immediate and marked improvement.

Consider now from this day forward — consider it.... From this day forward I will bless you.

God wants us to be aware that we will be more fruitful on our jobs when our lives are dedicated to Him.

There are two complementary forces that come to bear on our financial prosperity. The first is positive confession of the mouth; the second is diligent effort of the hands. **Proverbs 12:14** states:

A man will be satisfied with good by the fruit of his mouth, and the recompense of a man's hands will be rendered to him.

We need both faith confession and work. Faith confession without the work ethic will be superficial and lack the perseverance to bring true prosperity. On the other hand, the work ethic without the spiritual power of faith confession will lack the grace and anointing to bring about all the prosperity that God intends for us. If we combine faith and diligence, we will be operating under God's covenant and receive His full blessings.

26

FAMILY PRIORITIES
Part 1

The Transgenerational Link

Of all the interpersonal covenants, the one of highest priority is marriage. Family has the highest priority because one spends more time with his family than with anyone else. There must be corresponding commitment with every degree of intimacy. Since a husband and wife have absolute intimacy, they must have absolute covenant. Covenant is the bond of love; where there is greater love, there must be greater covenant. There is long-term intimacy and trust connected with the members of one's family. Therefore, there must be the corresponding covenant to match those relationships.

I used to think that putting emphasis on one's family was a diversion from commitment to the kingdom of God. After all, Jesus said that we must even hate our family members in comparison to our commitment to Him. If we see the family as a separate sphere from that of ministry, there will always be a dichotomy in our priorities. If we see commitment to the kingdom of God as one of being faithful to covenant, then commitment to one's family becomes a direct expression of one's kingdom of God priorities. The family may be seen as a mini-congregation, with the father as the pastor.

Marriage Fidelity

Marriage and children are high priorities in the kingdom of God. **Malachi 2:14-15** states:

> **The Lord has been a witness between you and the wife of your youth, with whom you have dealt treacherously; yet she is your companion and your wife by covenant. But did He not make them one, having a remnant of the Spirit? And why one? He seeks godly offspring. Therefore take heed to your spirit, and let none deal treacherously with the wife of his youth.**

The wife of one's youth points to the faithfulness over the long period from youth to old age. Because a man has known his wife from the time they were married in their youth, he should be ever faithful to her through the years. It was by covenant that the woman became the man's wife. God is calling the man to loyalty to his marital vows. His marriage is not based upon feelings of romantic attraction, but on the solid rock commitment of covenant.

We are not to violate the vows of our marital covenant. If we treat our wives treacherously, we have violated a fundamental covenant and have disqualified our integrity before God. If we are to be successful in spiritual life, we must give attention to the faithfulness of our marriage relationship.

God's Offspring

God's stated purpose in marriage is to bring about godly offspring (Malachi 2:15). The production of children who will follow in the footsteps of the covenant is immensely important. Most people underestimate the vital reasons for producing godly offspring. Biblical covenants depend on transgenerational commitment. Biblical covenants demand a link by which God can transfer His covenant to the succeeding generation (Genesis 17:7). Men live one generation at a time, but God lives over the span of many generations. If God is to have a covenant with mankind, He must make that covenant span more than one generation. A single-generation covenant falls short of a relationship with God because He is eternal. All of God's covenants with mankind must have a provision for carrying that covenant to unlimited generations in the future.

I Chronicles 16:15-16 states:

Remember His covenant always, the word that He commanded for a thousand generations. The covenant which He made with Abraham and His oath to Isaac, and confirmed it to Jacob for a statute to Israel for an everlasting covenant.

God describes His covenant as covering a thousand generations. The covenant that He made with Abraham had to be reconfirmed to Isaac, and then reconfirmed to Jacob again. A covenant is everlasting on God's side because He does not change. If it is to be everlasting for the subsequent generations of mankind, the covenant must be reconfirmed by each new group of people.

Children of the Covenant

If Satan can ruin the children of the covenant, he can foil God's plan in the earth. Attacks of Satan always come against the children of the covenant. Pharaoh tried to kill the male babies at the time of Moses. Herod tried to kill the male babies at the time of Jesus. The ancient pagan religions tried to intermingle their women with the covenant men in order to turn the children away from following the Lord. In modern times, such phenomena as the Holocaust, drug abuse, and abortion are aimed at destroying the potential progenitors of the everlasting covenant.

Covenants between people in society need only last during the time those individuals are alive. A covenant with God must extend beyond one's lifetime because God continues to be alive. Establishing a transgenerational link is essential to making a covenant with God. When God looks for a man with whom to establish His covenant, He looks for the character quality in that man to be committed to train and raise his children after him in the covenant. **Genesis 18:19** says of Abraham:

> For I have known him in order that he may command his children's household after him that they keep the way of the Lord, to do righteousness and justice, that the Lord may bring to Abraham what He has spoken to him.

Abraham is the father of our faith. We walk in the footsteps of Abraham. The reason that we walk in the footsteps of Abraham is that he understood how a covenant works. God picked Abraham to be the father of all covenant-making people because God knew he could trust Abraham not to abandon his children. Since Abraham's character was such that he would be committed to his children after him, God was able to set in motion through Abraham a covenantal pattern that would bless all succeeding generations.

The Link of Generations

The key to making covenant with God is to understand the link between one generation and another. The issue is the link itself. The covenant goes in both directions, backward and forward. God is committed to past generations and future generations. We must be equally committed both toward our ancestors and toward our descendants. This revelation will help us in understanding the language of covenant in the Bible. I must be committed to my children and to my forefathers. God is committed to my children and my forefathers because I have made covenant with Him. God is committed to me because my forefathers made covenant with Him. If I have a friend that is a close covenantal partner, I must be equally committed to his children and he to mine. There is spiritual power in the agreement between two people. There is also spiritual authority inherent in the link between one generation and another.

God said in Malachi 2:15 that He seeks godly offspring. God is always in intensive search for offspring of the next generation with whom to establish His covenant. Godly offspring are needed if the everlasting covenant is to continue.

Another reason that God seeks covenant-making offspring is that all covenants are patterned after the relationship between God and His Son Jesus. The blessings of a covenant are manifest through a faith promise. The manifestation of the faith promise comes through the figure of the Son. God desired to work with mankind on the earth, but He did it through the figure of His Son Jesus. Spiritual power is contained in the words of a promise. A promise is a group of words with a future fulfillment. A promise demands an exercise of hope and faith to see it fulfilled. God makes a promise with a man and it is manifest through the man's son. The man exercises hope and faith that the words of the promise will be fulfilled in the future in his son.

Promises Fulfilled in the Next Generation

God had a covenant with King David. David asked for a temple to be built. God promised that David's temple would be built. In the spirit, the temple was established at the moment of the promise between God and David. In the earth, the temple was manifested during the time of King Solomon. Although the temple is referred to as Solomon's temple, it was really David's temple. The temple was manifested here on earth as a fulfillment of the promise between God and David. The figure of the son is the one who bears the manifestation of previous covenantal promise.

God made promises to Abraham. They were to be fulfilled through his children and his children's children. One generation makes a covenant with God. The covenant bears with it promise of future blessing. The blessings are manifested fully in the generation that follows. The second generation goes deeper in covenant with God and receives even greater promises. These promises are then fulfilled and manifested in that next generation. Whenever faith can be sustained through more than one generation, the power and magnitude of the vision of the kingdom of God will grow to ever greater dimensions.

We as believers walk in the footsteps of those that have gone before us. We have learned through reading the books of those of the previous generations. They may have taken a lifetime to glean a revelation from God in a certain area. We of this generation, as their spiritual heirs, receive those revelations in a moment of time and go on to believe for even greater things. If we read the faith revelations of those who have gone before us, we will be in position to receive even more. I can read in a matter of hours what it might have taken a man of God in previous generations a lifetime to learn and compile. A covenantal heart appreciates those who have gone before and paved the way.

The Revelation of Respecting Parents

We can gain revelation about the future of our ministry if we respect and honor our parents. It is often through an act of appreciating our parents that the callings upon our lives are made obvious to us. I recall a time early in the ministry when I reached a log jam in the direction to which God was calling me. I prayed and prayed, but there seemed to be no door of understanding. I felt stuck. I wanted to serve the Lord, but there seemed to be no revelation as to which direction to go. The only perception that continued to come into my heart during this period was that I was supposed to respect and honor my parents more. I did not see how this was an answer to my prayers. However, since I could think of nothing else to do, I proceeded with acts of covenant obedience to be reconciled to my parents in deeper ways.

As I began to appreciate my parents even more, I had a growing understanding of who I was as a person. It became more clear to me, as I looked at my parents, the purpose for which God had created me. I could see elements in my parents that God had placed deep within my life. The more I appreciated my parents, the more I was able to understand the inherent callings and instincts within my own life that God had ordained. The more I appreciated my parents, the more obvious it became what direction I was being called in for ministry.

Many believers say they do not know in what direction God is leading them. If they would remove barriers between themselves and their parents, the answers to their questions would become apparent. Confusion about one's callings in God often stems from a lack of covenantal commitment to his parents. My friend Sid Roth, a radio host and Jewish evangelist, recently had the opportunity to spend time with his father at a traditional Jewish synagogue. Sid did this in covenantal honor and respect for his father. During these visits, there were major breakthroughs for Sid in understanding direction for the ministry. He also received revelations about the powers and principalities of rejection that were keeping Jewish people away from receiving their Messiah.

Spiritual power is released when children turn their hearts to their parents, and when parents turn their hearts to their children:

> **Behold, I will send you Elijah the prophet before the coming of the great and dreadful day of the Lord. He will turn the hearts of the fathers to the children, and the hearts of the children to their fathers (Malachi 4:5-6).**

This verse was partially fulfilled by the ministry of John the Baptist in introducing the coming of Jesus. There is enough revelation among the Body of believers today that the second coming of Jesus could be effected within a generation. A widespread reconciliation between parents and children of believers is coming. Spiritual power will be released. The children will receive revelation as to the purpose of their ministry here in the end times. Authority of covenant will be exercised, and the Body of believers will be able to pray effectively to call forth the kingdom of God and introduce the second coming. The children of the covenant will be a prophetic generation in the spirit of Elijah and John the Baptist.

Commitment to a covenant partner's son or daughter is described in the story of Mephibosheth. Mephibosheth was a son of Jonathan, the son of King Saul. He was crippled in his feet and lived in obscurity and disgrace. When David and Jonathan made their famous covenant, they committed themselves to be loyal to the other's children. After Jonathan's death, David searched to find if one of Jonathan's children might still be alive. When Mephibosheth was brought to David, he thought that David was intending to kill him. In **II Samuel 9:7**, David says to Mephibosheth:

> **Do not fear, for I will surely show you kindness for Jonathan your father's sake, and will restore to you all the land of Saul your grandfather; and you shall eat bread at my table continually.**

David tells Mephibosheth that he is going to be kind to him not for Mephibosheth's own sake, but because of the covenant he had with his father Jonathan. It is important to notice the phrase "for your father's sake." It was not a question of whether Mephibosheth was a worthy person or not. David directed special attention toward him because of David's own character of keeping covenant. Mephibosheth then had a choice as to whether he would of his own right enter into a covenantal loyalty with David. If Mephibosheth desired, he could have become a covenant partner with David. If he did not, however, David would still have directed kindness toward him because of his previous covenant with Jonathan. There is a difference between making a covenant with a person and showing kindness toward the descendants of a person with whom one already has a covenant.

I have this relationship with the children of my special covenant brothers. My friend Paul Wilbur, leader of Israel's Hope worship ministries, has two sons, Nathan and Joel. When Paul is on the road, traveling in ministry, I have blessed opportunities to spend intimate time with them. They see me as a kind of second daddy. There is a bonding between his sons and my sons, Yehezkel and Frederick. They are close in age, and whenever they get together, there is a supernatural favor between them.

Another dear friend, Andrew Shishkoff, pastor of Beth Messiah Congregation, has an older son David. David has been a student in the Christian high school where I am principal. He is a particularly spiritual, well-behaved, and intelligent young man. David and I have a kinship with one another, knowing that our lives are to be bound up in a united purpose for a long time in the future. This covenant that I have with the son of a covenant friend is precious to me.

Circle of Trust

There is a deeply touching and meaningful encounter at the cross between Jesus, His mother Mary, and His best friend John.

When Jesus therefore saw His mother, and the disciple whom He loved standing by, He said to His mother, "Woman, behold your son!" Then He said to the disciple, "Behold your mother!" And from that hour the disciple took her to his own home (John 19:26-27).

This is not merely a scene of compassion and charity. Deep covenantal intimacy and loyalty are being expressed. John is Jesus' closest covenant partner. The covenant demands that John, as a spiritual kinsman-redeemer, provide for the members of Jesus' family. Jesus is stripped, beaten and hanging upon the cross in shame. It is a moment of excruciating vulnerability. This is Jesus' innermost circle of covenantal warmth and intimacy. They are prepared to deliver themselves into one another's hands. The beauty of their mutual trust is overwhelming.

It is worth reviewing here in the shadow of the cross the primary principle of discipleship that we discussed earlier. Although Jesus loved the whole world and was willing to die for everyone in it, He could not entrust Himself into the hands of men because He knew they were untrustworthy. Jesus then picked out a group of men, whom He called disciples, to train to keep covenantal trust. This training took place over a period of three years. First He chose them; then they became His servants; then they became His trusted friends. **John 15:15** states:

No longer do I call you servants, for a servant does not know what his master

**is doing; but I have called you friends, for all things that I have heard from
My Father I have made known to you.**

The group of disciples became the covenant friends of Jesus because He was
able to trust them with His most intimate revelations. Among those disciples, Judas
eventually betrayed that trust. John, on the other hand, became the one who grew
closest to Jesus. At the cross, the covenantal relationship between John and Jesus is
being acted out. Not only did John receive into his house Jesus' mother, but he was
also privileged to receive into his heart some of the most outstanding revelations of
Scriptures that were ever given to a man.

Covenant and Jewish History

Covenant keeping with God requires a commitment to a transgenerational link.
God's dealings with the Jewish people throughout history involve a covenant that
spans many generations. In the example of Mephibosheth, David showed special
kindness and attention to him because he was Jonathan's son. It was not dependent
upon Mephibosheth's own worthiness, but rather, as David said:

For your father's sake.

In **Romans 11:28-29**, Paul speaks of the Jewish people who do not believe in
Jesus:

**Concerning the gospel, they are enemies for your sake, but concerning the
election they are beloved for the sake of the fathers. For the gifts and the
calling of God are irrevocable.**

There is a special covenant priority in directing love toward the Jewish people for
the sake of the covenant which their forefathers made with God. The gospel should
be preached to them first (Romans 1:16). Prayer intercession should be concentrated
for them (Romans 10:1). The restoration of the Jewish people in the end times
bears with it the promise of the fullness of God's kingdom to come (Romans 11:12
and 15).

We are not racially prejudiced either for or against the Jewish people. Every
individual is created equal before God and is equally beloved of Him. On the other
hand, all love that is flowing on the earth today is a result of the legal ground that
was won by keeping covenant. Commitment to covenant is what allows for love to
exist here. It is a desire for God's purposes on the earth that leads us to a special
overflowing compassion toward the Jewish people. As commitment to loyalty to
our families causes our ministries to be valid, so does commitment to loyalty to the
Jewish people make the preaching of the gospel valid. Love and faith are birthed
through faithfulness to all previous covenants.

My Family History

Most Jewish people who live in America today have their ancestry in Eastern

Europe. My family was no exception. Recently, a genealogical study was compiled of our family, and I was able to gain a fuller understanding of who I am and where I came from. Jewish people whose roots are in Eastern Europe do not know anything of their ancestry before two or three generations ago. The past is obliterated by the black pool of the Holocaust. The survivors are those who emerged out of that dark pit. There is no past beyond it. Since then, family lines are drawn from the memory of those who escaped.

I am named after my great-grandfather Asher David, whom I never met. He lived in a small village on the border between what is now Russia and Poland. The village life was that of what is popularly depicted in the style of "Fiddler on the Roof." He was comparatively well-to-do in the sense that he owned some land and even had some Polish people working for him. He was an elder in the community and also a "shochet" (one who does the work of a butcher according to the laws of traditional ritual purity).

Apparently, there was one large family with the name Intrater, whose relatives extended over several villages in the area. Everyone with that name was part of the same umbrella family. Only a few, however, survived the Holocaust. My grandfather Yehezkel Intrater, decided to immigrate to America after World War I, acting on the premonition of impending disaster in Eastern Europe. My firstborn son is named after him. Yehezkel is the name in Hebrew for what is known in English as Ezekiel. It means "the strength of God." My grandfather came to America alone and sent for his wife to follow a few years afterward.

My grandfather worked as a cantor and a mohel. A cantor is the worship and song leader in a traditional synagogue; a mohel is a man who performs ritual circumcisions. My grandfather worked in several cities in the United States before settling in the Washington, D. C. area. I am told that he had a magnificent voice, that people loved to hear him chant the traditional melodies. On the eighth day after my birth, he circumcised me according to the covenant of our forefathers.

My father Samuel was raised in that Orthodox Jewish home. During his childhood, he was reared to be a cantor to follow in the footsteps of my grandfather. I have a photograph of my grandfather and father leading the men's choir at the synagogue. My grandfather is tall and erect with a dignified air of authority and moral destiny. My father is standing in front as the child-soprano in knickerbockers and tallis (fringed prayer shawl).

Graduating from high school, my father entered World War II as a bombardier, flying combat missions over Germany. The events of World War II caused change in my father's Orthodox lifestyle and religious beliefs. My father was a brilliant student and, after World War II, matriculated at Harvard College, where he graduated with honors. He went on to become a well-known trial lawyer and civil plaintiff in the Washington, D.C. area.

I have an appreciation for the history of my family and my people. Covenant calls us to respect our parentage, both physical and spiritual. We owe much of who we are to them. My sense of God's purposes and destiny upon me and upon the lives of my children blossoms as I am aware of God's workings in covenant down through the ages. We serve the kingdom of God in the context of the moment in history in which we live. We stand where we are as the fruit of fathering and covenant-keeping that preceded us.

27

FAMILY PRIORITIES
Part 2

Husbanding

If we look at family life from a covenantal viewpoint, we will be able to reconcile our priorities with God and the ministries for the kingdom of God. The family is not a separate sphere from ministry. Rather, the family unit is the immediate, closest subsection of the Church. The family is a ministry. The family is a subsection of the worldwide congregation of believers. It is a group of people joined together in covenant.

Our first priority in ministry should be that of creating unity with our spouse. The husband and wife have become one flesh. One has to give equivalent attention to the edification of his spouse as he does to building himself up in the Lord. We are part of the same dual-person before God. For one spouse to try to get far ahead spiritually of his partner would be like a runner building up the muscles in one leg more than the other one. The one leg might look strong, but it would not be any good when it came time for the race.

Joint Heirs

A husband should view his wife as a joint heir or co-partner with him of the blessings that God intended to bestow upon them. **I Peter 3:7** describes husband and wife as:

being heirs together of the grace of life.

A husband can also see his wife as his co-pastor in the family. For those men who actually have the job of being the pastor of a congregation, it is easy to see the wife as the co-pastor to the women in the congregation. In another sense, however, each family is a subsection of the congregation; the husband is the pastor of the family and the wife is the co-pastor. Being a father and a mother is a ministry. Parenting is the central ministry in the kingdom of God. The husband and wife are in spiritual ministry together as co-pastors.

A husband should treat his wife as his most important disciple. Jesus had different levels of disciples. Some were closer to Him than others. A husband may see his wife as his innermost circle of discipleship. Discipleship is a process of building trust toward intimacy. One must have the greatest discipleship trust with the person who is the most intimate companion. Since a man's wife is his closest companion, she is rightly the highest priority for building trust and discipleship.

As a husband sets the vision for the family, he must be sure to communicate to his wife and draw her into unity with that vision. A wife should know about all the direction of the family and of her husband's ministry. She should be a living example of the values that her husband holds.

If a wife does not want to submit to the authority of her husband, it is unlikely that any other people outside the family will want to submit to his authority either. If the wife is not prospering and fruitful under the pastoral care of her husband, it is unlikely that others will be attracted to becoming his disciples either. I am so very proud of my wife, as I see her as a shining example of all that we believe in. I am blessed to see her fruitfulness, as she is the deposit of all the loving attention that is in my heart. I am blessed not only by her submissive, cooperative and hard-working nature, but also by her joyful, bold and victorious walk with the Lord. Along with being delicate and sensitive, she is also a strong and courageous partner in spiritual warfare.

All ministry is the extension of covenant keeping. The marriage covenant is our highest priority of interpersonal relationships. A man's outward ministry, therefore, is an extension of his covenant faithfulness to his wife. Ministry that goes beyond the bounds of covenantal loyalty to one's spouse is not valid ministry.

The Difference between Men and Women

Men and women are extremely different, much more different than many people would suppose. **Genesis 2:18** states God's desire to make woman as a companion for man:

It is not good that man should be alone; I will make him a helper comparable to him.

The words "helper comparable to him" in the Hebrew are "ezer k'negdo." This expression literally means a helper that is opposite to him. In many ways, men and women are opposites.

God sees a husband and wife as two members of a composite team. God will often draw together a man and a woman whose personal qualities are directly in contrast to one another. In this way the marriage partner will fill in the complementary personality gaps of the other. The two of them together will reflect the whole character of God.

Because men and women are so different, it is not surprising that a successful marriage requires many hours of communication. **I Peter 3:7** directs:

Likewise you husbands, dwell with them [your wives] with understanding.

Men need to approach their wives with much understanding. Because the wife's perspective is so very different, wisdom and understanding is needed to bridge gaps in communication. A man may often find himself vexed at the thought patterns, emotional responses and motivations of his wife. Today's science tells us that in every cell of every organ in man's body there are an "X" and a "Y" chromosome. In every cell of every organ in a female's body are an "X" and an "X" chromosome. Even in physical composition, a man and a woman are almost a different species.

A man needs to pull away from his objective, goal orientation to understand his wife's personal, relational orientation. A man tends to communicate about a specific matter at hand, while a woman prefers to communicate for the relational interchange itself.

Early in our marriage, I made all the classic husband mistakes. My wife came to me one day and said, "Honey, I would like to have some time to talk with you." I put down whatever I was doing at the moment and said in a controlled voice, "Well, what is it that you want to talk about?" To my astonishment, she burst into tears and said, "You just don't understand." It took me a while to figure out where I had missed our communication.

If a husband only wants to talk with his wife when he has an objective matter to deal with, he has devalued her as a person. The greater the matter at hand, the less emphasis there is on relating to one another personally. When a husband communicates to his wife that the main reason he wants to talk to her is that he enjoys and appreciates her companionship, he has affirmed her as a person. He blesses her to fulfill her role as a wife. Husbands need to invest time in listening to their wives and communicating with them.

The Security Factor

A man primarily ministers to his wife and children in the areas of stability, security, protection and provision. **I Peter 3:7** continues its description of a proper husband's attitude as:

giving honor to the wife as a weaker vessel.

Sometimes men do not feel that their wives are really the weaker vessel. It takes faith for a man to stand in his position as the source of security to the family. He may not feel all that stable himself. God's personality is described as being that of a rock. The husband should express that rock-like dependability to his wife and children. God's personality is also described as a tower of refuge. A man should be like a fortress of protection for his family. They should see him as a sturdy wall that keeps away all harmful enemies.

If a woman acts pushy and manipulative, she is often struggling with fear and insecurity. If the husband reacts defensively, he will only cause her to be more insecure, which will create even more pushiness. If a husband remembers to minister to his wife's sense of security, she will be able to relax. She can then return to him the blessing of being a submissive and supportive wife.

As the woman's primary need is for security, the man's primary need is for ego reinforcement. He needs to be the hero in his wife's eyes. The more she is submissive and supportive, the more he will feel like a champion. The more confident a man feels, the more he will be able to relax. A man's ego is delicately balanced and his wife holds the sway.

Wholesome Perspective on Sexuality

The spiritual dynamics between a man and a woman manifest themselves in a similar way in their sexual relationship. A woman's sexual response depends upon her feeling relaxed. She can only feel relaxed if she is secure and safe. A man's sexual response is dependent on his experiencing a feeling of power and dominion. A man needs to feel confident before he can be relaxed. A man is confident to the extent that his wife is acting submissive and supportive toward him.

I Peter 3:5-6 describes attractive and holy women as:

being submissive to their own husbands, as Sarah obeyed Abraham, calling him lord.

The sexual response is partly an expression of the flow of authority between a man and a woman. **Genesis 3:16** states:

Your desire shall be for your husband, and he shall rule over you.

The dynamics of sexuality are more spiritual and psychological than they are physical. If a husband will minister security to his wife, she will be able to relax. Everything about their marriage, including their sexual relationship, will improve. If a woman will yield to her husband's authority, he will feel more confident and there will be greater harmony in the home.

The sexual relationship is the privilege of intimacy that is earned by commitment to the marriage covenant. My wife and I see our sexual relationship as a periodic renewing of our marriage vows. As the Lord's supper is a communion that renews our covenant with Jesus, so is physical intimacy a communion that renews the covenant between husband and wife. In a marriage between believers, God should be seen as the mediator of the marital covenant. The Spirit of God should be an intimately involved third party in all the interactions of a marriage. Our marriage is a triangle that includes God Himself. God is with us when we talk, when we pray, when we eat together and even when we share sexual intimacy.

The world views sexuality as an uncontrollable desire. Religious hypocrisy views sexuality as dirty and degrading. Scriptures take the covenantal viewpoint that sexuality is a wholesome expression of physical intimacy as long as it is safeguarded under the commitment of marriage. **Hebrews 13:4** states:

Marriage is honorable among all, and the bed undefiled.

The feeling that marital relations are dirty is unscriptural. We can live in the freedom and cleanliness of God's forgiveness. The spirit of condemnation can make a person feel dirty, even though that is not God's view. **Proverbs 5:18-19** tells a husband to:

Let your fountain be blessed, and rejoice with the wife of your youth. As a loving deer and a graceful doe, let her breasts satisfy you at all times; and always be enraptured with her love.

Scriptures see sexual pleasure as a positive physical blessing when it is confined to marriage partners. The fact that God created food to taste good and to be enjoyed does not condone a spirit of gluttony. The fact that God made sexuality for pleasure and enjoyment does not condone a spirit of lust or adultery.

Prayer Partners

A husband and wife's highest calling is to pray and minister together. **I Peter 3:7** calls for harmony between a husband and wife:

as being heirs together of the grace of life, that your prayers may not be hindered.

We are called to be co-heirs and co-ministers of the gospel. We are to receive together the glorious inheritance of the kingdom of God. A husband's and wife's prayers, working in cooperation, have an exponential power of agreement. If there is division between a husband and wife, their prayers will be hindered. One cannot be effective for the kingdom of God if he is at odds and in disharmony with his wife. The key to a good marriage is being able to pray and communicate together.

My wife and I plan most evenings to get out for a walk around the neighborhood. We hold hands, enjoy the quiet of the evening, and pray in tongues together. This is our special time. It is the crown and reward of our day. All of our success in ministry and family is born out of this time.

For if a man does not know how to rule his own house, how will he take care of the Church of God (I Timothy 3:5)?

All ministry is an outward expression of the inward harmony of the home. The fruit of a man's ministry is connected to the fruitfulness of his relationship with his wife.

Maturity through Relationships

A man's ministry goes through a juvenile stage in which he sees himself as a lone star, performing great feats for God. In a more mature stage, he puts away his previous thoughts and sees his ministry as an expression of his personal relationships. True faith exploits are motivated by the desire to help others. **I Corinthians 13:11** states:

When I was a child, I spoke as a child, I understood as a child, I thought as a child; but, when I became a man, I put away childish things.

Even a famous preaching ministry, if it is not based in covenantal relationships, begins to sound hollow and superficial. **I Corinthians 13:1** states:

Though I speak with the tongues of men and of angels but have not love, I have become as a sounding brass or clanging cymbal.

When we understand covenantal relationships, we do not measure a man of faith according to his accomplishments. Even miracles seem unimpressive if there are no meaningful relationships to make those miracles worthwhile. Our estimation of people is not in what they achieve but in how they relate.

Though I have all faith, so that I could remove mountains, but have not love, I am nothing (I Corinthians 13:2).

We should desire to see all the miracles and all the power of God. We should actively pursue the faith capacity to explode with fiery power from the Holy Spirit. Yet we need to do so with our priorities first on grooming covenantal relationships. **I Corinthians 12:31** states:

Earnestly desire the best gifts. And yet I show you a more excellent way.

I Corinthians 13:13 says:

The greatest of these is love.

The most excellent way of running a ministry is to make covenantal relationships the center of God's will in our lives. Love drives us to lay hold of the power of God to set people free. **II Corinthians 5:14** states:

For the love of Christ compels us.

28

FAMILY PRIORITIES
Part 3

Fathering

God is a father. There is no greater calling in life than to be a father. Since God is a father, fathering is a central expression of His nature. Fathering imprints God's personality and inculcates spiritual values in a child. Fathering entails living as a physical image of God before young people so they can experience His presence. Pastoral ministry and discipleship are an expression of the fatherhood of God. Paul describes his ministry in **I Thessalonians 2:11:**

As you know how we exhorted, and comforted, and charged every one of you, as a father does his own children.

A father encourages, challenges, rebukes, hugs, instructs, commands and comforts. As fathers, we are called to restrain our children from doing wrong, to show them solace and to comfort them when they are hurt. We set goals to challenge the youngsters to fulfill their potential.

Fathers mold their children through the constant pressure of their words and presence. The parent is a picture image before the eyes of the child of what the child is to become when he grows up. **Isaiah 45:9-10** states:

Shall the clay say to him that forms it, "What are you making?"...Woe to him who says to his father, "What are you begetting?" Or to the woman, "What have you brought forth?"

Parents are the image of God to their children. Parenting is like forming wet clay.

Bible Tapes

One technique of parenting that has been quite successful for us is the use of cassette tapes to record conversations and Bible stories with the children. I gather the children together on the couch, snuggle up and read them stories out of the Bible. The children ask me questions, and I add comments and fatherly advice during the telling of the story. What is recorded on the tape is not only the episode from Scriptures itself but also a warm dialogue between father and sons. The tapes are then listened to by the children as they lie on their beds, waiting to fall asleep. They enjoy hearing the same stories repeatedly. They are taught the words of Scripture, while being bathed in the voice of their own father. They relive the time spent with me with each replaying of the tape.

The use of homemade Bible tapes helps to write the Word of God upon their hearts and to transfer our values to the children. It also has the side benefit of helping the children to fall asleep. **Deuteronomy 6:6-7** states:

And these words which I command you today shall be in your heart; you shall teach them diligently to your children and shall talk of them when you sit in your house, when you walk by the way, when you lie down, and when you rise up.

These verses are part of the command that Jesus said was the most important in all of Scriptures (Mark 12:29). Teaching our children takes an enormous investment in time, energy and money. The Hebrew word for "you shall teach them diligently," is "shinantam". "Shinantam" means to repeat a second time or to engrave with a sharp point. The words are to be repeated often to engrave them indelibly in the hearts and memories of the children. The words will be memorized through daily use and repetition.

Investing in our Children

Parents invest their hopes for the future in the lives of their children. John 3:16 says that God gave His Son to all of us in the world so that we could be saved by Him. All the destiny of the kingdom of God was deposited in Jesus. God's only means of rescuing the planet Earth was to believe that His Son would be successful in His task. Jesus, in turn, chose to invest His entire mission into the hands of a small number of men who were His spiritual children.

Adam was also called God's son (Luke 3:38). God invested in him all dominion and authority over the universe that God had created. The human race, as the offspring of God, has fallen short of God's plan for us. God, as a parent, is working with his wayward children to redeem our lives. Love and investment in children is a risky affair, but there is no other recourse.

It takes faith to believe that our children will grow up to be godly and successful. **Proverbs 22:6** states:

Train up a child in the way he should go, and when he is old he will not depart from it.

Abraham was chosen to be the father of faith because God knew that he would train his children to follow the ways of the Lord (Genesis 18:19). The investment of time, money and effort that a parent gives to his children seems almost overwhelming. To love is to give. Parenting is an essential part of demonstrating God's love upon the earth.

Many congregations today are faced with the challenge of establishing a biblically-based day school for their children. While there are many practical and administrative obstacles to starting a school, it is a covenantal imperative to guarantee a godly environment for the growth of our children. One cannot afford to turn his children over to an educational system that purposely denies godly values. A young person cannot be expected to respond to a biblical message on the weekend if he has been receiving a worldly message all during the week.

Covenant requires that our children be placed in some kind of schooling that has a biblical orientation. If a public school can be influenced to have godly values, we can enroll our children. If the public education system refuses to allow biblical standards, we must seek to enroll our children elsewhere, and even to start our own schools where necessary.

Consistency

A father must show consistency in the time he spends with his children. They need to feel his presence at regular intervals. My father was very consistent in his time coming home from work and in his presence at home on the weekends. He was a successful lawyer, and long hours of overtime could have meant an additional rise into even higher earning spectrums. My father decided to resist that temptation in order to have regular quantities of time with the family. This consistency produced in me a subconscious sense of his reliability and dependability. A father should use consistency as a tool to create security in the lives of his children.

My father was able to earn a stable income, and we never lacked anything as we grew up. Reliability of financial provision is another way in which a father generates security for his family. A wife and children do not need to see vast sums of money coming in. They do need to experience steadiness and regularity of income. Some men, particularly in sales and investment, tend to latch onto big "make it rich quick" schemes. Sometimes they make lots of money, and other times they are broke. This does not create security in the wife and children. These men think that if they could just make it big, they would be able to give security to their family. This illusion keeps them from providing the simple reliability that the family needs.

Get-rich-quick schemes are a deception from the devil. They are tantamount to a form of gambling.

An inheritance gained hastily at the beginning will not be blessed at the end (Proverbs 20:20).

He who tills his land will have plenty of bread, but he that follows frivolity will have poverty enough. A faithful man will abound with blessings, but he who hastens to be rich will not go unpunished (Proverbs 28:19-20).

The frivolity of get-rich-quick schemes generates fear and insecurity within the family. A man who is regular and faithful in his job will allow his family to abound with blessings. The man who flatters himself that he is just about to make the big deal may be avoiding the responsibility to be consistent over the long run. Families need dependability, not bonanzas.

Affection and Discipline

A father should offer his children a balance of physical affection and firm discipline. For young children, that balance is about nine parts affection to one part discipline. My children have a saying that daddy likes three things: hugs, kisses and spankings. When I come home from work, I pick them up, hug them, kiss them and pat them on the rear with playful spankings. When I come in the door, my five year old son runs up to me and says, "Daddy, play that game where you won't let me go." As I hug him, he squeals with delight, "Let me go! Let me go," while I growl, "No, never!" When I let him down, he says, "Do it again."

Disciplining a child must be done as a step of covenantal love toward him. The Scriptures are clear that spanking is an appropriate tool with which to discipline. Spanking is a time-tested method to turn children away from wrongdoing, particularly in the early years. **Proverbs 13:24, 19:18,** and **23:13** read as follows:

> **He who spares his rod hates his son, but he who loves him disciplines him early.**

> **Chasten your son while there is hope, and do not set your heart on his crying.**

> **Do not withhold correction from a child, for if you beat him with a rod, he will not die.**

Discipline is not done for the sake of anger or punishment. Discipline is a covenant step of correction to teach the child the difference between right and wrong. If spanking is done in frustration or loss of temper, its redemptive purpose will have been lost.

Spanking is an unselfish act of love on the part of the parent to expend time and energy to educate the child. Spanking is not lashing out in vengeance on the part of an emotionally upset adult. Discipline is the calm and determined instruction of the child, accompanied by measured physical spanking. The mood of the parent must communicate to the spirit of the child that he cares enough about the child to take this firm stance. Spanking is done to help the child and to prevent him from doing further wrong.

Spanking is a positive opportunity to bring loving, forceful authority into the child's life. We must control any emotions of anger or frustration before initiating a spanking. If we are upset, we will only cause the child to react vindictively. **Ephesians 6:4** states:

> **Fathers, do not provoke your children to wrath, but bring them up in the nurture and admonition of the Lord.**

We should never act in wrath. We are not seeking to hurt or destroy the children; we are seeking to change them toward what is correct. Provoking anger in the process of discipline will sow seeds of wrath and revenge in the child. Discipline that involves spanking, verbal instruction and affectionate affirmation will cause the child to be trained in the positive direction of the Lord.

Spanking requires self-control and courage on the part of the parent. He must control his own emotions, and he must not be afraid of a negative reaction on the part of the child. It is easier to avoid proper discipline or to discipline abruptly without the accompanying self-control and instruction. True covenantal discipline takes time and effort.

The parent should first make sure that he is calm and that he has his emotions under control. He must then do some brief investigation to make sure that he has all the facts in the situation. There is nothing more embarrassing than to discipline a child for the wrong reason. One time in a restaurant I lost my temper with my son. He had slipped under the table, and I thought he had pulled a piece of bubble gum from under the table and had begun to chew it. When I started to raise my voice and make a scene, he managed to communicate to me in a whimpering voice that I had not understood what had happened. He took a little box of raisins out of his pocket and told me that his mother had given them to him to keep for a snack. It is always worthwhile to take a little extra time to gather all the facts about a situation before starting to discipline.

Whenever I make a mistake with my children or lose my temper, I make it a point to go to them and apologize in an adult manner. While their minds may not completely understand what has happened, their spirits perceive that a reconciliation has been made. Children will not forget if they have been wronged. A covenant apology on the part of the parent will remove any grounds for resentment and set a good example for the child.

The spanking itself should be surrounded on both sides by words of instruction and reconciliation. The physical part of the spanking itself is only a brief moment in a rather extended time of covenantal dialogue. The child is ministered to with instructions and corrections of which only a part is the actual spanking. Correction is loving and covenantal. The time immediately following the spanking is a receptive one for tenderness and reassurance. The whole process from fact finding to instruction to spanking to the time of reassurance might take approximately twenty minutes. The parent and child experience a closeness and intimacy with one another as they leave a time of correction. Peace is restored to the home in the ensuing period.

Teenage Transitions

A different mode of correction is appropriate as the child reaches the teenage years. The adolescent is neither a child nor an adult. The word adolescent means "one who is becoming an adult." This stage of becoming an adult is full of seemingly awkward transitions. Certain God-given dynamics turn on inside a young person when he reaches the age of twelve. Parents need to adapt themselves to handle these changes. Many parents misunderstand the new set of reactions they see going on inside their children during this age period. Parents need to adjust their techniques in approaching teenage discipline.

I am again indebted to my friend Thurlow Switzer for guiding my understanding of teenage transitions. Luke 2:40-52 contains a classic passage on parent-teenage interactions: the interaction between Jesus and His mother. In verse 40 Jesus is referred to as a child. During this first stage of His life, He is growing up in grace and stature. Verse 42 notes that Jesus has reached the transition age of twelve years old. **Luke 2:40, 42** states:

And the child grew and became strong in spirit... And when He was twelve

years old, they [His parents] went up to Jerusalem according to the custom of the feast.

In verse 43, Jesus is referred to as a boy instead of a child. The boy stage is the adolescent transition between the child and the man. **Luke 2:43** states:

As they returned, the boy Jesus lingered behind in Jerusalem. And Joseph and His mother did not know it.

Jesus moves now naturally in new-found independence. He goes off in His own direction without telling His parents. In His sense of adolescent identity, He does not feel that He needs permission from His parents to act independently. Teenagers often see themselves as quite mature and expect to be treated as adults.

After three days they found Him in the temple, sitting in the midst of the teachers, both listening to them and asking questions (Luke 2:46).

A new dimension of inquisitiveness opens up during the teenage years. A mechanism goes on inside the adolescent in which he needs to know the reasons why a certain thing takes place. This is a God-given function of mental analytical skill. The teenager will ask why he is told to do certain tasks. A teenager should not use his inquisitiveness as a justification for rebellion or disobedience. On the other hand, the parent cannot simply deny the teen's desire to know and understand. A teenager cannot forever be told to obey just for the sake of obedience without explanation.

In our covenant high school, the teenagers are given opportunities to discuss the reasons behind our rules. They must never disobey a teacher and they cannot act disrespectfully. Questioning the teacher must be done privately and politely. If the teenager violates this attitude of respect, he loses the privilege to have his point heard. On the other hand, we look for opportunities to draw the teenager into the heart perspective of the reasons behind the rules. In addition to requiring obedience, we also invite them to agree with the spirit of the law. If a parent refuses to deal with the adolescent's questions, he will force that inquisitiveness to turn into rebellion.

Luke 2:47-48 states:

And all who heard Him were astonished at His understanding and answers. When they saw Him, they were amazed; and His mother said to Him, "Son, why have You done this to us? Look, Your father and I have sought You anxiously."

Parents are often shocked by the abrupt changes of the teenage years. Perhaps we can take some solace that even Mary and Joseph felt this way. Here it says they were astonished, amazed and anxious. Being anxiety ridden is not the way to win the loyalty or obedience of a teenager. Mary interpreted Jesus' natural independence as a personal attack upon herself; she felt hurt. The teenage years include major advancement in mental capacity; we must not act defensively at a teen's intellectual challenges. God is using this time to sharpen their mental skills to face challenges for the kingdom of God in their own generation. The teenager may come forth with a brilliant analysis one moment and then revert suddenly to some childish need or action the next.

Children are told exactly what to do. Teenagers are given clear rules and guidelines, but these guidelines include gradually increasing amounts of free choice as they grow older. The purpose of training teenagers is to prepare them to make the right set of choices when they are adults. We must draw them into the perspective of developing their own convictions about what is right. We must help their transition towards godly adulthood. An adolescent must continue to obey the authority of his parents. He should, however, be given increasing degrees of choice within the framework of his parents' rules.

In **Luke 2:49** Jesus answers His parents, asking:

Why is it that you sought Me? Did you not know that I must be about My Father's business?

It is during the teenage years that a young person begins to develop awareness of his own sovereign calling in God. A teenager's need for identity and independence can find its fulfillment in his unique destiny in God. In a brash way, he may be getting his first glimpses at God's special purpose for his own life.

While he is developing his own understanding about God's destiny in his life, and while he is growing in his freedom to make adult choices, the teenager must continue to submit to the authority of his parents. **Luke 2:51** states:

Then He [Jesus] went down with them [His parents] and came to Nazareth and was subject to them.

Even Jesus recognized the authority of His parents over His life. The balance between independence and submission is a godly dynamic within the teenager. The balance between demanding obedience and releasing freedom is a godly dynamic for the parent of a teenager.

Faith Words

A father establishes intimacy with his children by his words. We should talk to our children as God talked to Jesus. **Matthew 3:17** states:

This is My beloved Son in whom I am well pleased.

I often use this same expression on my sons. I hold them in my arms and say, "You are my beloved son in whom I am well pleased." Parenting requires faith confession. We speak over our children and name them to be the strong, spiritual and loving people that God desires. A father's purpose is not to entertain, but to establish foundations of steadiness and reliability in the child.

Not Hyper-Entertainment

Once I took my children to a restaurant that specializes in entertainment, games and parties for children. Their behavior became particularly uncooperative in such a wild atmosphere. Entertainment that bombards all of the senses at one time increases the desire for more. An overload of entertainment breeds dissatisfaction and restlessness. Fathers should develop stability and peace within a child. An absentee husband who comes back occasionally to lavish extraordinary gifts upon his children is only making matters worse. The children may feel drawn to a hyperactivity of entertainment, but they have no base of stability and trust on which to build their lives. If the child is surrounded by a biblical worldview in the home, the church and school, he will have a consistent set of values to carry into his adult life.

The elements of godly fathering are the following: verbal intimacy, physical affection, firm discipline, consistency of time and presence, moral integrity and joyous faith. We as adults must be victorious examples of the life of Jesus. We must stand in the gap and shepherd our young people with steadiness of hand and stability of spirit. Fathering requires strength, courage and patience. Fathering is an act of covenantal faithfulness.

29

CONGREGATIONAL GOVERNMENT: ELDERSHIP

As a father is to his family, so are the elders to a congregation. The primary government of a congregation is invested in the eldership. The elders are the decision-making body for a local community of faith. Among the group of elders is a lead elder or head elder, who is called the pastor.

Headship with Plurality

There are varieties of interpretation on the relationship between a pastor, the elders, gift ministries and other leadership in the Body of believers. The foundational principle of pastoral authority in relationship with others is HEADSHIP WITH PLURALITY. Headship with plurality means that final authority is held by a group of people working together. This group has a clear leader, and the members of the leadership team see themselves submitted to that leader's vision and direction. One should not have plurality without headship, nor should there be headship without plurality. In a large congregation, decisions are not made by the whole group, with every individual having a vote. The authority to make decisions is invested in a group of trusted leaders.

There is a relationship of mutual submission between the pastor and the group of elders of which he is a part. The elders have enough humility to recognize that God has graced one of them with a clear anointing for leadership. There is a unity of authority because the primary direction of the congregation flows from the pastor. The overall vision, of course, comes from God, as discerned through prayer. There is a singularity of motion as the elders allow the pastor to be the frontrunner in enunciating and formulating that vision for the congregation. The elders rally around the pastor to support his authority. They covenant together for unity and mutual accountability.

While the pastor is the clearly designated leader of the elders, he does not see himself as above the possibility of making a mistake. He is not beyond the reach of others around him to speak correction and advice into his life. Proverbs tells us that in the multitude of counselors there is safety. Having primary leadership invested in one man allows for clarity, decisiveness and unity in the direction of the congregation. Having that leader accountable to the immediate group of co-leaders allows for safety that the leader will not go astray.

Relational Authority

All authority in Scripture is based on relationships. In relational authority, people in the community trust the group of leaders to make decisions. In relational authority, the group of leaders trusts the head leader to hear from God and set direction they will support. In relational authority, the head leader trusts those around him to hold him accountable and speak words of counsel and correction into his life. Everyone is submitted and supportive to the leader of the group he is in. Leaders are sensitive to listen to and respond to the needs and input of the people they are leading.

If there is plurality without headship, the group will degenerate into a state where everyone is doing what is right in his own eyes. God's will is not best determined by collecting opinions of the majority. Biblical authority is prayerful and relational, but it is not democratic. One of the themes of the book of Judges is that when there is no clearly designated, anointed leadership, the people fall into division and confusion. The result is that the people are not able to follow the will of God.

The last verse of **Judges** states **(21:25):**

In those days there was no king in Israel; and everyone did what was right in his own eyes.

The king in this passage refers to a prophetic leader such as Moses or Joshua. God has only one will for a group of people as a whole. If everyone insists upon holding his own separate opinion and not submitting to a group direction, there will be an inability to hear the single voice of God. When people sincerely want to submit to the will of God, they will give up stubborn independence and allow for a divinely appointed leader to arise in their midst.

When people appeal to democratic mandate to set up biblical authority, that authority will have in its foundation the seed of its own destruction. Since it is based on responding to the voice of the people instead of the voice of God, it is not ultimately responsive to divine calling and authority. Basing leadership on the sway of popular opinion is humanistic.

In spiritual authority, the people pray together and recognize that God has ordained a certain person to be a leader in their midst. There is a type of democratic confirmation, because spiritually sensitive people will swing in support of the divinely appointed direction. In this way, there is also the widespread support by the people as a whole. The difference is that in one model the people are generating the authority out of their own collective personal desires. In the other model, the people are responding to the voice of God and recognizing that the authority of the leader originates with God's will.

Man-Based Authority

I Samuel 8:5-7 illustrates the will of the people in demanding that Samuel set up a king for them:

> **"Now make for us a king to judge us like all the nations." But the thing displeased Samuel when they said, "Give us a king to judge us." So Samuel prayed to the Lord and the Lord said to Samuel, "Heed the voice of the people in all that they say to you; for they have not rejected you, but they have rejected Me, that I should not reign over them."**

By demanding that a leader be established in response to the voice of the people, they chose a model of authority copied from the world's system. In rejecting the concept of a divinely anointed leader, the people rejected God's spiritual authority. The people demanded the will of their own plurality instead of yielding to the sensitivity of spiritual headship. This plurality without headship led to eventual tyranny and widespread destruction.

The imbalance of plurality without headship often leads to the contrasting imbalance of headship without plurality. Saul, who became king out of the demands of people when they rejected Samuel, never felt completely confident that his anointing and authority came directly from God. He was always insecure as to whether he maintained popular support. His leadership, therefore, was always reactionary and self-justifying. He was never free to be creative, resourceful and inspired. He was actually enslaved by the opinions of the people. He feared that the people might reject him. He became defensive and paranoid that his leadership might be usurped at any moment. This paranoia led him to be tyrannical and coercive in maintaining his authority.

Authority that originates from people's opinion will eventually have to use force to maintain its position. Authority that receives its appointment from God is relaxed and confident enough to be sensitive to the people. Humanistically-based leadership swings from the whims and doublemindedness of public opinion on one side, to the tyrannical overlordship of military force on the other.

Divine authority is not fickle because it comes from God. Divine authority is invested in a leader who is responsive to meet the needs of the people whom he is responsible to serve. The people confirm the leader's authority as they rally in unity behind God's will. In **I Samuel 15:24**, Saul says to Samuel:

> **I have sinned for I have transgressed the commandment of the Lord and your words, because I feared the people and obeyed their voice.**

In **I Samuel 15:30**, Saul continues pleading with Samuel:

> **Honor me now, please, before the elders of my people and before Israel,**

Saul could not help being enslaved by a man-pleasing spirit, because his entire kingship was based on pleasing the will of men.

Harshness Is Tyranny

Saul violates the divine sphere of authority in Samuel by performing a priestly sacrifice. God then calls Samuel to anoint David to become the new king. Samuel anoints the new king because Samuel represents divine authority. Saul then swings compulsively to a wildly tyrannical spirit and tries to murder David. Saul refuses to listen to his closest companions, including his son Jonathan. He demands his headship by force and refuses to respond to the plurality of leaders holding him accountable.

Those who desire strong headship without the mutual accountability of other co-leaders often do so out of a spirit of insecurity. Headship without plurality is an overreaction birthed out of a fear of rejection. Saul's fear of rejection made him more and more tyrannical. He thought he could find security by being unaccountable. He insisted upon maintaining his own authority by coercion, even to the point where it almost destroyed the entire nation. Saul became deaf to those around him. His view of authority became self-centered and self-justifying.

Headship without plurality means that the leader can justify any wrong means of behavior by saying that it supports the continuance of his stay in power. Headship without plurality can lead to the dangerous view that the only good is to maintain the person's position in authority. Headship without plurality allows the option that the ends justify the means. Headship without plurality is ultimately a breakdown in covenantal relationships.

The same dynamic took place in the reign of King Rehoboam who refused to be accountable to the elders around him. Had he been responsive to his elders and the sincere needs of the people, his divine calling would have been supported and confirmed. Rehoboam saw himself as above the counsel of his elders. He also became harsh, tyrannical and defensive. His insistence upon headship without plural accountability caused the division and destruction of the nation.

Divine Authority

Many passages of Scripture indicate divine authority in a single leader. Many other passages of Scripture indicate the need for accountability from a group of co-leaders or elders. The sweep of Scriptures as a whole takes the balanced view of headship with plurality. This model is reflected in the spiritual government of our congregations.

Divine authority starts with headship and extends into plurality. God makes a covenant with a man to head a certain project; that man invites other co-leaders into covenant with him to see that project carried out. Headship with plurality is essentially a covenantal model because it involves committed relationships in both directions. God's authority always flows through covenantal relationships.

In Exodus 4:29, Moses and Aaron invite the elders of Israel to stand with them for the liberation of the people from slavery in Egypt. In Numbers 26:18 and Deuteronomy 31:3, Joshua receives divine ordination from the hands of Moses. Joshua then joins in covenant with the elders of the people to lead the conquest of the land of Canaan. In Joshua 8:10, for example, the elders of Israel join with

Joshua to muster the army for the attack on the city of Ai. In Judges 11, Jephthah makes a covenant with the elders of Gilead to lead the people in battle against the Ammonites. In **II Samuel 5:3**, David makes a covenant with the leaders of Israel to be instated as the new king:

> **So all the leaders of Israel came to the king at Hebron, and King David made a covenant with them at Hebron before the Lord. And they anointed David king over Israel.**

While there are variations on the model, the underlying principle is the same: headship with plurality. A divinely appointed leader makes covenant with a group of elders. Divine anointing is recognized, and mutual accountability is accepted. Each person is equal in standing before God. Everyone is submitted in humility one to another. Divine authority is expressed through clear leadership. Headship without plurality and plurality without headship are both wrong.

Collegiality and Spontaneity

No form of congregational government should become a dominating structure in and of itself. All authority flows from being responsive and sensitive to the leading of the Holy Spirit. Spiritual government has an inherent charismatic and spontaneous nature to it.

We do not start with structure. We start and move with the direction of the Holy Spirit. Structure simply emerges as an effective expression of the Spirit's direction. Any structure that is not facilitating dynamic life in God should be trimmed away. **John 15:2** states that:

> **Every branch that does not bear fruit He takes away**.

Leadership, in turn, emerges out of collegial relationships. Brothers submit to the leadership of certain ones in their midst as spiritual strengths and leadership qualities emerge. Legal authority remains with the group of elders, while the group submits to direction of the leader that God anoints.

Elders

The same principles of authority flow through every group that is spiritually covenanted together. Whether it be a family, a congregation or an apostolic movement, the dynamics of headship with plurality remain the same. **I Peter 5:1-4** states:

> **The elders who are among you I exhort, I who am a fellow elder and a witness of the sufferings of Christ, and also a partaker of the glory that will be revealed: Shepherd the flock of God which is among you, serving as overseers, not by constraint but willingly, not for dishonest gain but eagerly; nor as being lords over those entrusted to you, but being examples to the flock; and when the Chief Shepherd appears, you will receive the crown of glory that does not fade away.**

Peter, who is clearly more than an elder, refers to himself as a fellow elder. In the U. S. Congress, for example, a certain member might be the Speaker of the House or the head of a committee, but he is still a congressman. Peter, who is a head-elder and even an apostle, is still an elder. It is to this group of men, called the elders, that Peter addresses the command to shepherd the flock. It is the eldership that has been invested and entrusted with the authority to govern a congregation of believers and to shepherd them. The elders, therefore, are the final decision-making body for a local community of faith.

Elders and other spiritual leaders do not see themselves as humanly better than anyone else. They are ambassadors and stewards of the true leader, who is Jesus. An elder is actually a sub-elder under the Great Elder, Jesus. Pastors are under-shepherds under the Great Shepherd, Jesus. Congregational authority is a humble and sensitive transfer of the spiritual authority of God Himself. We do not lord it over one another in pride, but seek to express the ministry of the pastoral heart of God.

Shepherding: Personal Care

The job of the biblical elder is to shepherd the flock. Shepherding the flock means to give personal care to the believers in a congregation and to get involved in their lives. We must do away with the view that an elder is like a board member in a worldly organization. Being an elder is a functional role more than an organizational position. Elders should be the ones who are actually doing the shepherding of the flock. There is a temptation for an elder to see himself as an executive board member. A board-of-directors mentality is dangerous for the congregation and unhealthy for the members.

Shepherding is a people-involvement task. The prophet Ezekiel rebuked the false shepherds who tried to keep themselves aloof from the work of nurturing, correcting and healing the flock. **Ezekiel 34:3-4** contains this indictment against hypocritical elders:

You eat the fat and clothe yourself with the wool; you slaughter the fatlings, but you do not feed the flock. The weak you have not strengthened, nor have you healed those that were sick, nor bound up the broken, nor brought back what was driven away, nor sought what was lost; but with force and cruelty you have ruled them.

A false shepherd does not think he is being cruel. The subtlety of pride in his position may cause him to be stand-offish from the messy relationships and needs of the people. Non-involvement is cruelty by its abdication. One cannot be a shepherd without touching the sheep; one cannot be a shepherd without getting his hands dirty with involvement in the personal care of the flock.

A Good Shepherd

John 10 refers to Jesus as the ideal pastor. It also presents guidelines for the proper qualities of pastors and elders within the body of believers. **John 10:11-14** states:

> **I am the Good Shepherd. The Good Shepherd gives His life for the sheep. But he who is a hireling and not the shepherd, one who does not own the sheep, sees the wolf coming and leaves the sheep and flees; and the wolf catches the sheep and scatters them. The hireling flees because he is a hireling and does not care about the sheep. I am the Good Shepherd; and I know My sheep, and am known by My own.**

A hireling attitude holds people at distance and wants to be respected because of outward credentials. An ownership attitude makes a covenantal commitment to people and desires the opportunity to help them.

In our high school, we instruct our teachers to treat each student as if he were his own child. They are to exercise the patience and commitment that knows no cost or compromise when dealing with a student. They are not to treat teaching as a job but as a covenantal ministry. To treat and care for people as if it were a job is to have the attitude of a hireling. A hireling does not go beyond what is required of him. When one feels that he is part of spiritually owning a ministry, he puts his whole heart into the effort. Problems and difficulties do not cause him to run away. His own life is covenanted with those of the flock. He cannot abandon those he is caring for, because his life is wrapped up with their success.

An elder must take the time to know the members of his flock personally. A good elder can say that he really knows the people he is working with.

Be diligent to know the state of your flocks (Proverbs 27:23).

A good shepherd must also allow his congregants to get to know him. His life is an open book before them. It takes courage to open oneself up to intimacy to a group of people. A good elder can say that he is known personally by the people he is serving.

A good pastor gives his life for the sheep. The Hebrew expression for this phrase means to give one's soul or life's energy to help others. It means more than being willing to be martyred for the sake of the ministry. A good elder or pastor gives his soul in shepherding. He gives his heart, his time, his energy, his effort, his prayer and his emotions for the benefit of others.

When the elders stop seeing themselves as a board, aloof from the people, and begin to care for the personal needs of the flock, there will be a breakthrough in congregational growth. In the last two decades, the revelation of home groups has swept the worldwide Body of believers. These cell groups allow for the shepherding responsibilities to be subdivided, and for as many people as possible to become involved in the pastoring process. One of the beauties of home groups is that they demand for all the upcoming elders to have direct involvement with people. The subdivision of pastoral responsibility allows for multiplication and reproduction to take place within the congregation. Home groups are an essential part of covenantal community. The elders together are the home group of the pastor.

Home Groups

The term "home group leader" probably conveys to the modern mind a meaning closer to the biblical concept of shepherding than the now religiously-coated terms "deacon" and "elder." Home groups allow everyone to be immediately involved in the growth of the congregation. All believers can be trained to participate in teaching Bible studies, reaching out to new people, serving others and practicing the gifts of the Holy Spirit. The genius of home groups has revolutionized the structure of the modern Church. Nothing has done more to bring us back to the organic form of the first-century community of faith.

Philemon 2 states:

To my beloved Apphia, Archippus our fellow soldier, and to the church in your house.

Romans 16:3 and **5** state:

Greet Priscilla and Aquila, my fellow workers in Christ Jesus.... Likewise greet the church that is in their house.

Aquila and Priscilla here are referred to as fellow workers. The emphasis is on how they serve, not what position they hold. **Colossians 4:15** states:

Greet the brethren who are at Laodicea, and Nymphas and the church that is in his house.

Since covenant is based on personal relationships, the small group setting of the home does much to foster covenant within a congregation. Without small group meetings, it is difficult to establish deeper relationships.

Congregants should be encouraged to join a home group and stay with it. Moving from home group to home group does not allow for longer term commitment and trust to develop. Congregants should be encouraged to relate to one elder and stay with him. Relationships take time. Switching from one elder's care to another disrupts the consistency of counsel which comes from knowing one another over time.

No matter how much business knowledge or organizational skill a man might have, he should not become an elder unless he can prove himself in the circle of small group relationships. Home groups are the proving ground for potential elders. If people cannot be drawn and attracted to a man within a small group setting, he will not be good at making decisions which affect the body as a whole. If a man wants to be an elder and avoids the process of grooming through homegroup leadership, it is probable that he has a wrong view of what eldering is. Home groups keep all positions of authority within the congregation connected to personal relationships and actual care for the people. A potential elder who makes excuses for not being involved in a home group may have need of personal healing.

Character Qualities

I Timothy 3:1-7 contains the prerequisites or qualities for an upcoming elder:

If a man desires the position of an overseer, he desires a good work. An overseer then must be blameless, the husband of one wife, temperate, sober-minded, of good behavior, hospitable, able to teach; not given to wine, not violent, not greedy for money, but gentle, not quarrelsome, not covetous; one who rules his own house well, having his children in submission with all reverence (for if a man does not know how to rule his own house, how will he take care of the Church of God?); not a novice, lest being puffed up with pride he fall into the same condemnation as the devil. Moreover he must have a good testimony among those who are outside, lest he fall into reproach and the snare of the devil.

It is probable that no one in the congregation lives up to all these qualifications perfectly. These prerequisites are not a legalistic test, but guidelines for understanding the type of heart attitude and proven character that should be developed in a man before he receives responsibility over others.

An elder must show drive and initiative to put energy into the work of the kingdom of God. He is supposed to be self-motivated enough to desire to be an elder. A passive, unmotivated person will not be able to overcome the fatigue and discouragement that hinder the ministry. An elder must be the type of person who will not lose his temper with others. When a person is in a position of spiritual authority, it is easier to hurt someone else's feelings than would normally be the case. He must be controlled enough to be polite at all times.

An elder's family life must be in good order. If his relationships with his wife and children are rewarding and satisfying, he will not be tempted to be imbalanced in his work for the ministry. If his family relationships are harmonious, he will reflect a good model to those in the congregation. A man reproduces who he is. If a man's family is in good order, the families of those he is pastoring will begin to reflect such good fruit.

Being able to offer hospitality in the home is important, because the home is the setting for pastoral relationships. Love is communicated to others through hospitality. Much of pastoral ministry takes place through inviting others into one's home. The ingredient of hospitality expresses the warmth of pastoral care.

If a man receives enough respect and submission within his own home, he will not feel the psychological need to make others in the congregation demonstrate their respect and submission to him. If a man's ego is satisfied within his family life, he can approach relationships in the ministry with a freedom and generosity that is not subtly self-serving. An elder must not form an ego attachment to the ministry.

One of the qualifications that separates an elder from a deacon is the ability to teach and verbalize concepts from Scriptures. A man does not have to be eloquent or quick-tongued to be an elder, but he must be able to understand the principles of Scripture and to convey them in words systematically to instruct others. An elder must be well-versed in the Scriptures. He must have an established habit of daily meditation in the Word of God. A man whose mind has not been renewed by regular Bible study will bring forth wrong attitudes in making decisions. An elder must be submitted to Scriptures as the final authority in his life. A man must have consistency in Bible study before he is made an elder. If he has already been teaching Bible studies in the home group setting, the evidence of his commitment to Scriptures should be clear. We are not seeking men of worldly wisdom, but men whose first priority is the Word of God. Elders are to be men of spiritual discernment, not men who impress others by the abilities of the soul.

Maturity

A man must show a certain degree of success in his job and in dealing with people in the secular community. Many aspects of character that are needed for an elder are not normally challenged within the scope of the spiritual life of the congregation. Certain spiritual characteristics only come to light when one is dealing with the rude and objective reality of the business world. An elder must have practical wisdom as well as spiritual insight. If a man cannot demonstrate integrity in his dealings with unbelievers in secular society, how much less will he be able to work with congregational government. Eldership requires too many practical decisions to have people who have their heads in the clouds in an unrealistic way. A young man being groomed for eldership may need to work at a secular job for a period of time before becoming an elder. The experience of practical wisdom will prevent the error of phony mysticism in the future.

Even if a new believer shows great signs of giftedness and anointing, he should not be made an elder until a certain amount of time has passed. No matter how much energy a man might have, some fruits of maturity in the Spirit only come with time. **I Timothy 5:22** states:

Do not lay hands on anyone hastily, or share in other people's sins.

It is a mistake to ordain someone too soon. The subtleties of spiritual pride, particularly in someone who is naturally gifted, take time to die away. If someone becomes an elder too soon, he may think he is more spiritually advanced than he really is. A premature ordination can ruin what would otherwise have been a fruitful ministry. A little more time for the person to grow is like an ounce of prevention that will avoid future problems.

Faith Prerequisite

James 5:14-15 states:

Is anyone sick among you? Let him call for the elders of the church, and let them pray over him, anointing him with oil in the name of the Lord. And the prayer of faith will save the sick and the Lord will raise him up.

Another prerequisite of becoming an elder is being able to act in the power of the Holy Spirit. An elder must know how to pray prayers of faith that will be effective. He must believe that if he lays hands on the sick in the name of Jesus, they will recover. An elder should have operative faith in regards to divine healing, casting out demonic spirits, faith confession and charismatic gifts. Acting in these areas is part of the function of an elder. He must be an example of walking in the power of the Holy Spirit. An elder must not give these operations of faith mere theological mental assent, but must be willing to perform them.

30

RESPONDING TO LEADERSHIP

Leadership may be defined as taking responsibility for areas of service. Leadership is a good and necessary function, one that requires courage and integrity to face the challenge of helping others.

In recent years in our country, leadership has been cast in a negative light. The media would portray those in authority with disrespect. Labor forces portray themselves as righteous in opposition to management. Student unrest tried to justify philosophically any rebellion against governmental authorities. In the 1960's, a popular mistrust for military leadership spread across the country in the aftermath of the Vietnam War. A further breakdown of trust in the integrity of governmental leaders swept over the people in the wake of the Watergate hearings.

Servant Leadership

To see management as always evil and labor as always righteous is not correct. The spiritual motivation for being in leadership should be to help and serve others. Leadership has sometimes been termed servant-leadership to emphasize this point. Lordship is the opposite of leadership.

The kings of the Gentiles exercise lordship over them, and those who exercise authority over them are called "benefactors." But not so among you; on the contrary, he who is greatest among you, let him be as the younger, and he who governs as he who serves (Luke 22:25-26).

Matthew 20:25 and Mark 10:42 contain the same teaching by Jesus. Selfish lordship over other people is the carnal counterfeit to unselfish leadership.

The one who most desires to lead is the one most willing to serve. Politicians used to be called civil servants. A civil servant was one who had given up the greater riches of the business world to dedicate himself to serve unselfishly the citizens in his community. He had given himself to civic service.

The leader is the one who is willing to serve the most. The type of person who labors and serves the kingdom is the one to whom we should submit. All of us should train ourselves to submit joyfully to those leaders who have worked hard among us. **I Corinthians 16:16** challenges us:

That you also submit to such, and to everyone who works and labors with us.

Courage to Stand

Leadership is difficult enough without the people being unresponsive. We should endeavor to be people who are a joy to lead.

Obey those who rule over you, and be submissive, for they watch out for your souls, as those who must give account. Let them do so with joy and not with grief, for that would be unprofitable for you (Hebrews 13:17).

People underestimate the grief that goes along with being a leader. Since people often resent being told what to do, leadership bears feelings of hurt and rejection. People focus their complaints and irritations on the person in charge. At times a leader receives ingratitude in return for effort expended to help someone else. He may feel like the man in the folk tale who found an injured snake upon the road and brought it into his house to nurture it back to health. As soon as the snake felt better, it turned and bit the man who helped him. People sometimes focus their negativity and resentment on the one trying to help them.

As principal of a Christian high school, I often have to exercise authority by not letting the students have what they desire. Fulfilling those desires may be harmful to them. A leader may have to resist a wave of antagonism when he introduces a new directive. Leadership can be an uncomfortable position. Not only is one going out of his way to help someone else, but he has to fend off attacks of ingratitude while doing so. Lack of appreciation does not stop a leader who has come to serve. Servant leadership is an act of unselfish love. Servant leadership is an act of courage and covenant.

Not Being Offended

Because pride is a central ingredient in the sinful nature of man, people are easily offended at someone exercising authority. Even the disciples of Jesus struggled with this problem. When the mother of James and John asked Jesus to give her sons a special place of honor, the other ten disciples were highly offended. **Matthew 20:24** records their response:

And when the ten heard it, they were moved with indignation against the two brothers.

Mark 10:41 records similarly:

And when the ten heard it, they began to be greatly displeased with James and John.

The natural tendency of our pride is to become indignant, irritated and offended when anyone else is in a position of leadership over us. We need to recognize that tendency quickly and purge it out of us before it poisons our relationships. When one is offended at a leader, he thinks he has a good reason for it. Whether there is a good reason or not is not the point; pride and offense are a wrong spirit and must be removed from us under any circumstances. There is never an excuse for yielding to a spirit of offense and unforgiveness.

There is a temptation to scrutinize someone who is in authority and to magnify any fault that can be found. We must resist receiving gossip about what a leader has done wrong. There is an evil fascination with negative reports about a leader. **I Timothy 5:19** warns:

Do not receive an accusation against an elder except from two or three witnesses.

Our congregants should not receive a negative report about someone who is leading a ministry. We should appreciate and be loyal to those in leadership. The leader in a group is the focal point of unity. If people support the leader, there will be unity in the group as a whole. Other focal points will cause a division of attention in the group. A group is unified by flowing with the direction of the leader.

Experience Appreciated

The leader usually started working in the particular ministry before the others in the group. Many areas that now seem easy were won and accomplished with great difficulty in the previous years. The freshness of a new person who is seeing the vision for the first time has not been worn and proven through the long period of applying himself to see that vision fulfilled.

There is a beauty in the calloused hands of a veteran worker. The Shulamite maiden in the Song of Solomon claimed that she did not appear as attractive as others because she had spent her time taking more care of others than herself. **Song of Solomon 1:6** states:

Do not look upon me because I am dark, because the sun has tanned me. My mother's sons were angry with me; they made me the keeper of the vineyards, but my own vineyard I have not kept.

The rough-skinned ruddiness of an experienced worker is more lovely than the fair-skinned freshness of one who has not done the work.

Spiritual Attack

There is also a greater spiritual attack that comes against one who is leading an area of ministry. There are different levels and ranks of satanic spirits, and they array themselves in an attempt to stop the kingdom of God. A more powerful enemy force is assigned to hinder those who are being more effective for the kingdom of God.

A demonic spirit was sent from Satan to attack Paul to hinder his ministry because Paul had received such powerful revelations. Satan had to focus increased attack upon this man who was leading the saints against the kingdom of darkness. Paul says in **II Corinthians 12:7:**

Unless I should be exalted above measure by the abundance of revelations, a

thorn in the flesh was given to me, a messenger of Satan to buffet me, lest I be exalted above measure.

When people find fault with a leader they should realize that they would probably not fare half as well themselves if they had to undergo the same amount of satanic opposition.

The Cares of the Ministry

In addition to satanic attack, leaders also bear the psychological weight of the concerns of the ministry. Although we are supposed to cast our cares and burdens upon the Lord, when one is sincere in desiring the best for the congregation, he tends to identify himself with the problems that are faced.

Besides the other things, what comes upon me daily: my deep concern for all the churches (II Corinthians 11:28).

Three things weigh upon ministry leaders: the counseling needs of the people, the build-up of administrative chores and the challenge of financial provision. If a leader is not strong, these concerns will begin to crush him. One is given more leadership to the extent that his faith can handle and have victory over the cares and burdens of the people, the administration and the finances.

Desire

God wants people to seek greater degrees of leadership. He wants us to expand our capacity for increasing spheres of responsibility.

If a man desires the position of an elder, he desires a good work (I Timothy 3:1).

It is a good quality to be willing to embrace the extra effort of added responsibility.

I Chronicles 4 contains the brief account of a man named Jabez. **Verse 10** states:

And Jabez called on the God of Israel saying, "Oh that You would bless me indeed, and enlarge my territory, that Your hand would be with me, and that You would keep me from evil, that I may not cause pain." So God granted him what he requested.

The name Jabez means "he will cause pain." Because of this, Jabez struggled with a negative self-image and feelings of rejection from his family. He wanted to serve God and have his area of responsibility enlarged so that he could be a blessing to others. He had to shake off all lack of self-esteem. He sought God to heal him from the hurts of his family background. His desire to be increased was seen as an honorable attitude by God. He may have seemed to be the one with the least potential among his brothers, but he exerted himself to be motivated to accomplish more for the kingdom of God.

God wants us to push through our personal shortcomings by faith to lay hold of the challenges of leadership in the kingdom of God. **Verse 9 of I Chronicles 4** contains this commentary on the story of Jabez:

Now Jabez was more honorable than his brothers, and his mother called his name Jabez, saying, "because I bore him in pain.

The more one is willing to be bold and grow in his spiritual authority, the more honorable he is in God's sight. God is looking for those who will be aggressive to attack the kingdom of Satan. He is looking for those who will wrest authority away from the enemy and gain territory for the kingdom of God. He is looking for those who will take the kingdom by force (Matthew 11:12).

Leading: Being in Front

In the army of ancient Israel as well as modern Israel, the one who leads the charge into the most dangerous area of battle will be the one who earns the greatest authority. God is looking for those with initiative, resourcefulness and creativity to bring victory for the kingdom of God in the name of Jesus. David won the loyalty of the people by leading the battle charge, going out and coming in before them. Joab won his place as commander-in-chief of the armies of Israel by leading the attack against the fortress city of the Jebusites, which later became Jerusalem (I Chronicles 11:6).

The tribe of Judah won its place as leader among the tribes even though Judah was not the first born son. Judah won the right to be the line of the coming messianic king because it was willing to lead the battle against the Canaanites (Judges 1:1, I Chronicles 5:2). Judah became the tribe from which Jesus would come, because of its boldness to lead in battle. It is commendable to desire to be a leader if one has godly motivations.

Dynamics of Leadership

In the book of Ecclesiastes, Solomon gives many clues to understanding the dynamics of leadership. Let us look at a few examples. **Ecclesiastes 5:8** states:

If you see the oppression of the poor, and the violent perversion of justice and righteousness in a province, do not marvel at the matter; for high official watches over high official, and higher officials are over them.

People get upset when they see something happen that is unfair. They think that those in management positions are getting away with evil without having to be accountable. Solomon says we are not to be upset about such things, because there are higher levels of supervision that we may not be aware of. Everyone has a boss over him somewhere. Everyone will eventually be held accountable for how he has exercised authority. We do not have to be frustrated or to complain about someone doing wrong in a position of authority because we know that he has a supervisor over him somewhere. Ultimately, God is supervising and holding everyone accountable.

We are also not to be frustrated or to complain if someone under our leadership says negative things about us. **Ecclesiastes 7:21** states:

Also do not take to heart everything people say, lest you hear your servant cursing you. For many times, also, your own heart has known that even you have cursed others.

A leader hears people complaining about him all the time. These complaints feel very unnerving. One's sense of self-confidence can be undermined by the murmuring. One might desire to take vengeance upon the person who is complaining against him. After a while, the leader begins to relax a little and not feel so threatened.

Most people's negative comments are rather superficial. Negative comments are usually made in moments of frustration and do not represent deep-seated rebellion. If the leader can train himself not to worry about complaints made against him, he will be able to overlook the insignificant matters and deal with the more objective problems. We should not be overly tense if people complain about our leadership. Complaints come with the job.

When a person comes into a new position of authority, he may feel threatened. His defensiveness may cause him to act somewhat rigidly or stiffly. After a while, however, his defensiveness will soften, and he will show more graciousness in his interactions with people.

A man's wisdom makes his face shine, and the sternness of his face is changed (Ecclesiastes 8:1).

As one gains experience in exercising authority, his face softens a bit. A new leader may see every situation as a challenge to his authority; he may act stern and officious. With wisdom however, he learns to handle situations with people without making every case one of rebellion. New leaders should try to stay relaxed and calm. They should recognize that there is a tendency to be defensive in the first period of time in a new position.

Sometimes one's boss loses his temper and directs a flood of angered emotions at the person who is trying to submit to him. At that moment, the one trying to be obedient will experience an inner turmoil. He will not know whether to run away, defend himself, apologize, or explode in anger. **Ecclesiastes 10:4** states:

If the spirit of the ruler rises against you, do not leave your post. For conciliation pacifies great offenses.

If our superior loses his temper, we must stay in our post until the wave of emotion has past. One should keep himself calm and respond slowly with measured words. One must not flee or try to defend himself in the middle of such turmoil.

If he can maintain his post without overreacting, he will win great confidence from the one in charge. One should take a deep breath and allow for the storm to pass by. He should use that moment of turmoil as an opportunity to prove and demonstrate his steadiness under fire. If one reacts emotionally at such a time, he may lose years' worth of work and effort. Standing still will be a great act of faithfulness.

How, then, should a responsible leader act? And how should people who want to be cooperative react to that leadership? The leader must be both directive and deferring. The people must be both strong and submissive. Both sides must be responsive to the other.

King David had a great capacity for personal leadership. He had a style of relating to people that drew loyalty to him. One of the most joyful moments in the history of Israel was when David was reconfirmed as king and made reconciliation with the Israelite tribes. **I Chronicles 13:1-4** is an example of masterful and responsive leadership:

> **Then David consulted with the captains of thousands and hundreds, and with every leader. And David said to all the congregation of Israel, "If it seems good to you, and if it is of the Lord our God, let us send out to our brethren everywhere who are left in all the land of Israel...that they may gather together to us; and let us bring the ark of our God back to us"....Then all the congregation said that they would do so, for the thing was right in the eyes of all the people.**

David gives a clear directive for a specific course of action. Notifications are sent throughout the land informing people of an assembly. He makes a major change in the religious structure by ordering the ark to be moved. He consults with leaders around him for their confirmation. He wins the heart of the people toward his plan. He appeals to their conscience by having his action be one of moral conviction and righteousness. He seeks God's will in prayer to gain divine wisdom and direction. He exercises a huge amount of authority, but is very gentle and affirmative in the process.

David has demonstrated here the three principles of responsive leadership:

(1) A clear course of action (*"let us send out and bring"*)
(2) Confirmation of the people (*"if it seems good to you"*)
(3) Spirit-led direction (*"if it is of God"*).

The people, in turn, respond to David's leadership in a true covenant attitude. **I Chronicles 12:38** states:

> **All these men of war, who could keep ranks, came to Hebron with a loyal heart, to make David king over all Israel; and all the rest of Israel were of one mind to make David king.**

These men were men of strength, self-discipline and military experience. They knew how to fight and to hold their ranks when the attack was on. They came to David with a loyal heart. Loyalty and faithfulness are central to a covenantal attitude. They were determined to make David king. Not only were they willing to submit to his authority, but they were seeking to reinforce it for the greater good of the nation. Because of this attitude, they were able to come to complete unity of mind. We need to train ourselves to be strong and loyal, to support authority and to seek unity. This is how a covenant people will respond to leadership in a positive and cooperative spirit.

The Mind of Christ

Unity of mind is the central factor in covenant decision making. A group of men can come to unity of mind if each one gives up his insistence upon his own viewpoint. We seek the will of God for the greater good of the group as a whole. Each one must seek God's point of view, since God sees all the parts together.

For "who has known the mind of the Lord that he may instruct Him?" But we have the mind of Christ (I Corinthians 2:16).

God has only one mind, one will, in a given situation. When we are in disagreement, it is because we are outside of His mind. It is possible for a group of people to discern the mind and will of God if they will seek Him in prayer. As we divest ourselves of self-interest, the mind of Christ becomes more and more obvious. The key is seeking His will instead of our own and to look at the whole picture instead of our part of it.

When I was an elder under Pastor Dan Juster, we had a policy that we would not make decisions by majority vote. There were five of us, and we sought to have a unanimous agreement on every decision. The word unanimous actually means "one soul." Uni means one, and animus, from which we get the word animated and animal, means soul. It is possible by faith to come to one mind together. That one mind has to be the one mind of Christ.

What precedes a policy of unanimous agreement is a commitment to unity, covenant, and the will of God. Some decisions would take hours of prayer or discussion before coming to agreement. A completely Spirit-led decision will be brought to unanimity. Spiritual decision making is based on gaining the will of God instead of holding on to our own will. God's wisdom and His perspective are available to us. If we are willing to do the will of God, we will know what that will is (John 7:17). If it is really God's wisdom that we are seeking, we can find it (James 1:5).

Sharing Rewards

In being loyal and submissive to someone else's authority, we must believe that we will be part of receiving the reward for the same ministry. If we give our life for a certain ministry, it will be given back to us. In ancient Israel, a person who even watched over the baggage would receive an equal share in spoils of the war (I Samuel 30:24). If one is loyal to someone else's leadership, he will in time be promoted. What one sows, one also reaps. If he is loyal and submissive to someone else's authority, people will eventually be loyal and submissive to his authority.

When we give up our selfishness in order to serve, we can be sure God will reward us with a spiritual inheritance.

A little-known biblical hero is the Egyptian servant Jarha. **I Chronicles 2:34-35** tells of him:

Now Sheshan had no sons, only daughters. And Sheshan had an Egyptian servant whose name was Jarha. Sheshan gave his daughter to Jarha his servant as wife, and she bore him Attai.

Jarha seemingly had no inheritance, no possessions and no reward. He gave up his life to serve his master Sheshan. He served in obscurity without even being part of the family or the family's name. Because Sheshan had no sons, he allowed his daughter to marry Jarha. This marriage made Jarha the equivalent of a son and now heir to Sheshan's entire property. God rewarded Jarha's service with promotion, honor and great possessions. He received a new name.

God knows everything that we do and is sure to give us a gracious reward. God is able to bring us from obscurity to renown in a moment of time. He can bring us from rags to riches, from disgrace to glory. Even as He took Joseph out of the dungeon and Daniel out of captivity, God is able to raise us up to prominence and authority. **Proverbs 22:29** exhorts:

Do you see a man who excels in his work? He will stand before kings; he will not stand before unknown men.

We learn to be responsive leaders by responding in a supportive way to others' leadership. God desires to bless us through one another.

31

DELEGATION: THE GIFT OF ADMINISTRATION

In traditional religious circles, a professional clergyman is hired to do the work of the congregation. He is a priestly performer whose ritualistic movements are observed weekly by the members of the congregation. In covenant circles, however, all the members of the congregation are encouraged to be involved in the spiritual activity. The minister seeks to share the work of the congregation with as many people as possible.

No Clergy and Laity

The lead pastoral figure is not seen as a freakish religious species. There should be no distinction between clergy and laity. The ministry leader is seen as a leader among peers; he coordinates and directs the involvement of everyone. The leader tries to maximize the capacity of every member to join in the ministry. **Ephesians 4:12-13** states that the reason to have full time apostles, prophets, evangelists, pastors and teachers is:

for the equipping of the saints, for the work of the ministry, for the edifying of the Body of Christ, till we all come to the unity of the faith and the knowledge of the Son of God, to a perfect man, to the measure of the stature of the fullness of Christ.

Who Does the Work?

The purpose of a minister is not to do the work of the ministry, but to prepare, equip, enable and involve the members of the congregation to do it. The work of a congregation is to be done by the congregants. The role of the minister is to facilitate their doing of the work. In this way, the congregation as a whole is built up with strength from within. If the minister ministers for the congregants, they have not been allowed to participate. As each member does his share, he is made strong by the practice and exercise of spiritual work. In this way, the whole community develops a grass roots maturity. The corporate identity of the individual members together grows to be one man in the full stature of Jesus.
Ephesians 4:16 states:

From whom the whole body, joined and knit together by what every joint

supplies, according to the effective working by which every part does its share, causes growth of the body for the edifying of itself in love.

It is the whole body that is to grow, not just the minister. As the body grows, it is to be more and more interconnected. It becomes interconnected by the fact that every part and every joint is active. Everyone is participating in the effective work. The members of the body are not joined and knit together by someone ministering at them or ministering for them. The body is to exercise the ministry of edifying love upon itself. The different members cause each other to grow by ministering one to another.

The role of the minister is to direct the work of the members ministering to one another. A congregation in which the minister does all the work is in a weakened state. When the minister can get the work away from himself and into the hands of others, the ministry will begin to grow strong.

The minister is not to do the work of the congregation but to cause others to do so. He must develop a mechanism to transfer that work into their hands. There must be a spiritual flow for getting the work to be shared, a process for shifting the responsibility for the work into the hands of others. The anointing to delegate spiritual authority into the hands of others is an essential part of covenantal leadership. Delegating is a primary function of leadership.

The Need to Delegate

The ability to delegate is referred to as the gift of administration or the gift of leadership. It is a supernatural spiritual gift, an expression of the indwelling grace of God. **Romans 12:6** and **8** state:

Having then gifts differing according to the grace that is given us, let us use them...he who exhorts, in exhortation; he who gives, with liberality; he who leads, with diligence.

If one is to be a leader, he must manifest the charisma of leading by delegation.

Pastor Cho of Korea has said that his primary gifts are faith and administration. The gift of administration is necessary if a congregation is to grow. If a congregation is very large, the head pastor cannot do all the work. Unless the pastor develops the gift of administration whereby he can parcel out the work of the ministry, the congregation will be limited in size. If a pastor can develop the ability to delegate spheres of responsibility to others, the congregation can grow unlimitedly.

Many ministers find themselves in the middle of a swirl of activity. All the work of the congregation seems to be piled up on top of them. They work longer and longer hours but cannot seem to get themselves out of the hole. As they become weary, the congregation begins to wane in spiritual vitality as well.

Pastoral overload was a familiar experience even to the great leader Moses. By the advice of his father-in-law Jethro, Moses was able to change his style of

ministry. Through delegation, he rescued the congregation. **Exodus 18:13-26** represents a major turning point in Moses' career. The principles of delegation can
launch a ministry into successful and effective reproduction.

> **On the next day Moses sat to judge the people; and the people stood before**
> **Moses from morning until evening (verse 13).**

Here we have a typical schedule for the overloaded minister. His hours run from
first thing in the morning until last thing at night. He is not able to do anything
productive or forward moving, because he spends all his time dealing with the
counseling emergencies that are lined up in front of him.

With a quick glance, Jethro is able to get a common sense perspective on
Moses' modus operandi. From this fresh point of view, Jethro sees the obvious
problem. He says to Moses in **verse 14:**

> **What is this thing that you are doing for the people? Why do you sit alone,**
> **and all the people stand before you from morning until evening?**

Jethro notes that Moses is doing all the work for the people. Moses is not getting
them to help themselves. He is sitting alone, and no one else is involved in the
ministry.

Moses replies that the people need him to minister to them. No one else seems
to be in touch with God enough to meet the people's needs. In **verse 15-16**, Moses
answers:

> **The people come to me to inquire of God. When they have a difficulty they**
> **come to me, and I judge between one and another; I make known the**
> **statutes of God and His laws.**

There is a temptation for a minister to be trapped into thinking that he is the only
one who can help the people. Anyone who has a problem, if he knows that he can
get to the top man, would rather see him than someone else. Moses thinks that he
is being sincere, but he is being unwise.

Tyranny of the Immediate

I worked in a biblical counseling center for several years. There I learned that
there is no such thing as an emergency in counseling. People want to make the
counselor feel that their problem is more urgent than anyone else's. They say that
they cannot wait another moment; they have to see the most anointed counselor.
However, they have lived with the same set of problems for decades until now.
They will continue to live their lives in the future.

Counseling and administrative needs seem to pile up on their own. They try to
demand more and more attention. The minister must not allow his every move to
be governed by the tyranny of the immediate needs. If he allows the tyranny of the
immediate to dominate him, he will be diverted from accomplishing that which the
Lord has given him. Any administrative chore or any counseling problem will

demand as much urgency upon the minister as he allows it to. By faith, the minister must get on top of the urgencies of the immediate moment. He must become the head and not the tail in regards to his daily schedule.

Jethro responds to Moses in **verses 17** and **18:**

> **The thing that you do is not good. Both you and these people who are with you will surely wear yourselves out. For this thing is too much for you; you are not able to perform it by yourself.**

God's opinion of this style of ministry is that it is wrong. Although it may come out of sincere intentions, it lacks knowledge and is ineffective. The minister who refuses to delegate and does not have the courage to stop trying to meet everyone's needs himself, will damage the congregation. He will become worn out, and the ministry will be weakened. Much is being written today about psychological stress and the syndrome of "burn-out." If a minister does not use the wisdom of God, he will not be exempt from the same pressures and hazards.

Jethro's Plan: Delegate Authority

Jethro brings Moses a prophetic word from God. Jethro presents to him a simple three-fold plan. The first part of the plan is that Moses should stand before God in prayer. As he gains understanding of the principles of a godly life, he is to teach the people in the larger assembly. In this way, Moses will be able to maintain his perspective and creativity over the whole situation. By teaching the group at large the principles of godly life instead of doing personal counseling, he maximizes his own effectiveness. Moses' unique role, which no one else can do, is to receive the primary vision from God and communicate it to the group at large. He must be willing to specialize in this role.

The second step of Jethro's plan is to set up leaders under Moses who have proven character and give them authority to deal with the matters involving the congregation. **Exodus 18:21-22** states:

> **You shall select from all the people able men, such as fear God, men of truth, hating covetousness; and place such men over them to be rulers of thousands, rulers of hundreds, rulers of fifties, and rulers of tens. And let them judge the people at all times.**

These men are the equivalents of the elders and deacons today. The brief list of the qualifications of these able men is parallel to what is more fully described in I Timothy 3. It is Moses, as the head pastor or apostle, who has the authority to appoint and ordain the leaders under him. The leaders are subdivided into several layers of expanding spheres of authority. They deal with people in groups of tens, fifties, hundreds, and thousands. Whether we call these people home group leaders or pastors, deacons or elders, is not that important. The principle is that there is a series of higher authorities that can be appealed to for more difficult matters. Into the hands of these men is given the authority to act with decisiveness in the matters of the people.

It is necessary to divert the counseling needs of the people to the lowest level of authority that can handle the needs effectively. It takes courage to require people to stay in a delegated sphere; they must not try to skip a level prematurely. Every matter should be handled on the lowest possible level. Congestion of problems must be kept away from the top figures. If the pilot of a ship is always in the galley, he will not be able to steer the vessel.

The leader should minister to his strongest members so that they in turn can minister to the weaker ones. If the leader spends all his time with the weakest members, the potentially stronger ones will also become weak, and the congregation will flounder. If the leader ministers to the strong, they will get stronger. If the stronger minister to the weaker, the weaker will get stronger. With this flow of divine counsel and authority, every member will maximize his own potential. In trying to reach a large number of people, we must make it our first priority to equip those who have the potential to help others. In this way the ministry will multiply.

The third part of Jethro's plan is that any matter that cannot be dealt with on a lower level, is allowed to move up the scale. Any situation that needs Moses' attention can be referred to him by his co-leaders. **Exodus 18:22** states:

Then will it be that every great matter they shall bring to you, but every small matter they themselves shall judge.

The leader does not want to detach himself from the needs of individuals. When matters have gone through the pastoral process, they should be gladly received by the leader. The leader can then look at every situation that is brought to him as a positive opportunity to touch the life of one of the individuals in the congregation. The purpose of pastoral delegation is not to avoid people's problems, but to spread the work to minister more effectively.

Structure is never made for structure's sake. Structure is only instituted to facilitate personal care and loving attention.

Monkeys

Administrative chores have been given the nickname "monkeys." Monkeys like to climb to the top of the ladder. Administrative chores and counseling needs will try to rise to higher levels within the congregation. We need to handle every problem on as low a level as possible. Monkeys need to be held firmly on a leash so that they do not run to the top. A monkey needs to be fed, or he will begin to chatter and complain. When someone has a chore in his sphere of responsibility, he must take care of it and not let it just sit there. If a chore is not completed, it will create problems for the future. It is irresponsible to leave a duty half finished.

On the other hand, a monkey wants to be overfed. A leader must not give a certain task more attention than it deserves. If a situation is draining time and energy, it may be a diversion from the progress of the congregation.

Sometimes it is necessary to shoot a monkey. If an administrative chore is no longer worth dealing with, it should not be allowed to linger. It should be officially concluded and removed from the agenda of things to do. If an administrative chore is to be terminated, direct notification must be given to the supervisor who assigned it. It would not be proper to terminate a task that was given by a superior without telling him, because he would be under the impression that work was continuing to be done on it.

Follow-Up and Accountability

It takes patience and sensitivity to shift responsibility into the hands of other people. One must first share the vision with them and get them involved in the work. Later, they are guided to shoulder the full responsibility for the area they have taken. There is a process of apprenticeship in which someone is trained to do a task. A person is first shown what to do; then he is allowed to try it himself under direct supervision. Finally he is released to operate in charge of his own sphere under periodic checks of accountability.

This is the way Jesus ministered. **John 4:2** states:

Jesus Himself did not baptize, but His disciples.

Jesus would meet with His disciples before He ministered and share with them about what they should do. When He finished preaching, His disciple would help Him minister to the people. The people would come forward to be baptized, to be prayed for, and to be healed. Sometimes Jesus would minister alone. Other times He would stand on the side, watching and directing His disciples. After the ministry time, He would take the disciples off alone and continue to train them and teach them how to minister.

The disciples were apprentices to Jesus. He spent the years of His ministry preparing them to continue His work after Him. He spent more time ministering to the twelve than He did teaching the masses. Within the twelve, James, Peter and John received even more close attention from Jesus. In addition to the twelve, there were seventy other disciples who also received training from Jesus. The three got more attention than the twelve, the twelve got more attention than the seventy, and the seventy got more attention than the masses.

After these things the Lord appointed seventy others also, and sent them two by two before His face into every city and place where He Himself was about to go (Luke 10:1).

In this process of apprenticeship, Jesus would send people out by pairs to help one another and hold one another accountable. Jesus had a planned itinerary where He was going to speak. He would send out His teams of advance men into a city where He was about to preach. They would prepare the area for Jesus' ministry. They would tell the people that He was coming; they would pray with the people; and they would share introductory teachings.

After their preliminary ministry, the pairs of advance men would report back to

Jesus. They would share with Him the successes of their ministry, and also their failures. Jesus would evaluate what they did and share with them new techniques. He would give them His discernments and spiritual insights. He would equip them with additional teachings to go out and minister again.

Luke 10:17-20 states:

Then the seventy returned with joy, saying, "Lord, even the demons are subject to us in Your name." And He said to them, "I saw Satan fall like lightning from heaven. Behold, I give you authority to trample on serpents and scorpions, and over all the power of the enemy, and nothing shall by any means hurt you. Nevertheless do not rejoice in this, that the spirits are subject to you, but rather rejoice because your names are written in heaven."

The seventy apprentices returned to Jesus and shared with Him the success of their deliverance ministry. In response, Jesus gave them some instruction as to the effect that ministry was having within the spiritual world in destroying the authority of Satan. Jesus then went on to give them some equipping teaching to increase their authority to do more deliverance ministry. He added an area of correction. They needed to watch out for the subtle temptation of getting into a wrong spirit by focusing on the ministry rather than on God. He evaluated, equipped, encouraged, and warned them. He prepared them to go on in the future. The process of apprenticeship requires patience and prolonged instruction. One can only delegate authority to the extent that he has drawn the person into taking responsibility for that sphere of authority. The shifting and re-shouldering of responsibility has to be observed and evaluated.

Choosing Disciples

One of the highest priorities in the ministry of Jesus was to train His disciples to carry on His work after Him. Jesus invested His life and work into the hands of these men. There could be no more important decision than determining which people are God's best choices to be trained as disciples. If a mistake is made in choosing a disciple, great time, effort and love will be wasted. Because the investment is so high, much prayer needs to go into identifying the right people.

Luke 6:12-13 states:

Now it came to pass in those days that He went out to the mountain to pray, and continued all night in prayer to God. And when it was day, He called His disciples to Him and from them He chose twelve whom He also named apostles.

Jesus spent all night in prayer, perhaps ten hours of solid intercession. What was He praying about? What was so important that it needed that much intense spiritual warfare? As He came out of the prayer time, He picked His twelve primary apprentices. In prayer, Jesus received the revelation about delegating authority to sets of sub-leaders. In prayer, He gained the discernment as to which men were to be His primary disciples. In prayer, He received the wisdom about how to go about training them and transferring His ministry into their hands.

One of the disciples whom Jesus chose was Judas Iscariot, who later betrayed Him. One young man I spent time discipling later betrayed the Lord and became a professional anti-missionary. Some young men I have discipled have gone on to thriving ministries. Reproducing the life of God through other trustworthy men is the central work of the ministry. **I Timothy 2:2** states:

And the things that you have heard from me among many witnesses, commit these to faithful men who will be able to teach others also.

Effort in Management

Delegating, administrating and coordinating people requires effort. Romans 12:8 says that when we exercise the gift of administration, we are to do so with diligence. The charisma of administration comes with the qualification that it requires diligence. Godly management and delegation require time and energy. We need to invest ourselves in planning, communicating, evaluating, motivating and decision making. Leadership is spiritual.

One invests in the spiritual work of management in the belief that it will produce good fruit in the effectiveness of the ministry. The relationship between effort and management is also stated in **Proverbs 12:24:**

The hand of the diligent will rule, but the slothful will be put to forced labor.

The demands of administration require self-initiative and self-discipline. An administrator who is lazy or comfort-seeking will harm the entire organization.

Communication

One area of administration that requires much effort is communicating. Communication must be reiterated and reemphasized until it sinks into consciousness of the hearers. The message must be repeated until it trickles down from the leaders into the reality of the lives of all the members.

Announcements should not be seen as an unspiritual part of the service. Announcements are part of preaching the practical aspects of the message for the week. Through the announcements, the gift of administration preaches. It communicates to the people how they are to be mobilized into action to fulfill the spiritual vision of the congregation. Announcements are a time of spiritual mobilization. We must listen as attentively to the practical directions of the announcements as we do to the spiritual exhortations of the sermon.

At the time of the Tower of Babel, the people were highly organized. Their outstanding administration produced such a unity between the men that they threatened the very authority of heaven. The potential is strong even for evil in the use of communication skills. Imagine how much more powerful it would be in harmony with God.

Indeed the people are one and they all have one language, and this is what they begin to do; now nothing that they propose to do will be withheld from them. Come, let Us go down and there confuse their language, that they may not understand one another's speech (Genesis 11:6-7).

The purpose of administration and communication is to produce unity. At Babel, the people were of one mind and of one language. Language is a system of communication. Unity produces unlimited effectiveness. Because the people were so well coordinated, there was nothing that they could not do. God's judgment on the human race was to cause a breakdown in their communication. Since that time, communication has been difficult between human beings. Communication is not only difficult between those who speak two different languages, it is even difficult to communicate meaningfully to someone who speaks the same language.

When we become believers, the curse of Babel should be reversed. It is reversed through speaking in tongues; it is reversed through our love for one another; and it is also reversed through the gift of administration in exercising anointed communication skills. All communication takes effort, because it must overcome the "Babel barrier." One has to communicate over and over again to solidify even the most simple of directives.

In working with high school students, I have seen that the classroom assignments must be manifestly clear and explicit. Even then, some students will say they did not know what the assignment was. We should train ourselves to pick up instructions quickly and respond at the first communication. When communicating to others, we must go the extra mile and repeat the instructions until the people grasp them.

Standards

Another area of the gift of management that requires diligence (Romans 12:8) is holding people accountable to objective standards of performance. Believers should not settle for a lower quality when doing something for the kingdom of God when they know that standard would not have been acceptable in their workplace. Although the work in the kingdom of God is voluntary, believers should not settle for a less than professional quality. If we are doing something for the Lord, we should do it with even higher standards. We should expect the best and demand the best from ourselves. We should have clear job descriptions, performance standards, and methods of accountability. We should have higher goals than the world around us.

Daniel was evaluated as being *"ten times better"* than all the professionals and experts of the king (Daniel 1:20). When a Roman military commander came to Jesus and said that he had learned how to give people administrative directives and hold them accountable for following through on an assignment, Jesus replied that

He had not found such faith and understanding among the covenant believers (Luke 7:8-9).

We should not make excuses to condone incompetence and irresponsibility. Believers need to put forth the effort to embrace management standards of excellence and quality control. We need to follow up our proposals and carry them out. God watches over His words to follow up on them and make sure they occur (Jeremiah 1:12).

Jesus has given us His name; He has delegated to us the authority to go out into the world around us and reproduce who He is and what He does. We incorporate in our ministries the principles of delegation. We transfer authority so that the life of Jesus can be reproduced in others. We will produce in others not only what we say but who we are. Whatever we do, we should do with all our heart and with the highest of quality because we are representing the Lord Himself.

32

DEACONATE: THE GIFT OF SERVICE

The worldly talent of administration seeks to place a person in an efficient organizational slot. The charismatic gift of administration seeks to release people into their divine callings. Godly delegation involves the discernment to perceive a person's divine anointing. People are most effective when they are doing what God calls them to do. People are most motivated when they are releasing the dynamic force of the gifts and calling that God has placed in them.

A covenant congregation is one in which everyone is doing his part. Every member should be participating in some aspect of spiritual activity. Everyone should experience the life of God and exercise the gifts that God has given. If everyone is to be involved, then each person must discover what his gifts and callings are. Ideally every person will operate in his own area of anointing.

Everyone Is Gifted

God has given to each person a measure of faith and an area of gifting. We are all cooperative partners in the congregation. The way we cooperate is to allow each person to release his gifting. **Romans 12:3-8** discusses the relationship between congregational cooperation and the release of motivational gifts:

God has dealt to each one a measure of faith. For as we have many members in one body, but all the members do not have the same function, so we, being many, are one Body in Christ, and individually members of one another. Having then gifts differing according to the grace that is given to us, let us use them: if prophecy, let us prophesy in proportion to our faith; or ministry, let us use it in our ministering; he who teaches, in teaching; he who exhorts, in exhortation; he who gives, with liberality; he who leads, with diligence; he who shows mercy, with cheerfulness.

There are seven giftings listed here. God has given each person a primary spiritual urge to fulfill. Within each person's spirit are these aspects of God's personality which desire to be expressed.

The seven motivational gifts are the following:

(1) prophecy—hearing from God in prayer and speaking out direction with a high concern for righteousness;

(2) service (ministry)—helping out with practical details and physical needs, getting things done;

(3) teaching—setting forth the truth of Scripture systematically for the renewing of the intellect;

(4) exhortation—encouraging and motivating others to do their best and fulfill their potential;

(5) giving—having the faith and generosity to receive and give money to bless individuals and ministries;

(6) administration (ruling or leadership)—coordinating people through delegation to have everyone help out and be involved;

(7) mercy—perceiving the hurt feelings of others and ministering compassion and comfort to them.

The Gift of Service

The gift of service is particularly important if every part in the body is to do its share (Ephesians 4:16). For example, in a worship service, while only one person ministers through teaching, there may be dozens who are involved in the ministry through practical works of service. The gift of service is the foundational gift for community life. Every member of the community should take on an area of responsibility.

The Deaconate

As a congregation grows, there are many practical chores and tasks that go along with that growth. The congregation must have an effective system for those tasks to be completed. **Acts 6:2-4** contains the apostles' directive to establish a deaconate board:

It is not desirable that we should leave the Word of God and serve tables. Therefore, brethren, seek out from among you seven men of good reputation, full of the Holy Spirit and wisdom, whom we may appoint over this business; but we will give ourselves continually to prayer and to ministry of the Word.

The deaconate has three primary purposes:

(1) To see that the practical business of the congregation is taken care of

(2) To involve all the members of the congregation in works of service

(3) To free the pastoral leadership for prayer and preaching.

The deaconate enabled the business of the congregation to be accomplished more smoothly, thereby allowing the ministry of the apostles to be more effective. The result of this functioning deaconate was to generate more evangelism in the city. **Acts 6:7** states:

And the Word of God spread, and the number of disciples multiplied greatly in Jerusalem, and a great many of the priests were obedient to the faith.

The outcome of a wise and helpful deaconate is revival in the community. The deacons get everyone involved in practical service. The people are edified by their participation in the activity of the congregation. The deacons allow the pastoral leaders to prepare better messages from the Word, which also edifies the congregation. The deacons create freedom for the elders to be more involved in evangelism, which increases the size of the community. The deacons are the link between the practical needs of the congregation and the spiritual vision of the elders.

The deacons should not be seen as men of practical experience alone, but also of strong spirituality. The deacons in Acts 6 were full of the Holy Spirit, faith and wisdom. Of both Stephen and Philip, there are recorded in Scriptures the testimonies of their ministries in evangelism and miracles. Deacons must be both practical and spiritual. If they are only spiritually inclined, they will not have the wisdom to handle the business. If they are only practically inclined, the workings of the congregation will take on a worldly manner.

The deaconate can be the proving ground for future elders. Not all deacons will become elders. The elders should have proven themselves in the practical wisdom and deaconate service of the congregation. If they have not, their vision for the congregation may lack reality and plausibility. Spiritual wisdom still includes common sense. The deacons are described as having practical wisdom and spiritual anointing. They also possess proven character and honorable reputations.

Ordaining Deacons

Let us examine the process of ordaining deacons. The deacons were chosen to meet specific needs among the people. The congregation had been growing, but the lack of a deaconate organization caused the practical administration to be neglected. This resulted in hurt feelings and complaining among the people. **Acts 6:1** states:

When the number of disciples was multiplied, there arose a murmuring against the Hebrews by the Hellenists because their widows were neglected in the daily distribution.

The burden for taking initiative and coming up with a plan lay with the elders. They prayed and presented a vision to the community. They responded to the complaints of the people but maintained their leadership in the process. The establishment of a deaconate board must be under the supervision of the elders. **Acts 6:2** states:

Then the twelve summoned the multitude of the disciples and said...

The vision and direction determined by the elders was communicated at a congregational assembly.

The first priority of the deaconate board was not to respond to the practical situation but to facilitate the ministry of the elder's vision. Practicalities do not lead the congregation. The workings of the deaconate fit into the definitions set by the elders. The apostles had demonstrated their priorities:

It is not desirable that we should leave the Word of God (Acts 6:2).

Every action of the community is done with the priority of seeking the kingdom of God first. The practical details are met in line with the purpose of the ministry.

The apostles then listened to the suggestions and discernments of the members. They wanted the members to be involved in the process. The input of the people was to give confirmation as to which men had earned a good reputation among them. They told the apostles which men were known by the group to have proven moral character. The input of the people was not so much to choose the deacons as it was to verify which men had earned and merited trust among them. **Acts 6:3** states:

Therefore, brethren, seek out from among you seven men of good reputation.

The elders should respond to the suggestions of the members. After receiving the input of the people, the apostles used their authority to make the appointments. **Acts 6:3** describes the appointment of the deacons by the elders:

whom we may appoint over this business.

The members then chose among themselves and nominated for the deaconate seven men that were trustworthy. **Acts 6:5** states:

They chose Stephen...Philip...Nicolas...

These deacon nominees were then set before the elders for their approval:

whom they set before the apostles (Acts 6:6).

The group then turns to a time of corporate prayer right in the middle of the nomination process. **Acts 6:6** states:

And when they had prayed...

There is a tendency for a nomination process to take on a worldly political air. It is important, therefore, to use prayer to gain the discernment to choose the right people. Politics must be avoided. Involvement in prayer is mandatory. If a person is not willing to pray and seek God's will, his opinion should not hold sway in determining the right choice.

The ordination is completed when the elders lay their hands upon the deacons. The laying-on-of-hands shows that the future decisions of the deacons will bear the authority of the elders. The congregation is placed in right order, and harmony emerges. The people are satisfied with this new organization and delegation of authority.

And this saying pleased the whole multitude (Acts 6:5).

The members are satisfied; the community is edified by the teaching of the Word and evangelism spreads to the surrounding neighborhood.

An added benefit of the ordination of deacons is the release of future gift ministers. Stephen, Philip and others of the seven went on to become pastors, prophets and evangelists.

Appointment and Confirmation

We see in Acts 6 a pattern that can be applied to appointments of leaders in other spheres of ministry.

(1) Individual members are given responsibility for service by the deacons.

(2) The deacons are appointed by the elders in response to the needs of the people.

(3) The confirmation of the members is sought in the process of appointment.

(4) Elders are ordained by the pastor under the oversight of the apostolic ministry (Titus 1:5).

(5) Apostles are set into ministry by direct prophetic mandate of the Holy Spirit with the confirmation, prayer and ordination of the pastors and prophets (Act 13:1-3).

Every level of ordination involves the seeking of God's will in prayer, the authority of appointment by the immediate supervisor and the receiving of input for confirmation from the congregants as a whole.

Appreciating Others' Gifts

Different people have different gifts and anointings. We need to yield to the strength in others. We should appreciate that other people have complementary gifts in areas that we lack. One with a gift of administration would have no one to coordinate if there were not a greater number of people moving in the gift of service. One whose gift is mercy should not be offended by the directive words of righteousness that come through the gift of prophecy. A prophetic-oriented individual should not belittle the ministry of mercy that provides the substance of love in the midst of a community. One who gives money should not think that other people are not as important as he is if they do not give as much money as he does.

Members of the community must see the one whose calling is in finances and business to be just as spiritual as one whose ministry is primarily in teaching. The giving of money is a spiritual calling to one as teaching is to another.

Some sermons will be given by those whose anointing is to encourage and motivate people toward the basics of Christian life. Other sermons will be given by those whose anointing is to set forth systematic truth to eliminate confusion over doctrine. Both are equally necessary. As we appreciate one another, the greater freedom we create allows a whole variety of spiritual gifts to be released.

Tribal Officers

The ministry of the deacon involves both administrative oversight and practical service. The word for the gift of service in Romans 12:7 is the same root in the Greek as the word for deacon. Deaconing is essentially the act of service. On the other hand, the Hebrew equivalent for the position of the deacon is "shoter," or officer. Numbers 11:16 refers to elders and officers. Deuteronomy 16:18 refers to judges and officers. The levels of spiritual authority in the New Testament are derived from the military model in ancient Israel. Structure within the church can be seen as a spiritual or allegorical application of the tribal battle formations. Congregational and apostolic leadership can be seen as a series of commanders over different size groups of people.

> I took the heads of your tribes, wise and knowledgeable men, and made
> them heads over you, leaders of thousands, leaders of hundreds, leaders of
> fifties, leaders of tens, and officers for your tribes (Deuteronomy 1:15).

A home group leader is a leader of a group of families. An elder is a leader of a
group of home groups. An apostle is the leader of a group of pastors. The Body of
believers is not a militia nor is the Church an institution of hierarchy. On the other
hand, every believer should be ready for mobilization and obedience to authority as
if he were a soldier in a spiritual militia. **II Timothy 2:3-4** states:

> You must endure hardship as a good soldier of Jesus Christ. No one
> engaged in warfare entangles himself in the affairs of this life, that he may
> please the one who enlisted him as a soldier.

An army has privates, sergeants, lieutenants and captains. We do not despise
authority, but rejoice in the order that authority brings. We have the spiritual
dedication of a soldier in the army of the Lord. It is not a coincidence that the
legions of angels under God are portrayed as an army: the "host" of heaven means
the army of heaven.

A deacon is a mid-level commanding officer in our spiritual team. The tribal
formation of ancient Israel combined the different aspects of life. The military, the
priesthood, the family and the judicial process were all interwoven together. There
was no separation of church and state. There was no division between what was
spiritual and what was secular. Everything in life was dedicated to God, and God's
authority was involved in every area of life.

Judicial Process

One of the aspects of the tribal system was the judicial process for religious,
civil and criminal cases. **Deuteronomy 16:18** establishes the authority of judges to
execute justice:

> You shall appoint judges and officers in all your gates, which the Lord your
> God gives you, according to your tribes, and they shall judge the people with
> just judgment. You shall not pervert justice; you shall not show partiality.

Deuteronomy 17:8 continues the mandate for judicial process:

> If a matter arises that is too hard for you to judge, between degrees of
> bloodguiltiness, between one judgment or another, or between one punish-
> ment or another, matters of controversy within your gates, then you shall
> arise and go up to the place which the Lord your God chooses. And you
> shall come to the priests, the Levites, and to the judge there in those days,
> and inquire of them; they shall pronounce upon you the sentence of judg-
> ment.

A similar passage establishing judicial authority can be found in Deuteronomy
1:16. Deuteronomy 20:1 describes the elders' investigation of an unsolved murder.
II Chronicles 19 describes the judicial reforms and the revival of King Jehoshaphat.
Ezra 7 records the establishment of just government in Israel under Ezra. Religious

judicial authority is what Jesus referred to in Matthew 23:3 when He commanded the people to obey the authority of the Pharisees.

There is a wide difference between covenantal judicial process and legalistic judgmentalism. In a sinful world, covenantal judicial process brings in the righteousness of God. Legalistic judgmentalism is a perversion of spiritual authority. Legalism turns revival into decaying religion. When there is criminal activity in the world, it is godly to establish a just system of judicial process. Witnesses and checks and balances help secure justice. Even within the Church, while people are still subject to temptation, an understanding of judicial process will safeguard us from divisions.

God is a just judge. Godly judgment with wisdom and discernment is not the same thing as hypocritical judgmentalism and condemnation. Believers should have a love and appreciation for justice and right judging. Because right judging has been confused with judgmentalism, many congregations have mistakenly avoided any concept of judicial process in their midst. Without just judging, there is no process for reconciling differences and no process for removing divisive elements. Without covenant judicial process, a congregation has no way to safeguard against major splits and divisions. Covenantal justice provides a godly recourse against rebellion and wrongdoing. Just judgment is the exercise of spiritual wisdom and discernment.

33

FINANCIAL ACCOUNTABILITY

One of the things that most easily causes offense among people is disagreement over money. As the love of money is the root of all evil, so is the temptation to be offended about the use of money in ministry a common source of offense. People can be very touchy in deciding how finances should be dispersed in the ministry. People are easily offended at how much money a pastor or evangelist earns.

The Greed-Betrayal Syndrome

Shortly before Jesus was to be crucified, a woman came and poured a flask of expensive perfume upon Him. Jesus' disciples thought that this was extravagant and became offended. **Matthew 26:8** states:

When His disciples saw it, they were indignant, saying, "To what purpose is this waste?"

Even though this money was used to honor Jesus, His own disciples became offended at Him. The disciple who was the most offended was Judas Iscariot.

Then one of His disciples, Judas Iscariot, who would betray Him, said, "Why was this fragrant oil not sold for three hundred denarii and given to the poor?' This he said, not that he cared for the poor, but because he was a thief, and had the money box; and he used to take what was in it (John 12:4-6).

Greed and desire for money makes it easier to become offended at money expended for the ministry.

All of us are attacked by the temptation to become irritated and offended at how money is used. One area of offense is the salary a full-time pastor receives. If we give the devil any ground, he is likely to sow seeds of resentment in us against whoever is receiving money from the congregational budget.

At the conclusion of the episode over the anointing with the expensive oil, **Matthew 26:14** records:

Then one of the twelve called Judas Iscariot went to the chief priests and said, "What are you willing to give me if I deliver Him to you?" And they counted out to him thirty pieces of silver. So from that time, he sought opportunity to betray Him.

It was in reaction to his offense about money that Judas decided to betray Jesus. It has profound significance for us that the cause of history's worst case of covenant betrayal was a disagreement over the spending of ministry funds. Since the other disciples did not have the same greed that Judas had, they were able to resist the temptation and evil thoughts about the money.

It is clear that greed was the source to Judas' betrayal since he asked the high priests to give him silver for the act of treachery. The greed-betrayal syndrome goes like this: first there is greed in the heart of a person. That greed gives ground to the devil to tempt him. The temptation is fueled by thinking begrudging thoughts about the money being spent for the ministry. The bad feelings grow into indignation. The offended party feels that he has well-justified reasons for being offended. The betrayer will then seek opportunities to make money for himself. Finally, since he has morally justified his actions in his own mind, he will betray the original minister. Greed causes offense; offense causes betrayal.

Record-keeping

Because money is a source of stumbling for others, ministers should go out of their way to handle their finances according to an external system of accountability. Peter, as a staff member of Jesus' ministry, was once questioned as to whether Jesus would cooperate with the secular tax collectors.

He [Peter] said, "Yes." And when he had come into the house, Jesus anticipated him, saying, "What do you think, Simon? From whom do the kings of the earth take customs or taxes, from their own sons or from strangers?" Peter said to him, "From strangers." Jesus said to Him, "Then the sons are free. Nevertheless, lest we offend them, go to the sea, cast in a hook, and take the fish that comes up first. And when you have opened its mouth, you will find a piece of money; take that and give it to them for Me and you"(Matthew 17:25-27).

The finances of Jesus' ministry were operated in accord with the bureaucracy of secular taxation. Jesus told Peter that although they were not really part of the world's monetary system, they should still act in accord with that system in order to give no offense either to believers or unbelievers. Spiritually, they were exempt from taxation and accountability; they submitted themselves to avoid any hindrance to the preaching of the gospel.

Jesus had faith that God would supply their needs, regardless of the financial demands. He did not want any matter having to do with financial accountability to create a barrier for people to receive the message. The appearance of the ministry's finances was of importance to Jesus.

Ideally, the ministry is a higher level of authority than the secular government. From God's point of view, ministers should be absolved from any financial encumbrance. Yet, the minister has to discern what the secular environment is concerning ministry finances and act appropriately. The only real priority is the furtherance of the gospel. Usually, seeking first the kingdom of God involves cooperating with systems of financial accountability to lessen stumbling blocks for other people's sake.

Ministers themselves are not exempt from the temptations of greed. Even if a pastor starts out with a right heart, he still may wind up falling into temptation if there is no financial accountability around him. The more financial accountability, the less possibility there is that a pastor or evangelist can be led astray to spend money on his own lusts. Anyone can make a mistake. No ministry leader should be beyond accountability in finances.

In today's society, it is a matter of covenantal integrity to make one's finances open to examination. We should desire to have accountability in order to demonstrate our moral convictions that ministries should be operated in righteousness. We are not submitting our ministry to secular authorities, we are displaying the upright standards we keep in our own self-discipline. Other ministries may operate dishonestly. Part of our witness for Jesus is that our business practices are done in honesty and with integrity. We are making a prophetic statement about our belief in honest weights and measures by demanding financial accountability.

Honesty and Prosperity

If we are upright in our financial conduct, God will surely bless us with every good thing. **Psalm 84:11** states:

No good thing will He withhold from those who walk uprightly.

There are four general principles of financial prosperity:
(1) Diligent work
(2) Positive faith confession
(3) Generous giving
(4) Honest accountability.

If one of these areas is missing, there will be a gap in our fulfilling the biblical plan. If these four legs are not in place, the table of prosperity prepared for us by the Lord will be wobbly. By diligent work, we produce and harvest the results of our labor. By positive faith confession, we use the supernatural blessing of God to make our seeds multiply one hundredfold. By generous giving, we set in motion the mechanism of measuring out to others; what we give will be measured back to us in a cyclical flow of generosity. By honest accountability, we use the law of righteousness to safeguard against the temptations of greed.

You shall not have in your bag differing weights, a heavy and a light. You shall not have in your house differing measures, a large and a small. You shall have a perfect and just weight, a perfect and just measure, that your days may be lengthened in the land the Lord your God is giving you. For all

who do such things, and all who behave unrighteously, are an abomination to the Lord your God (Deuteronomy 25:13-16).

The biblical principle of business is that it should be run with honesty and integrity. There is no difference in godly business for a believer or an unbeliever. Christian business practices are simply honest business practices.

A believer should operate his finances more honestly than a non-believer. If he is born again, his heart will be changed to want to make his business honest. The fact that a man is born again does not itself superimpose honesty upon a dishonest business. Sometimes unbelievers are more equitable in their business practices than believers. This should not be so, but believers sometimes make excuses to justify sloppy performance.

Holiness

Where there are strong moral convictions about honesty in financial disclosure, there will be greater holiness within the worshiping community. In Acts 5, a man named Ananias and his wife Sapphira acted with dishonesty in regards to a sizable contribution they were making to the congregation. They avoided financial disclosure and tried to make the records appear that they had given a larger percentage than they really had. The holiness of that community was so strong that a spirit of judgment fell, and Ananias and Sapphira died instantly. The result of such a powerful judgment was that a godly fear came upon the believers. Miraculous signs and wonders flourished in their midst. **Acts 5:11-12** states:

So great fear came upon the Church and upon all who heard these things. And through the hands of the apostles, many signs and wonders were done among the people.

Clear Statements

Lack of financial integrity is evil in God's sight. Whether in ministry or business, unjust weights and measures are an abomination to God. We maintain full financial accountability because we believe it is morally correct before God to operate our finances honestly. We use financial accountability to bear witness that we are honest.

The first principle of accountability is to issue clear financial statements. Exact recordkeeping prevents confusion. The Lord desires order in our affairs, not confusion. In today's ministries, a computerized monthly or quarterly statement is a necessity. The statement should have clearly labeled categories that are easy to understand. Everything we spend should come to light. It is a truth of God's kingdom that nothing is to be done in darkness or under cover. There is no reason for any item of spending not to be made available on open bookkeeping.

When Ezra returned with the remnant to rebuild the land of Israel, he was entrusted with large sums of money to be brought from Babylon. The money was to be deposited in the treasury as a donation to the ministry. When he arrived in Jerusalem, Ezra made sure that every item was clearly and exactly recorded as having been delivered. **Ezra 8:25** states that Ezra went to the priests:

> **And weighed out to them the silver, the gold, and the articles, the offering for the house of our God which the king and his counselors and his princes and all Israel who were present, had offered.**

Ezra was so concerned that the transaction be done with integrity that he made the transfer himself.

> **I even weighed into their hand 650 talents of silver...100 talents of gold... (Ezra 8:26).**

After he transferred the funds, Ezra warned the ministers to be attentive to their recordkeeping and keep exact statements of their spending. **Ezra 8:29** states:

> **Watch and keep them [the donations] until you weigh them before the leaders of the priests...in the chambers of the house of the Lord.**

Ezra asked for a formal receipt of the donations transferred. He asked for an itemized list of the articles donated and an official total of the accounting. **Ezra 8:30** states:

> **So the priests and the Levites received the silver and the gold and the articles by weight to bring them to Jerusalem to the house of our God.**

Different people have different types of anointing. Some people have particular wisdom in business, even though they are not called to preach or be elders. Although ministers should be mature in matters of business, it sometimes happens that in their concern for prayer and preaching they have lost some sharpness in financial management. If certain spiritual leaders have become lax in business practice, they should be open to receive advice from those with experience in that area.

Budgeting

Not only should exact records be kept of past spending, but clear statements of financial intentions for the upcoming fiscal period should be made available to the congregation. Budget projections should be established and confirmed. Percentages of spending should agree with the vision and purpose of the ministry. Budget projections are a way of stating in practical terms what the vision of the congregation is. These budgetary statements should be made available to the congregation in a way that they can be easily read and understood. The people will thus know the priorities of the ministry.

Money must be budgeted for discretionary spending by the leaders as needs and expenses arise. A leader should be given freedom within limits to write individual checks at his own will. A check exceeding the approved limit should be confirmed by more than one person. The leader should be given generous freedom to spend money at his own discretion, but there should be designated limits and categories to protect all involved. If the total of discretionary spending goes beyond the budgeted amount, an adjusted figure must be approved.

It may be wise to set up a deaconate-level advisory committee or to have the elders board handle all the financial decisions. If a financial committee is set up by the elders, it should have the following three purposes:

(1) To advise the pastor and elders of matters of business wisdom and accepted financial practices

(2) To carry out in practical ways the financial priorities set by the pastor and elders in their vision for the congregation

(3) To see that records are properly kept and that spending does not violate the budget guidelines agreed upon by the elders.

Any finance committee must be appointed by the elders and submitted to them. A financial committee is to help implement with business acumen the vision set by the elders. It is not to redirect or change the priorities of the spending.

Any action of the financial committee is subject to approval by the elders. The purpose of a financial committee, as in any other deaconate function, is to free the eldership to do more ministry in teaching, prayer and evangelism. Members of the finance committee must avoid political maneuvering and manipulation of the funds.

Worldly Wisdom

Wealthy and generous members of the congregation can be a great blessing by helping the congregation with their financial donations and with their advice on how to handle funds with more business savvy. On the other hand, wealthy and generous members can become a threat to the congregation if they do not understand the dynamics of spiritual authority. Congregations are not to be governed by donations. The ability to make large donations is not the same thing as being able to exercise spiritual authority. When a gift is given it must be done so with no strings attached. When a person gives a large donation, he must let go of it. He should not think that the size of his donation means that he should have more to say in how it is spent or what the direction of the ministry is. As long as the budget projections and percentages are clearly made known, anyone who is giving will be able to tell where the money is spent.

Business experience gained in the world is part godly wisdom and part carnal technique. The elders of a congregation need to listen to the godly wisdom that men of business experience have gained in the world. On the other hand, those with business experience must recognize that part of what they know is gleaned from an ungodly system and is not appropriate to congregational operations. **Luke 16:8** states:

So the master commended the unjust steward because he had dealt shrewdly. For the sons of this world are more shrewd in their generation than the sons of light.

Much godly wisdom is to be learned in the business world. Leaders of ministries should not be naive about their business practices. The toughness and shrewdness of those who have fought their way to be successful in the business world is often just what a ministry needs to accomplish its goals for the kingdom of God. Jesus was saying in Luke 16:8 that ministers should not avoid learning the shrewd tactics of contemporary business. If businessmen are willing to submit to the spiritual authority of their pastor, and if pastors are willing to learn from the wisdom and experience of their business friends, there will be a healthy balance in which the kingdom of God will be benefited. Meetings for financial disclosure and input should be regularly scheduled.

If the pastor has committed illegal actions, concerns can be brought to the board of elders. If the wrongdoing has not been redressed, an appeal can be made to a pastors' council or an apostolic team. Appropriating money for various ministry directions is not wrongdoing. Judicial challenge would be in the areas of immorality, occultism, decadence, falsifying records, and so on.

Vision for Budget Priorities

Each congregation must determine percentages of congregational giving. Biblical principles can be applied to modern day situations to arrive at appropriate allocations of funds. For example, in ancient Israel the people would tithe to the Levites. The Levites in turn would give a tithe of the tithe to the high priesthood. An application of the tithe of the tithe is a congregation's giving ten percent of its budget to its translocal apostolic ministry.

This apostolic ministry could be a council of cooperating pastors, a ministry led by an apostle, or an apostolic team which has involvement in the local congregation. As a congregation uses its money for pastoring and local evangelism, the tithe of a tithe can be used to promote the wider movement of which the congregation is a part. The apostolic movement can deal with issues of national and international concern to the Church and society. The apostolic tithe helps each congregation be committed to a world vision as well as to its local community.

A congregation can also budget money toward an equity fund. In ancient Israel the money brought into the Levites was not only used for their expenses but also to build up a central treasury for the temple. The congregational equity fund could be used toward the purchase of land, a building fund or a savings account. If a congregation will develop a habit of putting money toward savings, it will not find itself under such financial pressure at times that major expenditures are to be made. We should set aside small amounts on a regular basis toward a build up of savings that can be used in the future.

I Corinthians 16:2 states:

On the first day of the week let each one of you lay something aside, storing up as he may prosper that there may be no collections when I come.

In this case the planned saving was for a donation to the apostolic ministry.

Free Loans for Rehabilitation

Another possible area of budgeting is the establishing of a fund to lend money interest-free to members of the congregation who have fallen into need. **Leviticus 25:35** states:

If one of your brethren becomes poor, and falls into poverty among you, then you shall help him, like a stranger or a sojourner, that he may live with you. Take no usury or interest from him; but fear your God that your brother may live with you. You shall not lend him money for usury nor lend him your food at a profit.

It is an act of kindness to refrain from charging interest to a covenant brother; it is an act of prudence to give the money as a loan instead of an outright gift. In this way we can help our brothers who are in need without encouraging a cycle of welfare dependence.

Money can be made available through interest-free loans under the auspices of the congregation to be administered by the deacons. Individuals within the congregation may give free-will gifts to a needy person that are not on a loan basis at all. Money from the general budget can be dispersed on a free-loan basis unless there is a discernment from God to make it a donation.

Since this money is given on a no interest basis, it does not place an oppressive burden upon the person in need. Since it is lent, it allows the person the opportunity to pay the money back and free himself from dependence on others. The fact that it is a loan communicates the attitude that the person is to get himself back on his own feet in a productive earning cycle. Giving the money as a loan also prevents other people in the congregation from becoming jealous.

Free loans to persons with the capability to earn money does not invalidate the free gifts of charity to those who are unable to pay back. The congregation should feel free to give money however the Lord leads. There are many opportunities to give to the poor and needy, and widows and orphans. Discernment should be exercised as to the true level of need involved. For example, **I Timothy 5:3** and **9** state:

Honor widows who are really widows. Do not let a widow under sixty years old be taken into the number.

The family has the first priority to care for the widows and orphans. If someone really has been abandoned and is unable to care for himself and is sincerely committed to the Lord, he can be taken under direct care of the community. Usually, however, the church must defer the matter to the private family. **I Timothy 5:4-5** states:

> **If any widow has children or grandchildren, let them first learn to show piety at home and repay their parents. Now she who is really a widow, and left alone, trusts in God....**

The congregation must be prepared to face the broad issue of benevolence to the poor with both generosity and prudence.

There must be guidelines to determine whether a person is eligible. There must be full financial disclosure from the person before any money is lent or given. Sometimes it is not proper to lend or give a person money. If the person refuses to work, or refuses to be reconciled to his natural family, or refuses to let go of some area of unrepented sin, the lending or giving of money would be spiritually detrimental. On the other hand, there might sweep across the hearts of the congregation the desire to give the person the money simply as an act of mercy. If a person is a full covenant member, he should be eligible for a no-interest loan. The terms would be determined on a case-by-case basis.

Children's Education

Another major area of budgeting is children's education. As the rearing of children is the responsibility of individual parents, parents have to pay for the children's Christian education on a private offering basis. On the other hand, one of the functions of the Levites was to teach biblical principles to the community at large. To the degree that the Levites and the community of faith have a responsibility to give the children a biblical education, so should that portion of a Christian day school be paid for out of the tithes of the community.

Since both of these contrasting principles apply to the situation, the appropriate action might be to share the costs of a biblical day school between the tithes of the general community and the additional offerings of the individual parents. In this way the community at large takes up its responsibility to educate the next generation according to biblical principles, and the parents take up their individual responsibility to see that their own children are educated.

The cost of biblical education should not be underestimated. The needs for teaching staff, administration, classroom facilities, and operational overhead are quite expensive. Item for item they are more expensive than the equivalent needs for the congregation in worship and preaching. We need to prepare ourselves for the investment in the education of our children and teenagers. A biblically-based day school or high school is a major undertaking.

Local Evangelism

Funds should also be designated in the budget for the costs of local evangelism and outreach publicity. The money given to the translocal evangelists or the apostolic team does not replace the need for systematic saturation of the local community with gospel invitations. There may be a tendency for the pastoral staff to put more of an emphasis on the inside needs of the community.

Designating money in the budget toward local evangelism will express the priority of outreach and witnessing. Local evangelism is more of a priority than foreign missions. Jesus said in **Acts 1:8:**

You shall be witnesses to Me in Jerusalem, and in all Judaea and Samaria, and to the end of the earth.

The congregation should start with local evangelism and continue to expand its program until it reaches far flung areas. The distant missions are an extension of the commitment to local evangelism. Avoiding responsibility to evangelize those around us cannot be justified by sending money off to a stranger on a foreign missions field.

If the community emphasizes local evangelism, certain members will emerge as having a special gifting in witnessing. If they have been anointed of God, the congregation may want to invest money to back them in a missionary project to distant places. Missions are an extension and outgrowth of commitment to a program of effective evangelism in the local community. If a person does not show himself zealous and effective for evangelism locally, it does not make any sense to pay money to send him off to a distant place.

A congregation can raise up and equip evangelists to be sent out, rather than sending off money to foreign missionaries who are not related to the congregation. We invest our money in outreach as we can confirm the evangelistic anointing of the one being sent out. If one is being sent out as an evangelist, it should be discerned and proven that he can bear fruit in witnessing and bringing others to salvation.

There has been some debate as to whether an individual's tithe should go completely to his local congregation or be dispersed among different ministries. The root of the problem is that outreach ministries were never meant to be separated from local congregations. Paul's ministry was an apostolic outreach but he was covenantally connected to the congregations in Antioch, Rome, Ephesus, Philippi and Corinth.

If outreach ministers would keep their ministries under the cover of a congregational base, and if the local congregations would make the commitment to support financially the ministries they are backing, there would be no disagreement. An individual could give his tithe to his local congregation, and part of that money would be used to support the outreach ministries that the congregation is a covenant partner with.

As much money as possible should be budgeted for the hiring of more pastoral and evangelistic staff members. These people will be able to nurture the present flock and reach out to draw new people in. As these new people are brought in, the financial base of the congregation will grow.

If the congregation spends too much in the early stages in operational costs, buildings and equipment, it may overtax its small membership and drain their resources. If the members become spiritually drained as well as financially, the numbers in the congregation will dwindle as well. The overall growth of the community will be slow, and finances will be pressured. The emphasis must be on pastoral care and outreach. This priority should be reflected in the budget by hiring the people to do these tasks. Operational overhead should only be added as the growth of the community warrants it.

Administrative Expenses

Often a good secretary or an administrative staff person will be a better investment than a second minister. An efficient administrator or secretary may help make the pastoral staff and the volunteers of the congregation more efficient. Adding on a high paid minister when what is really needed is an aid to take care of the pile up of administrative chores would be a waste of money. Hiring an administrative person can free the minister into more direct pastoring and evangelizing.

A pastor needs to go to various conferences during the year. The costs of transportation, food and hotels for such conferences can be surprisingly high. The elders should determine with the pastor ahead of time which conferences are a priority and budget the money necessary to send him there. It is important for the pastor to attend these larger conferences to keep in touch with what is going on in the larger Body of believers. The choice of conferences should be discerned beforehand and given appropriate budgetary space.

There are also certain projects that a group of congregations locally need to support together. Pregnancy aid centers, abortion protests, social impact groups, Christian legal services, an area-wide Christian high school, missions to the poor and so on are particularly suited for cooperation between several congregations. An individual congregation is not likely to take on by itself a social issue that affects all of the churches. It is worthwhile to set aside money in the budget to support such issues and projects.

Faith for Finances

A challenge facing almost all ministries is the need for financial provision. We need to have major breakthroughs in faith to believe for large sums to finance the kingdom of God. Once we have set our house in order by arranging proper financial accountability, we can call our congregants to get serious about giving. For most ministries, the bottom line is money.

A feast is made for laughter, and wine makes merry; but money answers everything (Ecclesiastes 10:19).

When it comes to the practical ability to expand the operations of a ministry, it does seem that money answers almost everything. The reason that the Body of believers has been weak in the area of finances is that we have not sought the Lord sufficiently for wisdom about the nature of financial flow. The Bible has much to say about economics and prosperity. If we give enough prayerful attention to gaining revelation and anointing in God's financial provision, our ministries will be much more effective. If we continue to avoid divine wisdom about finances, we will always be hampered by lack of faith in this area. The silver and gold of this world should be used for the financing of the kingdom and the preaching of the gospel. **Deuteronomy 8:18** states:

It is He [God] who gives you power to get wealth that He may establish His covenant...

In times of revival, there is on outpouring of funds to give freedom for the ministry to move. **Ezra 1:6** states:

Those who were around them encouraged them with silver and gold, with goods and livestock, and with precious things, besides all that was offered willingly.

At the time of the return of the remnant to Israel, the hearts of the people were stirred with generosity.

II Kings 12:15 states:

They [the people at the time of Jehoash] did not require an account from the men into whose hand they delivered the money to be paid to workmen, for they dealt faithfully.

At the time of the restoration of the temple under Jehoash, more than enough money came in to finance the entire work. Trust, generosity and enthusiasm were running so high that no accountability at all was asked for the finances. Financial accountability is a facet of covenantal law keeping. Whenever there is a flood of revival, there will be no need for accountability.

II Kings 22:7 records a similar revival under King Josiah and Hilkiah the High Priest. Again more than enough money came into fund the ministry, and no accountability was needed. Actually, the accountability was there in the form of the extraordinary faithfulness among the people. In Acts 2:45 and Acts 4:34, large sums of money from the sale of houses, land, and possessions were simply laid at the apostles feet with no accountability asked for. At times of such outpourings of grace, the moral standards will be so high that integrity will be assumed.

Ideally, we should be in the middle of a wave of revival at all times. There is a balance between the law of financial accountability and the grace of freewill offering. The same integrity to institute procedures of financial accountability is that which is also worthy to be trusted when accountability is not needed. Covenant integrity demands trustworthiness of conscience on the part of each individual. Covenantal integrity also demands standards of financial accountability to those on the outside.

May God grant us the wisdom to walk in this balance of law and grace. A covenant person is committed to have the order of the finances of the ministry reflect his own convictions of integrity.

34

TRIBAL COVENANT: A CASE OF CORPORATE JUDICIAL ACTION

Covenantal integrity demands moral accountability on all levels: between individuals, in the family, in congregational government and in financial accountability for ministries. Occasionally a judicial confrontation arises between whole congregations or within a national movement. Entire congregations have fallen into doctrinal error and immorality. Sometimes a division splits a national movement in two.

Those are some of the most trying times for believers. History has shown how harmful these controversies can be. If foundational and irreconcilable errors occur in a large group, there must be divisions so that the righteous remnant may survive. **I Corinthians 11:18-19** states:

> **I hear that there are divisions among you, and in part I believe it. For there must also be factions among you, that those who are approved may be recognized among you.**

National Controversies

In ancient Israel there were times when whole tribes had major controversies with one another. There were even splits in the national kingdom when it was necessary for God's kingdom to flourish in the separate sections. Passages about tribal controversies contain biblical principles on how to handle major judicial confrontations within large sectors of the Body of believers.

Judges 20 involves a case where corporate judicial action was taken by all the other tribes against the tribe of Benjamin. An issue of moral accountability became so intense that they actually had to go to war over it. A criminal act of gang rape, homosexual attack, and murder had been committed against a citizen of the tribe of Ephraim by citizens of the town of Gibeah in Benjamin.

The man from Ephraim sent notice of the criminal action of the Benjamites to all the other tribes. He called them to preserve covenantal integrity in the nation of Israel and to handle the matter with corporate judicial process. **Judges 19:30** states:

> **No such deed has been done or seen from the day that the children of Israel came up from the land of Egypt until this day. Consider it, take counsel, and speak up!**

All of the tribes knew they had a moral responsibility to deal with this problem. They could not avoid it; the very integrity of the nation was at stake.

No one tribe wanted to deal with this matter alone. It was a matter for them as a nation of tribes together.

All of the children of Israel came out from Dan to Beersheba, and the congregation gathered together as one before the Lord at Mizpah (Judges 20:1).

Occasionally, an issue of immorality involves a major ministry leader. No one congregation will desire or be able to address the problem. What needs to happen is for the leaders of several congregations to band together to seek covenant reconciliation. Most congregational leaders avoid dealing with such a problem. They lack understanding of the biblical process of covenantal confrontation. If congregational leaders in an area had the working cooperation to deal with a matter of gross immorality, there would be much less immorality going on. Corporate accountability helps to prevent major wrongdoing.

The leaders of all the people, all the tribes of Israel, presented themselves in the assembly of the people of God (Judges 20:2).

The burden of responsibility lies with the representative leaders of each tribe or congregation. Pastors in a local area need to have the ability to gather together in prayer when there are major difficulties affecting the Body of believers as a whole.

Right Judicial Order

The first step of corporate judicial action is to make a thorough inquiry of the facts. **Judges 20:3** states:

Then the children of Israel said, "Tell us, how did this wicked deed happen?"

It is prudent to collect as much factual information as possible before a step of confrontation is made.

Because the matter involved an entire town, as well as members of two different tribes, there was no other recourse but to appeal the case to an intertribe council. The man submitted the decision to the board of tribal leaders. **Judges 20:7** states:

Look! All of you are children of Israel; give your advice and counsel here and now!

In American jurisprudence, a case involving two different states must be handled by a federal court. An interstate matter must be handled by an interstate level of authority. An intercongregational matter must be handled by an intercongregational board. If an entire congregation falls into error or if there is a division between two pastors, the situation must be appealed to a cross section of area-wide leaders.

When Paul's case about his disagreement with the Sanhedrin came up, he appealed to take the case to the highest court available, which was an audience with the emperor himself (Acts 25:10). This appeal was done on the basis of his being a Roman citizen from the separate territory of Tarsus. Since it was a matter involving two different territories, it could be appealed to a federal court.

Cooperation for Restoration

The intertribe council was not seeking so much to punish or condemn the offending tribe, as they were to make restitution for what had gone wrong. Biblical justice is done for the motive of restoring wholeness and integrity for the good of the greater community. **Judges 20:10** states:

That when they come to Gibeah in Benjamin, they may repay all the vileness that they have done in Israel.

If a group of pastors or apostles were to meet together to help adjudicate an intercongregational matter, their purpose would not be to point the finger at the guilty party, but to bring restitution and restoration to the greater Body of Christ. Their desire would be the health of the area-wide community of faith.

The leaders who would be willing to be involved in a covenantal judicial action might be accused of being divisive and judgmental. This is not true. The ones who are willing to be involved are courageous enough and care enough to take time out of their own schedules and risk their reputations in an unselfish effort to help the rest of the Body of believers. Abstaining leaders might say that they felt it would be a diversion from the ministry to be involved in such a matter. This also is not so. One of the duties of being a pastor is to offer authoritative counsel when there is controversy or dispute in the Body of believers.

Nehemiah refused to interrupt building the wall of Jerusalem to discuss the dispute with Sanballat and Tobiah:

I am doing a great work, so that I cannot come down. Why should the work cease while I leave it and go down to you (Nehemiah 6:3)?

Sanballat and Tobiah, however, were enemies of the kingdom of God. Their appeal to Nehemiah was a purposeful conspiracy to divert him and kill him. In dealing with other congregational leaders, we are not being diverted by an enemy; we are seeking to resolve a matter between members of tribes of the same nation.

There is a difference between forgiveness and restitution. In the Body of believers, forgiveness comes instantly whenever there is repentance. If, however, a previous sin has resulted in an ongoing injustice, those inequitable elements must be resolved. We can not proceed as a worshiping community if there are areas that lack restitution. Jesus said in **Matthew 5:23-24:**

If you bring your gift [worship] to the altar and there remember that your brother has something against you, leave your gift there before the altar, and go your way. First be reconciled to your brother, and then come and offer your gift.

Forgiveness of heart here is not the issue. Reconciliation and restitution with the offended party must be effected before worshipful communion with God can continue. We are given the mandate by Scriptures to interrupt our divine offering to ensure that an interpersonal offense is repaid.

It is important that an intercongregational matter be dealt with by united action; otherwise, even more division might occur. **Judges 20:11** states:

So all the men of Israel gathered against the city, united together as one man.

The unity of the other tribes in their commitment to judicial process created a covenantal base in which an eventual solution could result. When there is united action, attention can be focused on the real issues of the moral problem and the need for spiritual reconciliation. If there is not united action, attention may be diverted to interpreting the problem as a personality clash or a difference in style. United action keeps the covenantal process focused on the objective issues.

The first step in approaching the offending tribe was to ask for a full disclosure of what had happened.

Then the tribes of Israel sent men through all the tribe of Benjamin, saying, "What is this wickedness that has occurred among you" (Judges 20:12)?

Asking for disclosure of information allows for the other party to present its side of the story and any information that was not brought to light in the previous testimonies. Since we are interested in truth, information gathering is an essential part of covenantal process. Bringing facts to light generates much of the justice itself. **Ephesians 5:13** states:

All things that are exposed are made manifest by the light, for whatever makes manifest is light.

Bringing truth to light is part of spiritual justice. God is a God of light and truth.

Covenantal process is not vindictive; it does not seek to hurt anyone or to implicate those who are not involved. It does seek, however, to remove unrepentant men from the midst of the community of faith.

Now therefore, deliver up the men, the perverted men who were in Gibeah that we may put them to death and remove the evil from Israel (Judges 20:13).

In ancient Israel, legal and spiritual authority were combined. They would remove someone from the community by stoning him. In the Body of believers, we remove someone by having them leave the fellowship. The point here is not the death sentence. The intertribal council was not seeking vengeance on the entire tribe of Benjamin, but only to bring justice to the particular parties who had committed the crime. They wanted to eliminate the perverted people whose presence represented a cancer that might have eventually ruined the moral fiber of the entire nation. They were working toward righteousness, not condemnation. Justice works toward preservation of the greater good. Exercising justice is not being judgmental.

Had the tribe of Benjamin submitted to the intertribal council, righteousness could have been restored with relatively little harm to the nation as a whole.

Because the tribe of Benjamin refused to submit to corporate discipline, it escalated the problem to the stage where it injured thousands of innocent lives. **Judges 20:13** states:

> **But the children of Benjamin would not listen to the voice of their brethren, the children of Israel.**

When a group denies all covenantal jurisdiction, they have escalated what might have been an easily resolved problem. The nature of the problem has completely changed at this moment. The issue is no longer the original sexual abuse by the hoodlums of Gibeah, but rather the refusal of the leadership of an entire tribe to yield to the authority of the gathered translocal leaders. No group, no matter how large, and no person, no matter how important, has the right to deny all moral accountability from an appropriate body. To say that one has gotten beyond the point where any other group could adjudicate a matter towards him is a breakdown in covenantal foundations.

Divine Calling

There are times when a man receives such a sovereign call upon his life that even if a council of highly authoritative leaders were to tell him to cease his activities, he would have to obey his conscience and override their decision. Peter, James and John, for instance, did not stop preaching when told to do so by the Sanhedrin. Paul said that he received a command by God through revelation to preach the gospel to the Gentiles. He could not change that mandate even had the apostles directed him not to preach to the Gentiles. **Galatians 2:2, 5** and **6** state:

> **I went up by revelation, and communicated to them [the apostles] that gospel which I preach among the Gentiles, but privately to those of reputation, lest by any means I might run, or had run, in vain...to whom [false brethren] we did not yield submission even for an hour, that the truth of the gospel might continue with you. But from those who seemed to be something— whatever they were, it makes no difference to me—for those who seemed to be something added nothing to me.**

Paul, Peter, James and John were happy to bring their revelation before any authority or any group of people. If someone really has a call from God, he will look forward to making a full disclosure and full explanation whenever possible. If, after a person has made a full disclosure of his position, he has still the conviction in his conscience that he must not defer to his covenant brothers, he should go ahead and do what he believes to be right. If he is working for righteousness, he will be ever willing to make the facts of his position known. If a person or group is not willing to meet with covenant brothers and disclose all the information, they have sinned by rejecting covenantal process.

Refusing to be diverted from one's divine calling is not the same as refusing to talk with covenant brothers about alleged wrongdoing. No one pretends to be sitting in judgment over the direction of someone else's ministry. For instance, disagreement over the ministry of healing is not the same thing as an accusation of sexual misconduct. Every man can obey his own calling according to his own conscience. On the other hand, we are held responsible as covenant brothers to hold one another morally accountable, even if the other party is a nationally famous figure, and even if it deals with an entire congregation. Denying corporate judicial action by refusing to submit even to dialogue with covenant brothers is to reject God's own authority.

Difficulties in Dealing with the Issue

If controversy reaches such a broad scope of people, dealing with the matter is not likely to be comfortable. Times of controversy require in-depth prayer intercession. We must seek the counsel of God. **Judges 20:18** states:

And the children of Israel arose and went up to the house of God to ask counsel of God.

No one seeks to impose his own will on dangerous and difficult disputes. Everyone needs to put aside his own preconceived opinions and seek the Lord for righteousness. We need to seek the Lord not only about what is the right outcome, but how to go about approaching the problem to resolve it.

The cost of dealing with a major dispute will seem more than is worthwhile. Suffering is encountered when one stands up for principles of covenant righteousness. **Judges 20:21** states:

The children of Benjamin came out of Gibeah, and on that day cut down to the ground twenty-two thousand men of the Israelites.

When a controversy reaches translocal proportions, it is too late to be dealt with without pain and loss to those involved. Had the matter been handled earlier the cost would have been less. If the matter is dealt with in a later stage, the procedure will be more costly, but the movement still will be salvaged. If the controversy is not dealt with even at the later stages, the whole movement can be lost.

National ministries can be destroyed if issues of covenant reconciliation are not resolved. There are precedents in history where a national revival has lost its momentum because covenant standards were not maintained. We are on the verge of the greatest worldwide revival in history. If we can understand these principles of corporate judicial action, we will cause a breakthrough in the spiritual realm. Evil principalities will be torn down, and the power of righteousness will be released.

Covenantal process requires courage, consecration, and perseverance.

And the men of Israel encouraged themselves and again formed the battle line. Then the children of Israel went up and wept before the Lord and asked counsel of the Lord (Judges 20:22-23).

Revival on a national level will occur when the people of God are struck with a zeal to intercede before God that unrighteousness be removed. A spirit of repentance and dedication can sweep across the world of believers as it did in the church in Corinth (**II Corinthians 7:11**):

What diligence it produced in you, what clearing of yourselves, what indigna-tion, what fear, what vehement desire, what zeal, what vindication! In all things you proved yourselves to be clear in this matter.

The context of II Corinthians 7 is that the people were called to have the courage to stand up for corporate discipline in their church. What a wave and move of God's Spirit is at hand for us as we learn covenantal principles!

Attitude of Reconciliation

The only proper motivation for dealing with confrontation of such magnitude is a love for the Body of Christ at large. One must be moved by a desire to see the full restoration of the true Church of God. One must be grieved from deep within for any area that is missing from the worldwide Body of believers. **Judges 21:6** states:

And the children of Israel grieved for Benjamin their brother, and said, "One tribe is cut off from Israel today."

Our only desire from beginning to end is reconciliation. We want to heal the gaps and breaches, not create new ones. It is our love for the Body of believers that drives us to deal with covenantal process. Every shred of self-righteousness must be gone. We must weep at the loss that other brothers might incur. We must be grieved when any other part of the Body of believers is hurt.

Reconciliation creates peace between two parts of the Body of believers. In every aspect of the judicial process, we speak an invitation of peace to the other party. **Judges 21:13** states:

Then the whole congregation sent word to the children of Benjamin and announced peace to them.

We must constantly reaffirm our love for the other brothers during the dialogue. We must state openly that we seek restoration of relationships.

In an attempt to resolve conflict, we should extend ourselves in extra measures of affirmation toward the other party. We can make exceptions to our rules when necessary, in an effort to be kind to them. **Judges 21:22** states:

Be kind to them [the people of Benjamin] for our sakes, because we did not take a wife for any of them in the war.

If there is any way we can help people with their personal problems or family needs, we should do so. The covenantal process of God is filled with grace from first to last.

We seek not to tear down someone else's ministry, but to build it up. If loss has been incurred through the covenant process, it should be our desire to seek the speedy rebuilding of the previous ministry.

Then they [the people of Benjamin] went and returned to their inheritance, and they rebuilt the cities and dwelt in them (Judges 21:23).

Every ministry has a spiritual inheritance from God. If a brother has gotten off the track, we seek to restore him to his original calling. The more a brother enters into the full success of his ministry, the more we are delighted.

A major judicial action can take years to complete. It feels exhausting and seems as if there is no end to it. That is not true. Happy endings are designed by God. Major controversies can be reconciled after years of maintaining a covenant attitude. God gave us the process of covenant; we must believe that it will work. Eventual restoration is possible for everyone involved. **Judges 21:24** states:

> **So the children of Israel departed from there at that time, every man to his tribe and family; they went out from there, every man to his inheritance.**

There was a sense of covenantal kinship that existed between the tribes in ancient Israel. They saw themselves as linked with one another in bonds of blood and water, family and faith. God would instill in us today an inner sense of spiritual kinship and tribal loyalty.

35

TRIBAL LOYALTY

Some of the passages of Scriptures most difficult for the modern mind to fathom are those dealing with ancient tribal loyalty. If we miss the underlying theme of blood covenant between the tribes, the revelation of the passages will elude us. Many people would see the controversy between the Israelite tribes and the Benjamites to have been a case of heathenish civil war and internecine strife. The commitment of the leaders of Israel to establish restoration of covenant between the tribes is the very purpose of the passage.

The theme in the Old Testament of blood sacrifices for atonement has to do with the meaning of salvation in the death and resurrection of Jesus. The theme in the Old Testament of tribal blood covenants has to do with the full restoration of the Church as the bride of Messiah. The tribal covenants of ancient Israel lead symbolically to the full restoration of the Body of believers. The restoration of Israel runs parallel to the restoration of the Church. They are knit together as body and soul. Let us examine a few examples that show us how to interpret the Old Testament in terms of covenant and make applications to our lives today.

Abraham Rescues Lot

In Genesis 14, four kings from the Middle Eastern nations attack the area of Sodom and Gomorrah. In their attack, they carry off Abram's nephew Lot and all his possessions. When Abram hears that his nephew has been captured, he marshals his personal family militia to pursue the forces of the four kings. He routs them and wins back Lot and all the possessions of Lot's family. **Genesis 14:16** states:

So he [Abram] brought back all the goods and also brought back his brother Lot and his goods as well as the women and the people.

Abram risked this commando mission because his nephew, Lot, was in a position of tribal kinship to him. Abram had blood-covenantal responsibility to rescue him.

The Dinah Incident

In Genesis 34, Shechem, the prince of the neighboring Hivite tribe, falls in love with Dinah, Jacob's only daughter. Shechem sleeps with Dinah and comes to Jacob and the brothers to seek permission to marry her. The brothers plan a deception against Shechem and his people. The brothers tell them that they will allow Shechem to marry Dinah if the men of the tribe would be willing to be circumcised.

After the men are circumcised, while they are still incapacitated, the brothers attack the tribe, kill all the men, take their wealth, and return with Dinah. When Jacob hears what his sons have done, he is shocked. They have lied and stolen and murdered. When Jacob confronts them on this incident, they answer him in **Genesis 34:31**:

Should he [Shechem] treat our sister like a harlot?

To this remark, Jacob has no answer. In effect, they have said that they have a tribal, blood covenantal loyalty toward their sister Dinah. They have to defend the honor of their tribal loyalty. When Shechem slept with Dinah, he violated the basis of tribal loyalty that consumed their world view. The fact that Shechem loved her or that Dinah was willing to marry him could not undo this sense that the tribal blood loyalty had been violated. From their point of view, the honor of their tribal covenant was more important than the fact that they had deceived, murdered, and plundered the Shechemites.

The point of the story is not to excuse the actions of the sons of Jacob, but neither is it to demonstrate how vengeful and mean they were. The Bible is a book of covenant; the purpose of Genesis 34 is to underscore the fact that in the world view of the ancient tribes of Israel, the only issue of moral significance was keeping a blood covenant from being violated. Every act was seen as righteous or unrighteous only in relationship to loyalty to the covenant.

Judah and Tamar

In **Genesis 38**, Judah's widowed daughter-in-law Tamar asks him to find her a new husband. When Judah fails to do so, Tamar disguises herself as a prostitute, deceives Judah into sleeping with her, and becomes pregnant from the incident. Judah was completely unwitting to her ploy. When Judah finds out that Tamar is pregnant, he assumes that she has committed immorality and is about to have her executed. At that moment she indicates to Judah that it was he who fathered the child. As Judah realizes what has happened, he states in **verse 26**:

She has been more righteous than I, because I did not give to her Shelah, my son.

Tamar lied and committed immorality, yet Judah pronounces her to be righteous. Righteousness is only determined in relationship to loyalty to tribal covenant. Judah had a previous covenantal responsibility toward Tamar to find her a husband. He had a responsibility to the tribe as a whole to ensure that every healthy young woman would bear children to preserve the family line and continue the population of the tribe. Judah had violated his covenantal responsibility. Tamar called him back to loyalty to the tribe. Her deception was excused from the perspective of blood covenant.

Trans-Jordan Tribes

In **Numbers 32,** the tribes of Gad and Reuben appeal to Moses to let them settle on the east side of the Jordan without crossing over with the other tribes to the land of Canaan. Moses reacts in great indignation and accuses them of being sinful men and committing a heinous crime. What could be so terrible about settling peacefully on the east side of the Jordan? The crime is that the other tribes were about to go forward to face warfare in the land of Canaan. The tribes of Gad and Reuben owed them the covenantal loyalty to fight with them, even if they were not planning to inherit the land in that area.

The Gadites and Reubenites respond to Moses in **verses 17-18:**

We ourselves will be armed, ready to go before the children of Israel until we have brought them to their place; ...we will not return to our homes until every one of the children of Israel has received his inheritance.

They agree to remain loyal to their tribal covenant by crossing over the Jordan with the other tribes armed for battle. They would fight for the other tribes on behalf of their land and only return to their own homes when their tribal loyalty had been proven. When Moses hears this response, his attitude changes abruptly, and he grants them permission. The issue was not the place of settlement, nor the warfare, nor their courage. As long as they remained loyal to their covenantal responsibilities, Moses did not care where they chose to settle. If one reads Scripture with understanding, he will develop a consuming passion for covenantal loyalty.

Cities of Refuge

In Deuteronomy 19, Moses ordains that cities of refuge should be built in the promised land. In Joshua 20, Joshua sees that this plan is instituted. In the ancient world, safety was guaranteed for every person by the fact that the other members of his tribe would seek out and destroy anyone who injured one of their kinsmen. This system of vengeance was a crude but effective form of justice. The kinsman who would execute the retribution was known as the "avenger of blood." **Joshua 20:2-3** states:

Appoint for yourselves cities of refuge that the slayer who kills any person accidentally or unintentionally may flee there; and they shall be your refuge from the avenger of blood.

To guard against the imbalances of tribal vengeance, the Scriptures establish a form of judicial process in which an appeal could be made in a rudimentary courtroom. It was Scriptures that introduced the concept of equitable judicial process into a dark world filled with crime.

The avenger of blood would act out of a sense of tribal loyalty to find the manslayer and execute judgment upon him. This pursuit was seen not as a reaction of resentment, but rather one of moral responsibility. The avenger defended the honor and name of the person who was injured or slain. He was a criminal prosecutor employed by the life blood of the victim. He came with justice to punish wrongdoing.

The community set up these refuge cities as a covenantal protection for a possibly innocent defendant. Both the avenger of blood and the judges in the city were exercising tribal loyalty. Between the balance of the prosecuting attorney and the defending attorney as it were, covenantal justice would prevail. Only in a nation where tribal loyalty was intense would there have been such an institution as the cities of refuge. The Bible was written out of a society in which an avenger of tribal blood was a matter of common sense.

Jesus was acting out of tribal blood kinship when He offered His life on the cross for us. How does the perspective of blood loyalty, especially in the light of the blood of Jesus, alter our relationships with one another? We need to stretch our minds to grasp that ancient world view of covenant.

Rahab's Covenant

Tribal loyalty was based not only on family descent, but also on contract. Therefore, a person outside the family could enter the kinship of the tribe if special arrangements were made. In **Joshua 2**, the prostitute Rahab protects the two spies of Israel from the hands of her countrymen. She believes that the Israelites are about to conquer and destroy the city. She asks the two spies to make a covenant with her. She will protect them now, if they will protect them later. The spies make a covenant with her that they will trade their lives for the lives of Rahab and her family. This joining together for mutual protection is covenant. In **verse 14** the two spies say:

Our lives for yours, if none of you tell this business of ours. And it shall be when the Lord has given us the land, that we deal kindly and truly with you.

When the spies named their lives to be equal to the lives of Rahab and her family, they made covenant with her. Before departing, they sealed their covenantal agreement with an oath.

After the army under Joshua fulfilled its covenantal obligation by rescuing Rahab, she entered into further covenant with the tribes of Israel and dwelled with them as part of the covenant assembly. **Joshua 6:25** states:

And Joshua spared Rahab the harlot, her father's household, and all that she had. So she dwells in Israel to this day, because she hid the messengers whom Joshua had sent to spy out Jericho.

Her verbal covenant with Israel brought her an equal standing as any tribesman. She became an ancestor to King David and, therefore, even to Jesus Himself. Covenant is more a matter of loyalty than of physical parentage.

The Gibeonite Treaty

After the conquests of Jericho and Ai, a town called Gibeon lay not too far in front of the armies of Joshua. The people of Gibeon feared that they would be slaughtered. They knew that Joshua and the people of Israel were strong and loyal to their covenants. They knew if they could get the Israelites to make a covenant with them, even if by deception, that the Israelites would not violate that covenant. Therefore, the Gibeonites disguise themselves and pretend to be travelers from a distant country. They deceive Joshua into making a covenant with them and secure his promise not to harm them.

When Joshua finally realizes the deception, he knows that he cannot go back on the word of his promise to them. Had Joshua prayed to God before entering the covenant, the Lord would have told him that the people were deceivers. **Joshua 9:18-20** states:

> **The children of Israel did not attack them [the Gibeonites], because the rulers of the congregation had sworn to them by the Lord God of Israel. And all of the congregation murmured against the rulers. Then all the rulers said to all the congregation, "We have sworn to them by the Lord God of Israel; now therefore, we may not touch them. This we will do to them: we will let them live, lest wrath be upon us because of the oath we swore to them."**

Everything in the world revolved around keeping covenant for the tribes of Israel. Military strategy, settlement in the land, and sexual morality were all dependent upon loyalty to the blood covenant.

Years later there was a famine in the land of Israel under King David, and he asks the Lord why the nation is not being blessed. These same Gibeonites had been dwelling in the land all this time. During the reign of King Saul, Saul tried to kill the Gibeonites. Saul's actions amounted to a violation of the covenant between Israel and Gibeon, as established by Joshua. There was famine in the land because this violation of the covenant had not been rectified. Even though the covenant had been made years before under Joshua, and even though Saul, the man who violated the covenant was no longer alive, the spiritual results of the violation of that covenant were still in effect. The famine would stay until David took measures to rectify the previous violations of the Gibeonite covenant.

David goes to the Gibeonites and says:

> **What shall I do for you? And with what shall I make atonement, that you may bless the inheritance of the Lord (II Samuel 21:3)?**

David is at the mercy of the Gibeonites to set the terms for the reconciliation under covenant. David knows that he must reestablish covenantal loyalty with the Gibeonites at all costs. The Gibeonites propose to have seven men of the descendants of Saul executed. David says to them in **verse 4:**

> **Whatever you say, that will I do.**

No price could be too high. The only priority was to reestablish the covenant. When David turns over seven of Saul's descendants, he exempts Mephibosheth, the son of Jonathan, because of his previous covenant with Jonathan. He does not want to violate one covenant for the sake of another.

David's Loyalty

King David was a man who deeply understood covenantal loyalty. During the time that Saul was seeking to take David's life, David fled for refuge to King Achish of Gath and became a general in the Philistine army. Since the Philistines were at war with the Israelites, it was David's job to attack the Israelites. David obviously had a problem of split loyalties. David developed a plan in which he would divert the army division under him to raid the Amalekites. The Amalekites were one of the nations that God had told Moses to destroy.

David's policy was to kill every man, woman and child so that no one could escape to inform on him and bring a contradicting report. **I Samuel 27:10** states:

> **Then Achish would say, "Where have you made a way today?" And David would say, "Against the southern area of Judah...or the Jerahmeelites, or of the Kenites."**

David could not break his tribal loyalty with his people. He carried out raids well enough for King Achish, but he redirected them into a different area. Achish felt sure that the Israelites by now must have considered David to be an utter traitor. **I Samuel 27:12** indicates Achish's belief that David had:

> **made his people utterly abhor him; therefore he will be my servant forever.**

The lines of tribal loyalty are drawn deep.

The other generals of the Philistine army were not quite so convinced of David's conversion. When the time came for a mass attack by the Philistines on the Israelites at Jezreel, the other Philistine leaders demand that David leave the scene of the battle lest he remember his loyalty to his own people and betray them in the midst of the fighting. When David insists on his loyalty to Achish, Achish assures him of his personal trust. In **I Samuel 29:6**, Achish says to David:

> **Surely, as the Lord lives, you have been upright, and your going out and your coming in with me in the army is good in my sight. For to this day I have not found evil in you since the day of your coming to me. Nevertheless, the lords do not favor you.**

The counsel of the Philistine generals prevails, and David is sent away. They knew well enough how loyal David must have been in his heart to his own tribesmen. They reasoned that his military allegiance to them could not have been as strong as his blood-covenantal kinship with his own people.

On returning to Ziklag, the Philistine town where he and his men had been living, David found that the town had been raided and their wives and families captured. After some turmoil and prayer, David takes off with his men to rescue their families. This covenant rescue mission was successful, much in the way that

Abram's pursuit of the Middle Eastern kings was able to rescue Lot and his family. **I Samuel 30:18** states:

> **David recovered all that the Amalekites had carried away, and David rescued his two wives and nothing of theirs was lacking, either small or great, sons or daughters, spoil or anything which they had taken from them; David recovered all.**

Spiritual Warfare and Covenant Loyalty

Maintaining covenant loyalty to his tribe, to his family, and to his employer was a full-time occupation for David in the midst of such ongoing warfare. In the midst of the spiritual warfare of the kingdom of God, much of our efforts are directed toward maintaining covenantal relationships with our family, congregation and friends. It seems that every act of life is a step of preserving covenantal integrity. We bolster our relationships here; we fortify our integrity there. We prove our loyalty in one place, and we exercise our covenant in another.

As the Philistine forces defeat the Israelites, and the kingdom of Saul is destroyed, David is made ready to return to Judah to lead the country. David learns of the demise of Saul and Jonathan in a report from a young Amalekite refugee. Knowing of the war between Saul and David, the Amalekite boy feels sure that David will be happy to hear of Saul's death.

The Amalekite does not understand David's sense of covenantal commitment to whoever was the ordained king of Israel and also to his covenant partner Jonathan. Even though there had been enmity between Saul and David, David was completely loyal to him and only wished for his welfare. David is shocked that the Amalekite could think that the death of Saul and Jonathan would be a favorable report to him. After weeping, mourning and fasting, David commands for the Amalekite to be executed. **II Samuel 1:14** quotes David:

> **How was it that you were not afraid to put forth your hand to destroy the Lord's anointed?**

Abner's Leadership

One last example, that of Abner, should suffice to demonstrate the dynamics of tribal loyalty. We should learn from these examples how important it is that we be loyal to one another. We need to overcome differences of doctrine and seemingly opposing directions of ministry. Abner had a particular challenge in that he was a man of great integrity, but also the commander of the opposing army. We can learn from his good intentions, and also from his mistakes, how leaders should covenant together to form united authority within the kingdom of God.

The forces of David were now warring with the forces of Saul, and Abner was the commander of the remnant of Saul's forces. Ishbosheth, one of Saul's sons, is made king of the northern tribes in place of Saul. Although Ishbosheth is a man of low character, Abner continues to lead his army with faithfulness. **II Samuel 3:6** states:

> **While there was war between the house of Saul and the house of David, Abner was strengthening his hold on the house of Saul.**

Abner's strengthening himself means that he was solidifiying his position as the undisputed leader among the northern tribes, and also that he was working fully toward strengthening the kingdom under Ishbosheth. David appreciated Abner for being a man of such strength. If we are to be people of covenantal character, we must also be people of strength. If we are to deal with others of covenant character, particularly those who are in leadership, we must not be put off by others' strength. I enjoy seeing other men's strength of character and conviction, even when they have differences of opinion with me. Spiritual warfare for the kingdom of God can be scary at times and requires men and women of stern stuff. Covenant making is not for those who desire milk, but the solid meat of the Word of God.

Ishbosheth, even though he was king over Abner, was a man of weak moral fiber. He became jealous of Abner and sought to undermine him. Instead of talking to Abner, Ishbosheth spread a false rumor about an act of immorality on Abner's part. Political maneuvering, suspicions and negative talk that undercut a leader's honor are signs of weakness and cowardice. Honest and patient dialogue is a sign of strength.

Abner became indignant at the innuendoes and suspicions of Ishbosheth and said to him:

> **Am I a dog's head that belongs to Judah? Today I show loyalty to the house of Saul, your father, and have not delivered you into the hands of David; and you charge me today with faults concerning this woman (II Samuel 3:8)?**

Until this time Abner had been loyal to Ishbosheth. He was faithful to him as Saul's son, even though he knew that faithfulness was making him an enemy to David and the forces of Judah. Abner had continued to fight for Ishbosheth even though the tide of the war was turning against them. He had risked his life and honor for the sake of supporting the young man who, in return, did not have the character to keep from betraying him. At this point Abner decided to turn his support toward David.

In his conscience Abner knew all along that David was the better man. He was aware that David was God's choice to be the new king. Now he had the opportunity to swing his support along with what he knew God's will to be. In **II Samuel 3:9-10**, Abner says that he can now commit himself to do for David:

> **as the Lord has sworn to him, to transfer the kingdom from the house of Saul and set up the throne of David over Israel and over Judah.**

God had sworn and promised to make David king. Abner would now use his personal support to help establish that kingship. A covenant man will search his conscience to support God's will. A covenant man is willing to help establish someone else's authority.

Supporting Others' Leadership

Abner moves to establish David's throne by three actions. First, he announces his personal support for David and offers his own energies to help. Secondly, Abner goes to the other leaders who are aligned with him to communicate with them and persuade them to support David for the sake of unity. **II Samuel 3:17** states:

Now Abner had communicated with the elders of Israel, saying, "In time past you were seeking David to be king over you. Now then, do it!"

Abner uses his influence to garner support for a leader whose cause he perceives to be righteous. He appeals to the other leaders to do God's will. He persuades them not to insist upon their own separate authority, but to come over and support David. He shows them that their act of submitting to David will create a unity in the kingdom that will benefit everyone. Persuading leaders to submit one to another for the sake of unity is an act of courage and integrity. Abner knows that unified authority under David will cause great blessing to all the people. The leaders of Israel have enough character to cease this division and transfer their support to another man's leadership. Their willingness to do this brought a halt to what could have otherwise been many years of destructive civil war.

The third action that Abner takes is to gather the people together who are under his influence and sway their opinion toward supporting the plan of unity under David. **II Samuel 3:21** quotes Abner as saying to David:

I will arise and go, and gather all Israel to my lord the king, that they may make a covenant with you, and that you may reign over all that your heart desires.

Abner is a man of action; he is ready to arise and go to the people on his own initiative. Abner is a man whose heart desires unity; he gathers the people together for a common goal in the kingdom. Abner is a man of humility; he is willing to use his influence to support another man's authority. Abner is a man of moral conviction; he calls upon the people to cut a covenant of loyalty to David.

Abner wanted to give David enough support that David would feel secure to move easily as the Spirit led him. He told David that he wanted him to reign in any way that his heart desired. In this way Abner offered David a freedom of movement in his authority. Most leaders in ministry do not feel completely free to move with the authority and in the direction that God is leading them.

There is a spiritual attack of fear of man that will try to paralyze a leader's spontaneity in the Spirit. A leader will be made to feel he is being watched and judged at all times. If those around him will come and voice their unequivocal support, it will do much to help the leader fight off the paralysis that comes from fear of man. Leaders need to have their hands strengthened and their self-confidence bolstered by those around them.

> **Then Abner sent messengers on his behalf to David, saying, "Whose is the land?" saying also, "Make your covenant with me, and indeed my hand shall be with you to bring all Israel to you" (II Samuel 3:12).**

One of the most powerful actions in the kingdom of God is for leaders to covenant together to support a unified authority. Not only is Abner willing to support David, but he is willing to bring that support to covenantal commitment. He offers to cut the covenant with David. What a glorious moment! The integrity of this man has single-handedly brought unity, peace and authority to the kingdom.

David is delighted to make covenant with Abner, but he says he will do so only on one condition: that Abner bring back David's wife Michal, who was unlawfully taken away from him by King Saul. In **II Samuel 3:13**, David says to Abner:

> **Good, I will make a covenant with you. But one thing I require of you: you shall not see my face unless you bring Michal, Saul's daughter, when you come to see my face.**

Even though David wanted to make covenant with Abner, there was a moral issue left outstanding that prevented him from doing so. David felt that his scruples had been violated by the forced separation from his wife. David's integrity would not permit covenant with Abner until this moral liability had been taken care of.

Covenants must be made on the basis of moral uprightness. We cannot make covenants out of convenience no matter how much we might seem to benefit from them. If a moral issue is outstanding, covenant must wait until that issue is resolved.

II Samuel 3:18 states:

> **For the Lord has spoken of David, saying, "By the hand of My servant David, I will save My people Israel from the hand of all their enemies."**

David's authority came from God Himself. The nation knew that God's calling and anointing was upon David's life. We are not called to support man's authority, but God's authority. If we seek to support man's authority, our covenantal unity will degenerate into a form of political coalition. Man's authority leads to organizational structure that stifles spiritual life. Whenever we move to support someone in authority, we must do so with prayer and divine discernment. We are making an act of submission and support to God and God's authority through a particular man. We are not submitting to a man on his own standing.

We must ask ourselves the same question that Jesus asked of the Pharisees concerning the prophetic anointing of John the Baptist. In **Mark 11:29-30** Jesus says:

> **I will ask you one question; then answer Me, and I will tell you by what authority I do these things: the baptism of John—was it from heaven or from men? Answer Me.**

When we encounter leadership, we must ask ourselves whether the authority is coming from man or from God. Covenant making presumes that one is able to perceive the kind of anointing and authority that is divinely ordained. The success of our unity depends on our being able to see through human manipulations and to enter the flow of God's purity and authority. Political maneuvering will ruin our opportunity to yield to the grace of God.

The Joab Syndrome

Covenant making, when not understood spiritually, can be perverted into an oppressive militaristic spirit. This perversion of covenant making was demonstrated by the character of Joab. We all need to guard against the Joab syndrome. Joab was the commander-in-chief of David's army. In many ways, he was the most courageous and loyal supporter that David ever had. Joab had a marvelous extremism when it came to being committed to covenant loyalty. His problem, however, was that he allowed his radical commitment to become carnal and harsh. His loyalty had a certain overbearing, demanding nature to it that David could perceive was dangerous.

Joab was an outstanding soldier and absolutely fearless in warfare. In a battle no one could have been a better general than he. On the other hand, he lacked spiritual sensitivity and compassion. Eventually, his supposedly extreme loyalty led to treachery and rebellion.

Well-meaning believers who give themselves to a radical commitment to covenant need to guard themselves against developing a Joab spirit. There is nothing macho or domineering about covenantal courage. Covenantal character is patient, sensitive and yielding, while it maintains its firmness of conviction.

Joab missed the real issues of spirituality behind the flow of authority. He mistakenly took spiritual authority to be military and political power. He always pushed his own case and forced his own will. He ended up murdering Abner, murdering Absalom, and murdering Amasa. In the long run, he turned in rebellion against David's son Solomon. The Joab syndrome and the Joab spirit is a dangerous perversion of true covenant-making. Let us recognize it as a counterfeit, purge it from our midst, and not be diverted from wholesome and divinely-led commitment to covenant loyalty. God's love can be beautifully expressed when leaders submit themselves one to another to support a unified flow of spiritual authority.

36

THE NEW COVENANT
OF NEHEMIAH

God's promises to bring a Messianic king who would offer a covenant of salvation and eternal life were intricately knit together with His promises to restore a godly kingdom to the nation of Israel. The Messianic king and the Messianic kingdom are interrelated. Jesus came as the newborn, divinely-ordained King of the Jews.

The kingdom of Israel bore the promise of the coming kingdom of God. It reached a high point at the time of David and Solomon in which it was close to giving birth to the Messianic kingdom. Then the kingdom of Israel went through a stage in which it was divided in two, at the time of the split between Rehoboam and Jeroboam. Israel then went into a third stage, one of exile, in which anointed prophets spoke of the spiritual values of the kingdom. These prophets taught the difference between a worldly kingdom and a heavenly one. They promised a future restoration of Israel. The people would return to their land in unity. The prophets promised a new covenant and a new commonwealth. They promised a new kind of king, a Messiah, who would lead this heavenly kingdom and give eternal life to His people.

Jeremiah's Vision

Jeremiah was one of the prophets who preached these spiritual values to the children of Israel. **Jeremiah 31:31** states:

"Behold, the days are coming," says the Lord, "when I will make a new covenant with the house of Israel and with the house of Judah."

The new covenant is a covenant between God and the people of Israel and Judah. The promises of the new covenant involve a reunification between the tribes of Israel and the tribes of Judah. The new covenant of salvation involves restoration of the physical city of Jerusalem and the nation of Israel. **Jeremiah 31:38** states:

"Behold, the days are coming," says the Lord, "that the city [Jerusalem] shall be built for the Lord from the Tower of Hananeel to the Corner Gate."

Let us go back in time to view the unfolding of the meaning of the new covenant. Let us watch that unfolding from the point of view of the historical people of God. Discard for a moment the perception of the new covenant looking backwards through two thousand years of Western Christianity. Let us watch through the eyes of an ancient tribal people who saw their God, El Shaddai, carve and mold for them out of history the fulfillment of the promises He had made to their forefathers. Let us view through the eyes of the prophets the emerging of the revelation of this new kind of heavenly kingdom, one that will transcend and yet be closely involved with the restoration of their people.

David's Kingdom

At the time of King David, the kingdom of Israel was close enough to righteousness that God could introduce to them the promise of an eternal king. The prophet Nathan came to David with a prophecy that had a double meaning. One level of the promise had to do with David's son Solomon; another level of the promise had to do with David's greater son, the coming Messiah, Jesus. **II Samuel 7:12-17** states:

> **"When your days are fulfilled and you rest with your fathers, I will set up your seed after you, who will come from your body, and I will establish his kingdom. He shall build a house for My name, and I will establish the throne of his kingdom forever. I will be his Father, and he shall be My son. If he commits iniquity, I will chasten him with the rod of men and with the blows of the sons of men. But My mercy shall not depart from him, as I took it from Saul, whom I removed from before you. And your house and your kingdom shall be established forever before you. Your throne shall be established forever." According to all these words and according to all this vision, so Nathan spoke to David.**

This prophecy was given to Nathan by a direct revelation from God. He spoke the words exactly and the prophecy contained manifold levels of meaning. The primary double entendre was the overlaying of the vision of the Messianic King Jesus upon the image of David's immediate son and successor, King Solomon. This double photographic image in the Spirit is typical of the sweep of prophecies concerning the kingdom of God. Jesus Himself was not an angel. He was a man. He was the Son of David. He was the King of the Jews. In addition, Jesus was born as the divine Son of God, the fulfillment of the Word of God made flesh. Jesus was the fulfillment of the sum-total of all the prophecies concerning the coming of the kingdom of God. These words were rolled into one flesh and made manifest upon the earth.

During the reign of King Solomon, the kingdom of Israel reached fantastic proportions. The name Solomon comes from the Hebrew name "Shlomo," from which we also get the word "Shalom." The name Solomon means "peaceful one." In the reign of King Solomon, who is a type or precursor of the Messiah, there was peace, prosperity and majestic worship. Abundance flowed in every dimension of life. Tragically, the overflow of blessings turned to decadence in the hands of the people. The people were overwhelmed by the splendor of God's provision and worshiped their own prosperity and sensuality. They began to worship their own magnificence instead of the Magnificent One who gave it to them.

The Split Kingdom

In the time of King Solomon's son Rehoboam, the kingdom was divided in two as a judgment from God. The ten northern tribes were given into the hands of Jeroboam. The two southern tribes and the temple priesthood remained under the rule of Rehoboam. Dividing a nation in two is a classic form of divine judgment. This division is what is referred to by the prophets when they said that God would bring a plumbline. A plumbline is a string with a weight on it that is used to draw a vertical line or divide an area in half. Germany was divided in two after World War II. America was almost divided in two in the period of the Civil War. The division between the northern and southern kingdoms of Israel lasted for many centuries. The judgment of God held them split in two.

It is important not to underestimate the significance of this division. It lasted on and on into the years. The same judgment befell the ancient Babylonians under King Belshazzar, when the handwriting on the wall came and spelled out the words:

Mene, Mene, Tekel, Upharsin (Daniel 5:25).

The inscription may be translated as "Measured, Measured, Weighed and Divided." The word "Upharsin" is a play on words between two different roots which may mean "divided" and also "Persian." The kingdom was divided and given to the Persians.

What a woeful state that the centuries rolled on with the kingdom of Israel divided in two! There is a symbolic parallel with the worldwide Body of believers that has also been divided in two. The Scriptures see this primary division as between Jew and Gentile. **Ephesians 2:14-17** states:

For He Himself is our peace, who has made both one, and has broken down the middle wall of division between us, having abolished in His flesh the enmity, that is, the law of commandments contained in ordinances, so as to create in Himself one new man from the two, thus making peace, and that He might reconcile them both to God in one body through the cross, thereby putting to death the enmity. He came and preached peace to you who were afar off and to those who were near.

As the archetypal hope of ancient Israel was the reconciliation between the northern and southern tribes, so is there the ever expectant hope of the Church for the reconciliation between Jew and Gentile. The emergence of thousands of Jewish believers in Jesus in recent times heralds with it the ever hastening restoration of God's people.

Ezekiel's Vision for Restoration

The split in the nation of Israel represented a foundational spiritual challenge to the kingdom of God. It may be likened to what a divorce or division between husband and wife would do to the underpinnings of a family. The healing of the great split that started in the time of Rehoboam and Jeroboam had prophetic significance for the coming Messianic kingdom. Ezekiel prophesied about the coming of the new covenant kingdom as recorded in chapters 36 and 37. This sweeping prophecy contained three major categories:

(1) a spiritual renewal of heart;

(2) the regathering of the people of Israel;

(3) the healing of the split between Judah and Israel.

The promise of the kingdom of God and eternal life was wrapped up in these three themes.

Ezekiel 36:24-28 states:

For I will take you from among the nations, gather you out of all countries, and bring you into your own land. Then I will sprinkle water on you, and you shall be clean; I will cleanse you from all your filthiness and from all your idols. I will give you a new heart and put a new spirit within you; I will take the heart of stone out of your flesh and give you a heart of flesh. I will put My Spirit within you and cause you to walk in My statutes, and you will keep My judgments and do them. Then shall you dwell in the land that I gave to your fathers; you shall be My people, and I will be your God.

This prophecy contains the promise of spiritual rebirth. God says that He will give us a new heart and a new spirit. He will even cause His own Spirit to dwell inside us. The rebirth of one's own spirit and the receiving of God's Spirit are the first two steps of the walk of a believer in Jesus.

This promise of eternal spiritual life is sandwiched between the promises of the regathering of the people of Israel and the restoration of the land of Israel. God calls two peoples to be one in Ephesians 2; He calls Jew and Gentile to be united. God unites in this new covenant the promise of inner rebirth with the promise of restoration of the land of Israel. These two go hand-in-hand. The restoration of the Church and the restoration of Israel flow together toward the fullness of the kingdom of God.

In eye of the ancient prophets, there could not have been a separation between spiritual renewal and national restoration. As Ezekiel prophesied to the people in exile, the hope of a coming Messianic kingdom combined these elements. Like body and soul, the Messianic kingdom could not be conceived of without both the spiritual and the national.

Ezekiel 37:12-14 states:

Behold, O My people, I will open your graves and cause you to come up from your graves, and bring you into the land of Israel. Then you shall

know that I am the Lord, when I have opened your graves, O My people, and brought you up from your graves. I will put My Spirit in you, and you shall live, and I will place you in your own land. Then you shall know that I, the Lord, have spoken it and performed it.

The bones of the nation of Israel were to be regathered. The Spirit of God was to be breathed upon them as God breathed life into Adam's clay body. The promise of the breath of life is commensurate with the promise of the rejoining of the bones.

The United Kingdom

The ancient prophets saw the revelations of God as connected with God's covenants with Israel. The judgments of God were manifested in the disastrous effects upon the nation of Israel. Those judgments included the division in two at the time of Jeroboam and the later exile to Babylon. While the children of Israel were in exile, God promised them through the prophets a renewed covenant. A new restoration of God's covenant with Israel would be coming, and the heavenly kingdom would be birthed through that restoration.

Somehow the people would have to be regathered, and somehow the north-south split would have to be healed. Concurrent with that restoration would be the emergence of the spiritual Messianic kingdom. **Ezekiel 37:16, 17 and 22 state:**

As for you, son of man, take a stick for yourself and write on it: "For Judah and for the children of Israel, his companions." Then take another stick and write on it, "For Joseph, the stick of Ephraim, and for all the house of Israel, his companions." Then join them one to another for yourself into one stick, and they will become one in your hand. I will make them one nation in the land, on the mountains of Israel; and one king shall be king over them all; they shall no longer be two nations, nor shall they ever be divided into two kingdoms again.

In the new covenantal kingdom, the great judgment that God inflicted upon the nation at the time of Jeroboam and Rehoboam would be healed. The Messianic king was seen to be the king that would rule at the time of reunification and restoration. The great hope of the new covenant was that after all the centuries, the two sticks would become one.

The Returning Remnant

After the time of the fullness of exile, the prophets began to predict that the remnant of the exiles of Israel would return to the land. This return of the remnant happened in three waves of "aliyah," the Hebrew word for immigration, which means "to go up." The first wave of aliyah was led by Zerubabel in the reign of

King Cyrus. The second wave was lead by Ezra in the time of Artaxerxes. The third wave of return was led by Nehemiah. In these waves of immigration, people came whose hearts were tender toward God. This group of families and their children would soon receive the coming Messianic King.

All twelve of the tribes of Israel, as well as the Levites, were diligent to keep meticulous records of their genealogies during the years of exile. Their ancient sense of blood covenant kept their identity with each of the tribes strongly in their minds. Although these people knew what tribes they had come from, the years of exile and the difficult obstacles that faced them in returning to Israel made them forget any enmity between them. These were the hand-picked, tenderhearted remnant from each of the tribes. They had been sifted and refined and humbled. They were returning now, not to set up a carnal kingdom, as their forefathers had, but with love in their hearts and prayer in their mouths to pioneer a new common-wealth. They had a new sense of covenant with God to worship Him in spirit and truth.

This returning remnant could be likened to the first pioneers to settle in America. The pioneers escaped from the old world of Europe to start a new world and a new life that God had promised them. To the early pilgrims, America was a place where they believed they could live a true Christian faith in sincerity and love, having escaped the decaying religious institutions of Europe. They faced tremendous obstacles, but they bore the promises of God for a great new nation. They had to overcome almost overwhelming opposition, and though they seemed barely to succeed, they managed to found a nation that was destined to become the most prosperous, most powerful and most Christian nation the modern world has known.

The situation was similar with the exiles returning from Babylon to Israel. They faced natural obstacles and opposition from evil men. They barely seemed to succeed, but they did manage to found the nation that bore with it the promise of the restoration of Israel and the coming Messianic King. These people and their succeeding generations ingrained in their children the belief that a great Messiah would soon be born in their midst. The substance of that faith began to build and build. The Messianic hope grew even stronger in their hearts. The expectation of a glorious spiritual commonwealth was virtually tangible to them. It was to the children of these families that Jesus was to come.

The Twelve Tribes

The remnant of people who returned to Israel included members from all twelve tribes. (This fact may be seen by such verses as II Chronicles 10:17; 11:3; 11:16; 15:9; 30:21; 30:25; 31:6; Ezra 2:2; 2:59; 2:70; 6:16; 6:21; 7:7; 9:1; 10:1; 10:25; Nehemiah 7:7; 7:73; 9:2; 11:3; 11:20; and 13:3.) After the split between the northern and southern tribes, at various times of revival, people from the northern tribes came down to live in Judah. When Judah was taken into captivity, these people kept their tribal identities. When they came back into Israel after the exile, they continued their family listings. In the period of the New Testament, the people knew what tribe they were from and who their parents were, back to many generations. To say there are ten lost tribes of Israel floating around somewhere is patently unbiblical.

In Luke 2:36, the prophetess Anna is listed as coming from the tribe of Asher, one of the most northern and least populated tribes of Israel. In large sections of the books of Ezra and Nehemiah there are genealogical listings. These listings are subdivided into categories. One of these categories is the people who came from the tribes of Israel. In addition, the Apostle James writes his letter in the New Testament to all twelve tribes, now known as the Jews. Jesus' family certainly kept clear genealogical records on both His father's side and His mother's. Throughout the New Testament, there is no mention of any lost tribe of Israel. The people that Jesus addressed as the Jews were considered to have the remnant of the northern tribes within them.

The first wave of aliyah came under Zerubbabel, whose Persian name was Sheshbazzar. He was of the immediate line of the kings of Judah. Zerubbabel may be considered the king of Judah at that time. He had with him in leadership a man who was a direct descendant of Aaron, the high priest. His name was Jeshua, which is the same name that is translated in English in the New Testament period as Jesus. The name of Jesus in the New Testament could just as easily have been listed as Jeshua or Yeshua. This Jeshua, at the time of Zerubbabel may be considered as the high priest.

Although the returning remnant was small, the national structure was intact with the king, the high priest and the leaders from each of the tribes of Israel. **Ezra 2:2** states:

Those who came with Zerubbabel were Jeshua, Jeremiah, Seraiah...the number of the men of the people of Israel were...

This remnant was also accompanied by the prophets Haggai, Zechariah, and others. The king, elders, prophets, priests and representatives from all twelve tribes were present.

The Messianic Promise

To this small group of people fell all the promises of the new covenant. They were the heirs to the regathering of Israel, to the uniting of the northern and southern tribes, to the promised spiritual renewal and to the coming Messiah. The historical books of the Old Testament leave off with the remnant of people gathering together under Nehemiah to make covenant to serve the God of Israel. The history of the Old Testament ends with Nehemiah's covenant. It points the people in expectation toward the place where the gospels of Matthew and Luke begin.

The remnant returning from exile made a renewed covenant with the God of Israel. They had put away the carnal attitudes of the previous kingdom. They had died in the period of exile and were being raised anew to establish a commonwealth of devout people. The hopes and promises of past generations rested on their shoulders.

The later prophets of the Old Testament period prophesied that a great outpouring of God's Spirit would soon come to their descendants. These people renewed their commitment to God; they made a new covenant. They saw themselves as heirs to a new kind of kingdom according to the prophecies of Jeremiah and Ezekiel. They believed that God would make a new covenant with them. They joined their hearts in repentance and hope, searching the Scriptures to find clues about the coming Messiah.

Nehemiah's New Covenant

In chapters 9 and 10 of the book of Nehemiah, the people gathered together to pray, fast and commit themselves in a new covenant to God. **Nehemiah 9:3** states:

They stood up in their place and read from the book of the law of the Lord their God for one fourth of the day; and for another fourth they confessed and worshiped the Lord their God.

With prayer and fasting and confessing the promises of God's covenant, they stood before the Lord. They called upon God to make this new covenant with them. **Nehemiah 9:32** states:

Now therefore, our God, the great, the mighty, the awesome God, who keeps covenant and mercy: do not let all the trouble seem small before You that has come upon us, our kings, and our princes, our priest and our prophets, our fathers and on all Your people.

They believed that God was forgiving them for the past sins in the history of their people. All the sins that had resulted in the twin judgments of division and exile were now being forgiven. The sins of idolatry and witchcraft had been put away. They had been miraculously preserved as a remnant and brought back to the land of Israel. They were sure that God was hearing their prayers. They were sure that God would make a new covenant with them since He had so obviously forgiven their sins. They believed that a great outpouring of God's Spirit was soon at hand.

Nehemiah 9:38 states:

And because of all this, we make a sure covenant, and write it; and our leaders and our Levites and our priests seal it.

They enacted the covenant, made it formal, had it verified by their leaders and sealed themselves into it.

Waiting for the New Covenant

In the silence of the intertestamental period, the children and the children's children of this remnant kept up a faithful prayer vigil. They interceded for the promised revival of the new covenant to come. For four hundred years, these people spent days and nights interceding before God in the courts of the temple in Jerusalem.

There was in the days of Herod, king of Judah, a certain priest named Zacharias, of the division of Abijah. His wife was of the daughters of Aaron, and her name was Elizabeth. And they were both righteous before God, walking in all the commandments and ordinances of the Lord blameless (Luke 1:5-6).

Certainly, many of the priests and Israelites living in the land at this time were not truly devout; yet many of them were. This devout priest went in to offer incense for the multitude. As he offered the incense, he was interceding in prayer. Right in the middle of his prayers, the angel Gabriel appeared from God. The angel said to him in **Luke 1:13:**

Do not be afraid, Zacharias, your prayer is heard.

In answer to the prayers of these generations, the angel promised Zacharias that a prophet fathered by him would be the last great prophet and would introduce the soon-to-be-born Messiah. The angel appeared to Zacharias in answer to the prayers of those preceding generations. Luke 1 picks up where Nehemiah 9 leaves off. The people cut the covenant in hope in Nehemiah 9. They and their children interceded throughout all the intertestamental period. The answer to their prayers was announced to them by a miraculous appearance of the angel Gabriel. Gabriel spoke to one of their high priests at the moment of offering the sacrifice and sacred incense on the altar.

As the angel appeared to Zacharias on the inside of the temple, a crowd of people was standing around the courts interceding with all their hearts. **Luke 1:10** states:

And the whole multitude of the people was praying outside at the hour of incense.

This is how it should have been. The incense was being offered up as the covenantal symbol of the prayers. The people were praying at the same time in devout intercession. These people were spiritually attuned to what was going on. When Zacharias came out of the temple, they were able to perceive that he had seen a vision.

But when he came out, he could not speak to them; and they perceived that he had seen a vision in the temple (Luke 1:22).

The Birth of the King

Amazing signs and wonders began to break out among the people. Men and women had miraculous visitations from angels. Women had supernatural births, and shepherds saw visions while attending their sheep. Fishermen would spend their days, while mending their nets, talking about the promises of the Scriptures of the coming Messiah. Popular opinion was rising that great spiritual breakthroughs were happening.

Intense spiritual battles were going on. The secular authorities began murdering the covenant children. Wise men from distant countries were led to come to Israel by visions of glory. People filled the streets, praying and reading the Scriptures. People left their homes and their jobs to go into the wilderness to hear prophets preaching. Commoners on the streets would stop and have arguments as to which town the Messiah would come from.

It was into this explosive mixture of gas and air that the spark of Jesus the Messiah was born. The resultant explosion rocked the world and changed the course of history forever. God had been faithful to His promises. The new covenant had been fulfilled, and the kingdom of God is now being preached all over the world.

Additional copies of this book and other
book titles from DESTINY IMAGE are
available at your local bookstore.

For a bookstore near you, call 1-800-722-6774
Send a request for a catalog to:

Destiny Image® Publishers, Inc.
P.O. Box 310
Shippensburg, PA 17257-0310

*"Speaking to the Purposes of God for This
Generation and for the Generations to Come"*

For a complete list of our titles,
visit us at www.destinyimage.com

6B-2:87

MESSIANIC JEWISH THEMES

Jewish Roots, A Foundation of Biblical Theology

A significant book on Messianic Judaism which offers insight on many difficult questions. $17.00

Growing to Maturity, A Messianic Jewish Guide

This book is used by many congregations for membership classes. $10.00

Jewishness and Jesus

A booklet to help you share Messiah with your unsaved Jewish friends.
$1.00

OTHER BOOKS BY OUR AUTHORS

Asher (Keith) Intrater

The Apple of His Eye

Find out how your life can be transformed as you are bathed in the light of God's grace. $6.00

Covenant Relationships

A handbook on the biblical principles of intergrity and loyalty. This book lays important foundations for congregational health and right spiritual attitudes. $15.00

Dan Juster

Dynamics of Spiritual Deception

This book will help you to avoid demonic counterfeit in Spirit-filled congregations. $7.00

Due Process

This book reveals the need for God's people to pursue, in love, godly justice. $7.00

ITEM	COST/BOOK	NO. ORDERED	AMOUNT
		Subtotal	
Maryland residents add 5% Sales Tax (or send tax exempt certificate for our files.)			
15% P & H ($4.00 minimum)			
		TOTAL ENCLOSED	

Mail all orders with checks payable to:

Tikkun International
P.O. Box 2997
Gaithersburg, MD 20886